Y0-AGS-480

# The Complete Step by Step American Cookbook

**Compiled by Judith Ferguson**
**Introduced by Jane Adams**
**Photography by Peter Barry**
**Designed by Philip Clucas, Sally Strugnell and Alison Jewell**
**Recipes Prepared for Photography by Bridgeen Deery**
**and Wendy Devenish**

CLB 2206
This 1990 edition published by CLB Publishing, Inc.
Airport Business Center, 29 Kripes Road, East Granby, CT 06026

Color separation by Hong Kong Graphic Arts Ltd., Hong Kong.
Printed and bound in Cordoba, Spain by Graficromo, S.A.

ISBN 0 86283 767 7

# The Complete Step by Step
# American Cookbook

PUBLISHING

# CONTENTS

# INTRODUCTION

For many years Americans have been looking abroad for culinary inspiration. Stuck with a reputation for "fast food," gigantic steaks and fattening cakes and desserts, American cooking was out of tune with the trend towards fresher, lighter, more healthy eating. Now Americans are reawakening to the possibilities offered by their own "home cooking." These possibilities are not just confined to the best-known classics, such as Thanksgiving Dinner, with all its historical and patriotic associations, but include the enormous and varied repertoire of regional dishes which a country as vast as the United States can provide.

In rediscovering our own cooking, we Americans have also discovered that there never was any need to look abroad, because all those influences, East and West European, African and Far Eastern, were to be found here at home. Added to which was the native knowledge of the Indian and the inventiveness of successive generations of settlers.

For the history of American cooking closely reflects the country's pattern of colonization. From the Pilgrim Fathers onwards, regular influxes of immigrants from all over the world each brought with them their own familiar ways of cooking. These were adapted to the ingredients available wherever they eventually settled, native influences were absorbed and the resultant reinterpretation of the recipes they brought from home became part of the richness and diversity that is American cooking. All this means that the American cook can choose from a vast variety of dishes without ever venturing beyond his or her own shores.

In this book, we have chosen to present for you six of the distinct cooking styles from among all those that go to make up American cooking. They take us on a journey around the American seaboard linked via the Southwestern states. We begin our journey appropriately enough in New England, which saw both the beginnings of the United States and of that very process of immigrant influence and adaptation which is so typical of American cooking. This then is traditional cooking, with its sober reminders of the Pilgrim Fathers and their initial struggle for survival. Journeying south we stop to enjoy some legendary Southern hospitality.

The next stages of our journey take us through three of the most popular of America's rediscovered cooking styles, Cajun, Creole and Tex-Mex, each of which typifies the American immigrants' talent for adapting their recipes to the ingredients they found when they arrived in America. In each case the result is an exuberant style of cooking, and one which suits the present trend towards tasty but less heavy food.

Finally we reach the West Coast and journey's end in California. This is the culmination of our journey in every sense, for here is a style of cooking that is a truly cosmopolitan blend of all that's gone before, together with some Oriental overtones, and all transformed with more than a little Californian pizazz. And that's it: from the very source of American cooking to its most contemporary expression in one easy trip.

The format we have chosen for this culinary journey means that you are literally only a few steps away from discovering all the joys of our national cooking for yourself. Whether you choose the traditions of New England or the modern interpretations of Californian dishes, it is all there for you to try. It's not going to be an easy choice, with so many color photographs to tempt you, but it could be the start of a lifetime's exploration of your own backyard.

# New England Cooking

# INTRODUCTION

The recipes of New England are some of the oldest and most traditional in the country. Food played an enormous part in the founding of the United States, which began in this part of the country with the landing of the Pilgrims. During their first year they saw their crops, planted from seed brought with them from home, fail to take hold in the new soil and climate. They had to adapt to survive, and that meant relying on native foods, however strange these seemed. The Indians introduced the Pilgrims to maize, pumpkins, squash, cranberries and their own domesticated turkeys. The Pilgrims were soon using these North American ingredients in many of their favorite recipes from home. These foods that saved the settlers' lives also became part of the Thanksgiving menu that is still enjoyed today. Fish and seafood were important resources from the start and have remained so. But New England has contributed many other good things to American cooking – maple syrup, blueberries for pies, clams for chowder, to name just a few. As immigrants from other countries came to join that first band of settlers, they brought their own influences to bear on a cuisine that retains its traditional connections while being at the same time truly American.

SERVES 6-8

# CLAM CHOWDER

French fishermen invented this thick soup-stew, but New Englanders adopted it as their own, using the delicious varieties of clams found along their coastlines.

2lbs clams (1lb shelled or canned clams)
3oz rindless bacon, diced
2 medium onions, finely diced
1 tbsp flour
6 medium potatoes, peeled and cubed
Salt and pepper
4 cups milk
1 cup light cream
Chopped parsley (optional)

**Step 1** Cook the clams until the shells open. Stir occasionally for even cooking.

**Step 2** Cook the bacon slowly until the fat renders.

**Step 3** Cook the onion in the bacon fat until soft and transluscent.

**1.** Scrub the clams well and place them in a basin of cold water with a handful of flour to soak for 30 minutes. Drain the clams and place them in a deep saucepan with about ½ cup cold water. Cover and bring to the boil, stirring occasionally until all the shells open. Discard any shells that do not open. Strain the clam liquid and reserve it and set the clams aside to cool.

**2.** Place the diced bacon in a large, deep saucepan and cook slowly until the fat is rendered. Turn up the heat and brown the bacon. Remove it to paper towel to drain.

**3.** Add the onion to the bacon fat in the pan and cook slowly to soften. Stir in the flour and add the potatoes, salt, pepper, milk and reserved clam juice.

**4.** Cover and bring to the boil and cook for about 10 minutes, or until the potatoes are nearly tender. Remove the clams from their shells and chop them if large. Add to the soup along with the cream and diced bacon. Cook a further 10 minutes, or until the potatoes and clams are tender. Add the chopped parsley, if desired, and serve immediately.

## Cook's Notes

**Time**
Preparation takes about 30 minutes and cooking takes about 20 minutes.

**Cook's Tip**
Soaking clams and other shellfish in water with flour or cornmeal before cooking plumps them up and also helps to eliminate sand and grit.

**Buying Guide**
If fresh or canned clams are not available, substitute mussels or cockles instead.

SERVES 8-10

# A GREEN-PEAS SOUP

This is a summery version of a hearty winter staple. Green peas and mint add a freshness and a light, delicate taste to dried split peas.

¾ cup dried split peas
1¼lbs frozen peas
3oz fresh mint leaves
½ cup butter or margarine, melted
Pinch salt and pepper
Sprigs of fresh mint to garnish

**Step 1** Cook the split peas in water until very soft. Test by mashing some against the side of the pan.

**1.** Place the split peas with about 6 cups water in a heavy saucepan. Cover, bring to the boil and cook until very tender, about 40 minutes.

**2.** Strain the peas and reserve the liquid.

**3.** Pour the liquid back into the saucepan and add the frozen peas. Chop the mint leaves, reserving some for garnish, and add to the peas. Bring to the boil in a covered saucepan.

**Step 3** Cook the frozen peas in the reserved split pea liquid along with the chopped mint.

**Step 4** Puree the split peas and stir them back into the soup, mixing well.

**4.** Meanwhile, add the melted butter to the dried peas and push through a strainer or work in a food processor to form a smooth purée. Add the purée to the green peas, mixing well. Add salt and pepper to taste.

**5.** Pour the hot soup into a tureen and garnish with sprigs or leaves of mint. Serve immediately.

## Cook's Notes

**Time**
Preparation takes about 30 minutes, cooking takes 45-50 minutes.

**Variation**
Other fresh herbs, such as marjoram, chervil or thyme may be substituted for the mint.

**Buying Guide**
Dried split peas are readily available in supermarkets and health food stores.

SERVES 4

# Fresh Creamed Mushrooms

For a recipe that has been around since Colonial times, this one is surprisingly up-to-date.

1lb even-sized button mushrooms
1 tbsp lemon juice
2 tbsps butter or margarine
1 tbsp flour
Salt and white pepper
¼ tsp freshly grated nutmeg
1 small bay leaf
1 blade mace
1 cup heavy cream
1 tbsp dry sherry

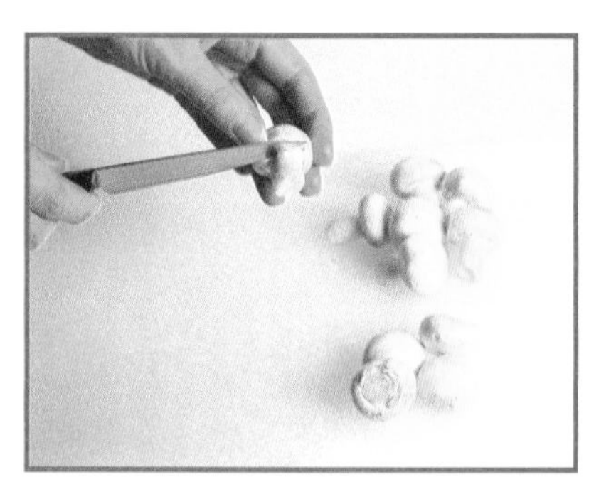

**Step 1** Trim the mushroom stems level with the caps. Do not use the stems for this recipe.

**Step 2** Cook the flour gently in the butter for about 1 minute.

**Step 3** Test with a sharp knife to see if the mushrooms are tender.

**1.** Wash the mushrooms quickly and dry them well. Trim the stems level with the caps. Leave whole if small, halve or quarter if large. Toss with the lemon juice and set aside.

**2.** In a medium saucepan, melt the butter or margarine and stir in the flour. Cook, stirring gently, for about 1 minute. Remove from the heat, add the nutmeg, salt, pepper, bay leaf and mace and gradually stir in the cream.

**3.** Return the pan to the heat and bring to the boil, stirring constantly. Allow to boil for about 1 minute, or until thickened. Reduce the heat and add the mushrooms. Simmer gently, covered, for about 5 minutes, or until the mushrooms are tender. Add the sherry during the last few minutes of cooking. Remove bay leaf and blade mace. Sprinkle with additional grated nutmeg before serving.

**Cook's Tip**
If the mushrooms are clean, do not wash them. If washing is necessary, rinse them very quickly and pat dry quickly. Mushrooms absorb water easily.

**Time**
Preparation takes about 20 minutes, and cooking takes about 7 minutes.

**Variation**
The recipe may be used as a sauce for chicken or ham as well.

**Serving Ideas**
Serve on hot toast or in individual custard cups or scallop shells, accompanied with hot buttered toast or melba toast. Serves 4 as an appetizer.

SERVES 6-8

# CREAM OF PUMPKIN SOUP

Pumpkins have an honoured place in American culinary history and show up in many different preparations. Their excellent colour and texture make a distinctive soup.

1 large pumpkin about 4-5lbs in weight
¼ cup butter or margarine
1 large onion, sliced
1 cup heavy cream
Pinch salt, white pepper and nutmeg
Snipped chives to garnish

**1.** Wash the pumpkin well on the outside and cut through horizontally, about 2 inches down from the stem end.

**2.** Carefully cut most of the pulp off the top and reserve the "lid" for later use.

**3.** Remove the seeds from the inside and discard them.

**4.** Using a small, sharp knife, carefully remove all but ½ inch of the pulp from inside the pumpkin. Work slowly and carefully to avoid piercing the outer skin of the pumpkin. Chop all the pulp from the top of the pumpkin and the inside and set it aside.

**5.** Melt the butter or margarine in a large saucepan and add the onion. Cook slowly until the onion is tender but not brown. Add the pumpkin flesh and about 4 cups cold water. Bring to the boil and then allow to simmer gently, covered, for about 20 minutes.

**6.** Purée the mixture in a food processor or blender in several small batches. Return the soup to the pot and add the cream, salt, pepper and nutmeg to taste. Reheat the soup and pour it into the reserved pumpkin shell. Garnish the top of the soup with snipped chives, if desired, before serving.

**Step 2** Using a large, sharp knife, cut the top off the pumpkin to serve as a lid.

**Step 3** Remove the seeds and stringy pulp from inside the pumpkin and discard.

**Step 4** Using a small, sharp knife, work slowly to remove the pulp from inside the pumpkin. Leave a layer of flesh on the skin to form a shell.

## Cook's Notes

**Time**
Preparation takes about 45 minutes, and cooking takes about 20 minutes.

**Preparation**
If desired, 2 pumpkins may be used, 1 for making the soup and 1 to serve as a tureen. The pumpkin used for cooking must be peeled first.

**Variation**
Canned pumpkin may also be used for the soup instead of fresh. Soup may be served in a tureen or individual bowls instead of the pumpkin shell, if desired.

SERVES 4

# Cape Cod Mussels

When seafood is as good as that from Cape Cod, even the simplest preparations stand out.

- 4½lbs mussels in their shells
- Flour or cornmeal
- 1 cup dry white wine
- 1 large onion, finely chopped
- 2-4 cloves garlic, finely chopped
- Salt and coarsely ground black pepper
- 2 bay leaves
- 1 cup butter, melted
- Juice of 1 lemon

**1.** Scrub the mussels well and remove any barnacles and beards (seaweed strands). Use a stiff brush to scrub the shells, and discard any mussels with broken shells or those that do not close when tapped.

**2.** Place the mussels in a basin full of cold water with a handful of flour or cornmeal and leave to soak for 30 minutes.

**3.** Drain the mussels and place them in a large, deep saucepan with the remaining ingredients, except the butter and lemon juice. Cover the pan and bring to the boil.

**4.** Stir the mussels occasionally while they are cooking to help them cook evenly. Cook about 5-8 minutes, or until the shells open. Discard any mussels that do not open.

**5.** Spoon the mussels into individual serving bowls and strain the cooking liquid. Pour the liquid into 4 small bowls and serve with the mussels and a bowl of melted butter mixed with lemon juice for each person. Dip the mussels into the broth and the melted butter to eat. Use a mussel shell to scoop out each mussel, or eat with small forks or spoons.

**Step 1** Scrub the mussels with a stiff brush to remove barnacles and seaweed beards.

**Step 1** To test if the mussels are still alive, tap them on a work surface – the shells should close.

**Step 5** Hold a mussel shell between 2 fingers and pinch together to remove mussels from their shells to eat.

## Cook's Notes

**Time**
Preparation takes about 30 minutes, and cooking takes about 5-8 minutes.

**Cook's Tip**
The beards are strands of seaweed that anchor the mussels to the rocks on which they grow. These must be removed before cooking. They can be pulled off quite easily by hand, or scrubbed off with a stiff brush.

**Variation**
The same recipe may be prepared with clams. Use the amount of garlic that suits your own taste or leave out the garlic, if desired. Chopped fresh herbs may be added.

SERVES 6

# HARVARD BEETS

One of the best known dishes using this readily available root vegetable. The color makes this a perfect accompaniment to plain meat or poultry.

2lbs small beets
Boiling water
3 tbsps cornstarch
½ cup sugar
Pinch salt and pepper
1 cup white wine vinegar
¾ cup reserved beet cooking liquid
2 tbsps butter

**Step 3** The peel should pull easily off the beets with a sharp knife.

**1.** Choose even-sized beets and cut off the tops, if necessary. Place beets in a large saucepan of water. Cover the pan and bring to the boil. Lower the heat and cook gently until tender, about 30-40 minutes. Add more boiling water as necessary during cooking.

**2.** Drain the beets, reserving the liquid, and allow the beets to cool.

**Step 3** Slice the beets into thin rounds.

**Step 4** Combine all the sauce ingredients and cook until the cornstarch thickens and clears.

**3.** When the beets are cool, peel them and slice into ¼ inch rounds, or cut into small dice.

**4.** Combine the cornstarch, sugar, salt and pepper, vinegar and required amount of beet liquid in a large saucepan. Bring to the boil over moderate heat, stirring constantly until thickened. Return the beets to the saucepan and allow to heat through for about 5 minutes. Stir in the butter and serve immediately.

## Cook's Notes

**Time**
Preparation takes about 20 minutes, and cooking takes about 30-40 minutes for the beets, 5 minutes for the sauce and 5 minutes to reheat.

**Preparation**
Canned beets may also be used. Substitute canned juice for cooking liquid. Omit the 30-40 minutes cooking time and simply reheat in sauce.

**Variation**
Orange juice may be substituted for part of the vinegar measurement, if desired. Garnish with fresh orange slices for color.

SERVES 4

# STUFFED ACORN SQUASH WITH A RUM GLAZE

Squash has a subtle flavor that blends well with other ingredients.

2 even-sized acorn squash
1/3 cup butter or margarine
2 cooking apples, peeled, cored and cut into 1/2 inch pieces
1/2 cup pitted prunes, cut into large pieces
1 cup dried apricots, cut into large pieces
1/2 tsp ground allspice
6 tbsps rum
1/2 cup chopped walnuts
1/2 cup golden raisins
1/2 cup packed light brown sugar

**1.** Cut the squash in half lengthwise. Scoop out and discard the seeds.

**2.** Place the squash skin side up in a baking dish with water to come halfway up the sides. Bake for about 30 minutes at 350°F.

**3.** Melt half the butter in a saucepan and add the apple, prunes and apricots. Add the allspice and rum and bring to the boil. Lower the heat and simmer gently for about 5-10 minutes. Add the nuts and golden raisins 3 minutes before the end of cooking time.

**4.** Turn the squash over and fill the hollow with the fruit. Reserve the fruit cooking liquid.

**5.** Melt the remaining butter in a saucepan and stir in the brown sugar. Melt slowly until the sugar forms a syrup. Pour on fruit cooking liquid, stirring constantly. Bring back to the boil and cook until syrupy. Add more water if necessary.

**6.** Spoon the glaze onto each squash, over the fruit and the cut edge. Bake for a further 30 minutes, or until the squash is tender.

**Step 2** Place the squash skin side up in a baking dish with water to pre-cook.

**Step 5** Heat the butter and brown sugar in a saucepan until syrupy. Add the liquid from squash, stirring continuously.

**Step 6** Spoon the glaze over each filled squash half, making sure to cover the cut edge.

## Cook's Notes

**Time**
Preparation takes about 30 minutes and cooking takes about 1 hour.

**Buying Guide**
Acorn squash is a winter variety of squash and should have a very hard rind. The recipe may be prepared with other varieties of squash, such as butternut. These vegetables are available in large greengrocers and vegetable sections of larger supermarkets.

**Serving Ideas**
Serve as a side dish with turkey, chicken, ham or pork. If desired, add chopped cooked turkey, chicken or ham to the fruit filling and bake as directed. Serve as a light main course.

SERVES 6-8

# CRANBERRY ORANGE SAUCE

This North American berry, with its crisp taste and bright hue, is perfect with ham, chicken, pork and, of course, Thanksgiving turkey.

3 cups whole cranberries, fresh or frozen
Juice and rind of 2 large oranges
1 cup sugar

**Step 2** Grate the oranges on the coarse side of a grater or use a zester to remove the rind.

**1.** Pick over the cranberries and remove any that are shrivelled or discolored.

**2.** Use the coarse side of the grater to grate the oranges. Take care not to remove too much of the white pith. Alternatively, remove the rind with a zester. Cut the oranges in half and squeeze them for juice.

**3.** Combine the sugar and orange rind in a deep saucepan and strain in the orange juice to remove the seeds. Bring to the boil and simmer for about 3 minutes, stirring continuously to dissolve the sugar.

**4.** When the sugar has dissolved, add the cranberries and cook until the skins pop, about 5 minutes. Remove from the heat and allow to cool slightly before serving. The sauce may also be served chilled.

**Step 3** Combine the orange juice, rind and sugar in a deep saucepan, bring to the boil and cook until the sugar dissolves.

**Step 4** Add the cranberries and cook until the skins pop.

## Cook's Notes

**Time**
Preparation takes about 15 minutes, and cooking takes about 10 minutes.

**Variations**
Cranberry sauce may be prepared without the orange, simply substituting water for the orange juice. Alternatively, cook with red wine. Add cinnamon, cloves or allspice, if desired.

**Preparation**
Cranberry sauce may be prepared up to 1 week ahead of time and kept in the refrigerator, well covered.

SERVES 4

# CREAMED ONIONS

Whole small onions in a creamy, rich sauce are part of Thanksgiving fare, but they are too good to save for just once a year.

1lb pearl onions
Boiling water to cover
2 cups milk
1 bay leaf
1 blade mace
2 tbsps butter or margarine
2 tbsps flour
Pinch salt and white pepper
Chopped parsley (optional)

**Step 2** Once the onions are boiled, put them into cold water and the peels should come off easily.

**Step 1** Trim down the root ends of each onion.

**Step 3** Place the blade of mace and bay leaf in a saucepan with the milk, and heat until just beginning to boil.

**1.** Trim the root hairs on the onions but do not cut the roots off completely. Place the onions in a large saucepan and pour over the boiling water. Bring the onions back to the boil and cook for about 10 minutes.

**2.** Transfer the onions to cold water, allow to cool completely and then peel off the skins, removing roots as well. Leave the onions to drain dry.

**3.** Place the milk in a deep saucepan and add the blade mace and the bay leaf. Bring just to the boil, take off the heat and allow to stand for 15 minutes.

**4.** Melt the butter in a large saucepan and, when foaming, stir in the flour. Strain on the milk and discard the bay leaf and blade mace. Stir well and bring to the boil. Allow the sauce to simmer for about 3 minutes to thicken. Add salt and white pepper to taste and stir in the onions. Cook to heat through, but do not allow the sauce to boil again. Serve immediately and garnish with chopped parsley, if desired.

## Cook's Notes

**Time**
Preparation takes about 30 minutes and cooking takes about 10 minutes for the onions and about 10 minutes for the sauce.

**Preparation**
Infusing the milk with the bay leaf and blade mace gives extra flavor to the sauce.

**Cook's Tip**
When adding onions to a white sauce, do not allow the sauce to boil as the onions can cause it to curdle.

SERVES 6

# SUCCOTASH

A tasty side dish with a strange name, this was inherited from the American Indians, who made it a full meal by adding meat or poultry to it.

4 oz fresh or frozen corn
4 oz fresh or frozen lima beans
4 oz fresh or frozen green beans
3 tbsps butter
Salt and pepper
Chopped parsley

**1.** If using frozen vegetables, bring water to the boil in a saucepan and, when boiling, add the vegetables. Cook for about 5-8 minutes, drain and leave to dry.

**2.** If using fresh vegetables, bring water to the boil in a saucepan and add the lima beans first. After about 2 minutes, add the green beans. Follow these with the corn about 3 minutes before the end of cooking time. Drain and leave to dry.

**3.** Melt the butter in a saucepan and add the vegetables. Heat slowly, tossing or stirring occasionally, until heated through. Add salt and pepper to taste and stir in the parsley. Serve immediately.

**Step 2** Cook all the vegetables in boiling water, adding them one after the other.

**Step 3** Melt the butter in a saucepan and toss the vegetables over heat.

## Cook's Notes

**Time**
Preparation takes about 10 minutes if using frozen vegetables and 25 minutes if using fresh vegetables. Cooking takes about 5-8 minutes for frozen vegetables and about 8-10 minutes for fresh vegetables.

**Preparation**
If using fresh vegetables, use a small, sharp knife to cut the kernels from the ears of the corn. Stand the corn on one end and cut down the length of the ear to separate the kernels. If using fresh lima beans, snap open the pods and push out the beans inside. If desired, the outer skin of the beans may be removed after cooking. Top and tail the fresh green beans and cut into 2 or 3 pieces.

**Variation**
Succotash can be made with just corn and lima beans or corn and green beans. Add red or green pepper, or chopped onion for flavor variation.

SERVES 4

# Poached Chicken with Cream Sauce

Plainly cooked chicken can be as flavorful as it is attractive.

4½lb whole roasting chicken
8-10 sticks celery, washed, cut into 3 inch lengths and tops reserved
4oz bacon, thickly sliced
2 cloves garlic, crushed
1 large onion, stuck with 4 cloves
1 bay leaf
1 sprig fresh thyme
Salt and pepper
Water to cover
⅓ cup butter or margarine
6 tbsps flour
1 cup light cream

**1.** Remove the fat from just inside the cavity of the chicken. Singe any pin feathers over gas flame or pull them out with tweezers.

**2.** Tie the chicken legs together and tuck the wing tips under to hold the neck flap. Place the chicken in a large casserole or stock pot. Chop the celery tops and add to the pot. Place the bacon over the chicken and add the garlic, onion with the cloves, bay leaf, sprig thyme, salt, pepper and water to cover.

**3.** Bring to the boil, reduce the heat and simmer gently, covered, for 50 minutes, or until the chicken is just tender.

**4.** Cut the celery into 3 inch lengths and add to the chicken. Simmer a further 20 minutes, or until the celery is just tender.

**5.** Remove the chicken to a serving plate and keep warm. Strain the stock and reserve the bacon and celery pieces. Skim fat off the top of the stock and add enough water to make up 2 cups, if necessary.

**6.** Melt 1 tbsp of the butter or margarine in the casserole and sauté the bacon until just crisp. Drain on paper towels and crumble roughly.

**7.** Melt the rest of the butter in the casserole or pan and when foaming take off the heat. Stir in the flour and gradually add the chicken stock. Add the cream and bring to the boil, stirring constantly. Simmer until the mixture is thickened.

**8.** Untie the legs and trim the leg ends. If desired, remove the skin from the chicken and coat with the sauce. Garnish with the bacon and the reserved celery pieces.

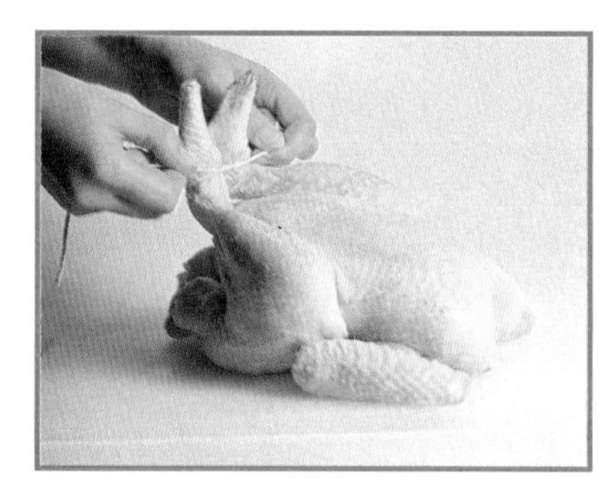

**Step 2** Tie the legs together but do not cross them over. Tuck the neck skin under the wing tips.

**Step 3** Arrange the bacon over the chicken, add the celery tops and the rest of the ingredients.

## Cook's Notes

**Time**
Preparation takes about 25 minutes and cooking takes about 1 hour 10 minutes.

**Serving Ideas**
The chicken may be jointed into 8 pieces before coating with sauce, if desired. Cut the leg joints in two, dividing the thigh and the drumstick. Cut the breast in two, leaving some white meat attached to the wings. Cut through any bones with scissors.

**Variation**
Sliced or whole baby carrots may be added with the celery. Small onions may also be cooked with the celery and peeled in the same way as for the recipe for Creamed Onions.

SERVES 6

# CHICKEN POT PIE

Not a true pie, this dish is nevertheless warming winter fare with its creamy sauce and puffy biscuit topping.

4 chicken joints, 2 breasts and 2 legs
5 cups water
1 bay leaf
2 sprigs thyme
1 sprig rosemary
1 sprig fresh tarragon or ¼ tsp dry tarragon
4 whole peppercorns
1 allspice berry
4 tbsps white wine
2 carrots, peeled and diced
24 pearl onions, peeled
6 tbsps frozen corn kernels
½ cup heavy cream
Salt

**Biscuit Topping**

3½ cups all-purpose flour
1½ tbsps baking powder
Pinch salt
5 tbsps butter or margarine
1½ cups milk
1 egg, beaten with a pinch of salt

**1.** Place the chicken in a deep saucepan with water, herbs and spices and wine. Cover and bring to the boil. Reduce the heat and allow to simmer for 20-30 minutes, or until the chicken is tender. Remove the chicken from the pot and allow to cool. Skim and discard the fat from the surface of the stock. Skin the chicken and remove the meat from the bones.

**2.** Continue to simmer the stock until reduced by about half. Strain the stock and add the carrots and onions. Cook until tender and add the corn. Stir in the cream and add the chicken. Pour into a casserole or into individual baking dishes.

**3.** To prepare the topping, sift the dry ingredients into a bowl or place them in a food processor and process once or twice to sift.

**4.** Rub in the butter or margarine until the mixture resembles small peas. Stir in enough of the milk until the mixture comes together.

**5.** Turn out onto a floured surface and knead lightly. Roll out with a floured rolling pin and cut with a pastry cutter. Brush the surface of each biscuit with a mixture of egg and salt. Place the biscuits on top of the chicken mixture and bake for 10-15 minutes in a pre-heated oven at 375°F. Serve immediately.

**Step 4** Rub the butter or margarine into the dry ingredients until the mixture resembles small peas.

**Step 5** Roll out the biscuit mixture on a floured surface, cut into rounds and place on top of the chicken mixture.

## Cook's Notes

**Time**
Preparation takes about 25 minutes and cooking takes about 20-30 minutes for the chicken, about 20 minutes to prepare the sauce, and about 10-15 minutes to finish off the dish.

**Preparation**
Once the biscuit topping has been prepared it must be baked immediately or the baking powder will stop working and the biscuits will not rise.

**Variations**
Diced potatoes and pimento may be added to the sauce along with other vegetables. Add chopped fresh parsley or a pinch of dried thyme as well, if desired.

SERVES 10-12

# NEW ENGLAND ROAST TURKEY

The Thanksgiving celebration would not be the same without a turkey on the table. Native Indians first domesticated the bird and introduced the early settlers to it.

1 fresh turkey weighing about 20lbs
⅓ cup butter

**Sausage Stuffing**
4 tbsps oil
4oz sausage meat
3 sticks celery, diced
2 onions, diced
1 cup chopped walnuts or pecans
1 cup raisins
1lb day-old bread, made into small cubes
1 cup chicken stock
¼ tsp each dried thyme and sage
2 tbsps chopped fresh parsley
Salt and pepper

**1.** Singe any pin feathers on the turkey by holding the bird over a gas flame. Alternatively, pull out the feathers with tweezers.

**2.** Remove the fat which is just inside the cavity of the bird.

**3.** To prepare the stuffing, heat the oil and cook the sausage meat, breaking it up with a fork as it cooks. Add the celery, onion, nuts and raisins and cook for about 5 minutes, stirring constantly.

**4.** Drain away the fat and add the herbs, cubes of bread and stock, and mix well. Season to taste.

**5.** Stuff the cavity of the bird using your hands or a long-handled spoon. Save some stuffing to tuck under the neck flap to plump it.

**6.** Sew the cavity of the bird closed, or use skewers to secure it. Tie the legs together but do not cross them over. Tuck the neck skin under the wing tips and, if desired, use a trussing needle and fine string to secure them.

**7.** Place the turkey on a rack, breast side up, in a roasting pan. Soften the butter and spread some over the breast and the legs. Place the turkey in a pre-heated 325°F oven and cover loosely with foil. Roast for about 2 hours, basting often.

**8.** Remove the foil and continue roasting for another 2-2½ hours, or until the internal temperature in the thickest part of the thigh registers 350°F. Alternatively, pierce the thigh with a skewer – if the juices run clear then the turkey is done. Allow to rest for about 15-20 minutes before carving. Make gravy with the pan juices if desired and serve.

**Step 8** Pierce the thigh with a skewer. The turkey is done when the juices run clear.

## Cook's Notes

**Variation**
Many different ingredients can be included in a turkey stuffing. Ham or crisply cooked bacon can be substituted for the sausage. A mixture of dried fruit may be used instead of all raisins. Chopped apple may also be included.

**Time**
Preparation takes about 25-30 minutes and cooking takes about 4-4½hours.

**Cook's Tip**
Leaving a turkey or other roast bird to stand for 15-20 minutes before carving keeps the natural juices in the meat.

**Watchpoint**
The stuffing may be prepared in advance, but do not stuff the bird until ready to roast. There is a danger of food poisoning if a turkey or any other bird is stuffed too long before cooking.

SERVES 4

# NEW ENGLAND BOILED DINNER

The "corning process" for preserving beef was a useful one in early America. The process took a long time, but fortunately we can now buy our beef already "corned"!

3lb corned beef brisket
1 bay leaf
1 tsp mustard seed
3 allspice berries
3 cloves
1 tsp dill seed
6 black peppercorns
2 potatoes, cut into even-sized pieces
4 small onions, peeled
4 large carrots, scraped
4 small or 2 large parsnips, peeled and cut into even-sized pieces
1 large or 2 small rutabagas
1 medium-size green cabbage, cored and quartered
Salt

**1.** Place the corned beef in a large saucepan with enough water to cover and add the bay leaf and spices. Cook for about 2 hours, skimming any foam from the surface as the meat cooks.

**2.** Add the potatoes and onions and cook for about 15 minutes. Taste and add salt if necessary.

**3.** Add the carrots, parsnips and rutabagas and cook for a further 15 minutes. Add the cabbage and cook a further 15 minutes.

**4.** Remove the meat from the casserole and slice it thinly. Arrange on a warm serving platter and remove the vegetables from the broth with a draining spoon, placing them around the meat. Serve immediately with horseradish or mustard.

**Step 1** Combine the corned beef, salted water and spices in the pan. Bring to the boil, skimming the foam that rises to the surface.

**Step 3** When the corned beef and root vegetables have cooked for 15 minutes, add the cabbage, pushing it under the liquid.

**Step 4** Remove the meat from the pan and slice thinly across the grain.

**Preparation**
The meat may be cooked for its first 2 hours in advance and refrigerated overnight if desired. Reheat and then add the vegetables according to the recipe.

**Time**
Preparation takes about 30 minutes and cooking takes about 3 hours.

**Economy**
Leftover corned beef is delicious for sandwiches, or for making corned beef hash.

**Variation**
Freshly-cooked beets may be added to the vegetable selection. Cook the beets separately or they will color all the vegetables and the meat. Substitute turnips for the rutabaga if desired.

SERVES 6-8

# YANKEE POT ROAST

This classic American recipe has its roots in French and German cuisine. It is an excellent way with economical cuts of beef.

3lb beef roast (rump, chuck, round or top end)
Flour seasoned with salt and pepper
2 tbsps butter or margarine
1 onion stuck with 2 cloves
1 bay leaf
2 tsps fresh thyme or 1 tsp dried thyme
1 cup beef stock
4 carrots
12 small onions, peeled
4 small turnips, peeled and left whole
2 potatoes, cut into even-sized pieces
2 tbsps butter or margarine mixed with 2 tbsps flour

**1.** Dredge the beef with the seasoned flour, patting off the excess.

**2.** Melt the butter in a large, heavy-based casserole or saucepan and, when foaming, brown the meat on all sides, turning it with wooden spoons or a spatula.

**3.** When well browned, add the onion stuck with the cloves, bay leaf and thyme and pour on the stock. Cover the pan, reduce the heat and cook on top of the stove or in a pre-heated 300°F oven. Cook slowly for about 2 hours, adding more liquid, either stock or water, as necessary.

**4.** Test the meat and, if beginning to feel tender, add the vegetables. Cover and continue to cook until the meat is completely tender and the vegetables are cooked through.

**5.** Remove the meat and vegetables from the casserole or pan and place them on a warm serving platter. Skim the excess fat from the top of the sauce and bring it back to the boil.

**6.** Mix the butter and flour (beurre manie) to a smooth paste. Add about 1 tsp of the mixture to the boiling sauce and whisk thoroughly. Continue adding the mixture until the sauce is of the desired thickness. Carve the meat and spoon over some of the sauce. Serve the rest of the sauce separately.

**Step 2** Place the meat in the hot fat to brown slowly and evenly. Use wooden spoons or a fish slice to turn.

**Step 6** If the sauce needs thickening at the end, add a small spoonful of flour and butter paste and whisk well.

## Cook's Notes

**Time**
Preparation takes about 30 minutes and cooking takes about 2-2½ hours.

**Cook's Tip**
The flour and butter paste or beurre manie may be prepared in large quantities and kept in the refrigerator or freezer to use any time thickening is necessary for a sauce.

**Serving Ideas**
This dish can be a meal in itself. If an accompaniment is desired, serve a green vegetable or a salad.

SERVES 4

# RED FLANNEL HASH

The name comes from the color of the dish, made bright with the addition of cooked beets. It frequently features on brunch menus.

1lb cold corned beef
3-4 cold boiled potatoes, roughly chopped
1 medium onion, finely chopped
Salt, pepper and nutmeg
1-2 cooked beets, peeled and diced
2 tbsps butter or bacon fat

**Step 1** Best results are obtained by chopping the meat into small dice by hand.

**Step 2** Spread out the mixture in the hot fat in a frying pan.

**Step 4** When a crust forms on the bottom, turn the mixture over to brown the other side.

**1.** Cut the meat into small pieces. If using a food processor, be careful not to overwork. Combine all the remaining ingredients except the butter or bacon fat.

**2.** Melt the butter or fat in a frying pan and, when foaming, place in the mixture. Spread it out evenly in the pan.

**3.** Cook over low heat, pressing the mixture down continuously with a wooden spoon or spatula. Cook about 15-20 minutes.

**4.** When a crust forms on the bottom, turn over and brown the other side. Cut into wedges and remove from the pan to serve.

## Cook's Notes

**Time**
Preparation takes about 20 minutes if using leftover corned beef and potatoes from the New England Boiled Dinner recipe. Cooking takes about 25-30 minutes.

**Serving Ideas**
A freshly-poached egg may be placed on top of each serving of Red Flannel Hash. Serve with a mixture of mustard and horseradish, or horseradish and sour cream.

**Economy**
Use leftover corned beef from the New England Boiled Dinner or leftover roast beef for this recipe if desired.

SERVES 6-8

# BOSTON BAKED BEANS

The first American "fast food", these beans were frozen and taken on long journeys to re-heat and eat en route.

1lb dried navy beans
5 cups water
4oz salt pork or slab bacon
1 onion, peeled and left whole
1 tsp dry mustard
1/3-1/2 cup molasses
Salt and pepper

**Step 1** Soak the beans overnight so that they soften slightly and swell in size.

**1.** Soak the beans overnight in the water. Transfer to fresh water to cover. Bring to the boil and allow to cook for about 10 minutes. Drain and reserve the liquid.

**2.** Place the beans, salt pork or bacon and whole onion in a large, deep casserole or bean pot. Mix the molasses, mustard, salt and pepper with 1 cup of the reserved bean liquid. Stir into the beans and add enough bean liquid to cover. Expose only the pork rind on the salt pork and cover the casserole.

**3.** Bake in a pre-heated 300°F oven for about 2 hours. Add the remaining liquid, stirring well, and cook a further 1½ hours, or until the beans are tender. Uncover the beans for the last 30 minutes.

**4.** To serve, remove and discard the onion. Take out the salt pork or bacon and remove the rind. Slice or dice the meat and return to the beans. Check the seasoning and serve.

**Step 2** Combine the beans, salt pork and onion with the molasses mixture.

**Step 3** After the beans have baked for 2 hours, add remaining bean cooking liquid and stir well.

## Cook's Notes

**Time**
Preparation takes about 20 minutes, with overnight soaking for the beans. Alternatively, bring the beans to the boil and then allow to stand for 2 hours. Cook as directed in the recipe. Total cooking takes about 3½ hours.

**Preparation**
The beans may be prepared well in advance and reheated just before serving. Leftovers may be frozen for up to 2 months.

**Serving Ideas**
Baked beans are traditionally served in Boston with steamed brown bread (see recipe). Sausages may be served with the beans, if desired.

SERVES 6-8

# Venison Stew

A recipe very similar to the country stews of France, this one made use of the abundant game found in the New England colonies.

3lbs venison shoulder or leg, cut into 2 inch pieces
2 cups dry red wine
4 tbsps red wine vinegar
1 bay leaf
2 tsps chopped fresh thyme or 1 tsp dried thyme
6 juniper berries, crushed
3 whole allspice berries
6 black peppercorns
1 clove garlic, crushed
4 tbsps oil
2 carrots, cut into strips
1 onion, thinly sliced
2 sticks celery, cut into strips
8oz mushrooms, sliced
Chopped parsley to garnish

**1.** Combine the wine, vinegar, bay leaf, thyme, juniper berries, allspice, peppercorns and garlic with the venison, and marinate overnight.

**2.** Remove the meat from the marinade and pat dry on paper towels. Reserve the marinade for later use.

**3.** Heat the oil in a heavy frying pan or casserole and brown the venison on all sides over very high heat. Brown in several small batches if necessary. Remove the venison and lower the heat. If using a frying pan, transfer the venison to an ovenproof casserole.

**4.** Lower the heat and brown the vegetables in the oil until golden. Sprinkle over the flour and cook until the flour browns lightly. Combine the vegetables with the venison and add the reserved marinade.

**5.** Cover and cook the stew in a pre-heated 300°F oven for about 2 hours.

**6.** Fifteen minutes before the end of cooking time, add the mushrooms and continue cooking until the meat is tender. Garnish with parsley before serving.

**Step 1** Combine the venison, wine, vinegar, herbs and spices in a polythene bag and tie securely. Place in a bowl to catch any drips and turn the bag often to marinate evenly.

**Step 4** When the vegetables and flour have browned, combine them with the browned meat. Gradually pour marinade over the ingredients, stirring well.

## Cook's Notes

**Time**
Preparation takes about 30 minutes, plus overnight marinating. Cooking takes about 10 minutes for the meat to brown and about 2 hours for the stew to cook.

**Preparation**
The stew may be prepared in advance and refrigerated, which will intensify the flavour. Reheat slowly, but bring briefly to the boil before serving.

**Serving Ideas**
Serve with chestnut purée, mashed potatoes or boiled potatoes. Add a green vegetable or salad if desired.

SERVES 4

# BOSTON SCROD

Scrod, or baby codfish, provides the perfect base for a crunchy, slightly spicy topping. Boston is justly famous for it.

4 even-sized cod fillets
Salt and pepper
1/3 cup butter, melted
3/4 cup dry breadcrumbs
1 tsp dry mustard
1 tsp onion salt
Dash Worcester sauce and tabasco
2 tbsps lemon juice
1 tbsp finely chopped parsley

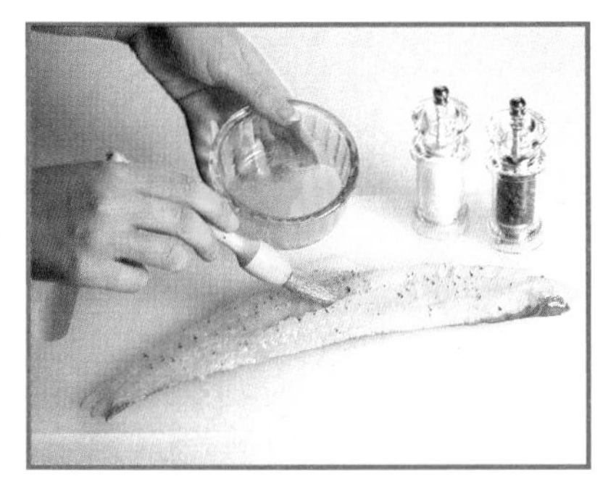

**Step 1** Season the fish lightly with salt and pepper and brush with some of the melted butter. Broil to pre-cook but do not brown.

**Step 3** Press the crumbs gently to pack them into place using a spoon or your hand.

**1.** Season the fish fillets with salt and pepper and place them on a broiler tray. Brush with butter and broil for about 5 minutes.

**2.** Combine remaining butter with breadcrumbs, mustard, onion salt, Worcester sauce, tabasco, lemon juice and parsley.

**3.** Spoon the mixture carefully on top of each fish fillet, covering it completely. Press down lightly to pack the crumbs into place. Broil for a further 5-7 minutes, or until the top is lightly browned and the fish flakes.

## Cook's Notes

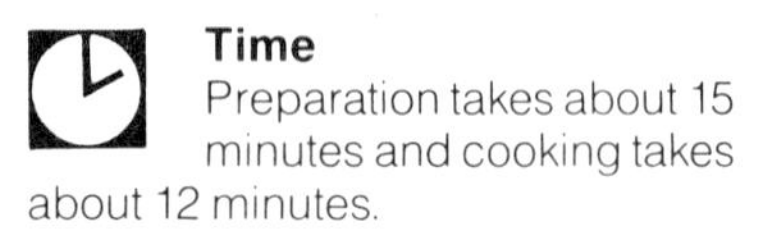

**Time**
Preparation takes about 15 minutes and cooking takes about 12 minutes.

**Preparation**
If desired, the fish may also be baked in the oven. Cover the fish with foil for first 5 minutes of baking time, uncover and top with the breadcrumb mixture. Bake for a further 10-12 minutes at 350°F.

**Variation**
The breadcrumb topping may be used on other fish such as haddock, halibut or sole.

SERVES 4

# NEW ENGLAND BOUILLABAISSE

French settlers brought this favorite recipe to the New World, and just as they would have at home, they used local, seasonal ingredients in it.

**Stock**
1lb fish bones, skin and heads
7 cups water
1 small onion, thinly sliced
1 small carrot, thinly sliced
1 bay leaf
6 black peppercorns
1 blade mace
1 sprig thyme
2 lemon slices

**Bouillabaisse**
⅓ cup butter or margarine
1 carrot, sliced
3 leeks, well washed and thinly sliced
1 clove garlic
Pinch saffron
⅓-½ cup dry white wine
8oz canned tomatoes
1 lobster
1lb cod or halibut fillets
1lb mussels, well scrubbed
1 lb small clams, well scrubbed
8 new potatoes, scrubbed but not peeled
Chopped parsley
8oz large shrimp, peeled and de-veined

**1.** First prepare the fish stock. Place all the ingredients in a large stock pot and bring to the boil over high heat. Lower the heat and allow to simmer for 20 minutes. Strain and reserve the stock. Discard the fish bones and vegetables.

**2.** Melt the butter in a medium-sized saucepan and add the carrots, leeks and garlic. Cook for about 5 minutes until slightly softened.

**3.** Add the saffron and wine and allow to simmer for about 5 minutes.

**4.** Add the fish stock along with all the remaining bouillabaisse ingredients except the shrimp. Bring the mixture to the boil and cook until the lobster turns red, the mussel and clam shells open and the potatoes are tender. Turn off the heat and add the shrimp. Cover the pan and let the shrimp cook in the residual heat. Divide the ingredients among 4 soup bowls. Remove the lobster and cut it in half. Divide the tail between the other 2 bowls and serve the bouillabaisse with garlic bread.

**Step 2** Cook the carrots, leeks and garlic in butter until soft but not colored. Combine all the bouillabaisse ingredients in a large stock pot.

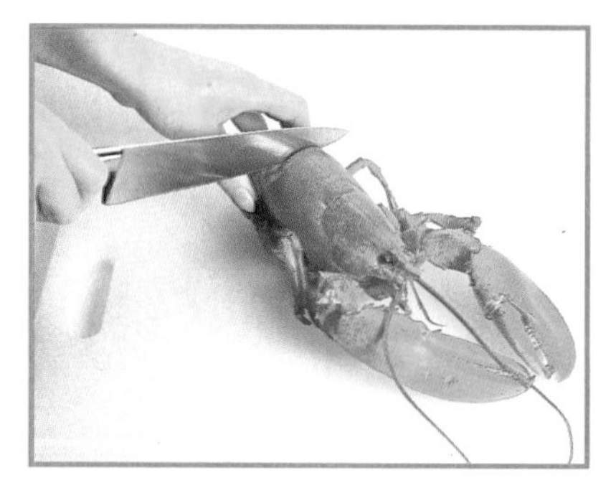

**Step 4** Remove the lobster and cut it in half using a large, sharp knife.

**Time**
Preparation takes about 35 minutes and cooking takes about 30 minutes.

**Watchpoint**
Leeks must be split in half first and rinsed under cold water to remove sand and grit before slicing.

**Variation**
Use whatever shellfish or fish is in season or suits your taste. Lobster is not essential.

SERVES 4

# Whole Baked Fish with New England Stuffing

A whole fish, perfectly cooked, never fails to impress. With a stuffing of oysters, it is certainly grand enough for an important dinner party.

4¼lb whole fish, gutted and boned (use salmon, salmon trout or sea bass)

**Stuffing**

8oz savory cracker crumbs
¼ cup butter, melted
Pinch salt and pepper
2 tsps lemon juice
¼ tsp each dried thyme, sage and marjoram
1 shallot, finely chopped
10 oysters, shelled

**Step 2** Place the prepared fish on lightly-greased foil, shiny side up.

**Step 3** Spoon the stuffing into the cavity of the fish.

**Step 4** Pat the fish to distribute the stuffing evenly.

**1.** Have the fishmonger gut and bone the fish, leaving on the head and tail. Rinse the salmon inside and pat dry.
**2.** Place the fish on lightly oiled foil. Combine all the stuffing ingredients, mixing so that the oysters do not fall apart.
**3.** Open the cavity of the fish and spoon in the stuffing.
**4.** Close the fish and pat out gently so that the stuffing is evenly distributed. Close the foil loosely around the fish and place it directly on the oven shelf or in a large roasting pan. Cook at 400°F for about 40 minutes. Unwrap the fish and slide it onto a serving plate. Peel off the top layer of skin if desired and garnish with lemon slices.

## Cook's Notes

**Time**
Preparation takes about 25 minutes and cooking takes about 40 minutes.

**Preparation**
If asked, the fishmonger will gut and bone the fish for you. Fish may also be stuffed with the bone in, but this makes it more difficult to serve.

**Variation**
Substitute mussels, clams or shrimp for the oysters in the stuffing. Add chopped celery or red or green pepper, if desired.

SERVES 4-6

# Boatman's Stew

This quick, economical and satisfying fish dish will please any fish lover for lunch or a light supper.

6 tbsps olive oil
2 large onions, sliced
1 red pepper, seeded and sliced
4oz mushrooms, sliced
1lb canned tomatoes
Pinch salt and pepper
Pinch dried thyme
1½ cups water
2lb whitefish fillets, skinned
½ cup white wine
2 tbsps chopped parsley

Use a sharp knife to cut the onion into thin crosswise slices.

**1.** Heat the oil in a large saucepan and add the onions. Cook until beginning to look transluscent. Add the pepper and cook until the vegetables are softened.

**2.** Add the mushrooms and the tomatoes and bring the mixture to the boil.

**3.** Add thyme, salt, pepper and water and simmer for about 30 minutes.

**4.** Add the fish and wine and cook until the fish flakes easily, about 15 minutes. Stir in parsley.

**5.** To serve, place a piece of toasted French bread in the bottom of the soup bowl and spoon over the fish stew.

**Step 1** Cook the onions in the oil along with the peppers until soft.

## Cook's Notes

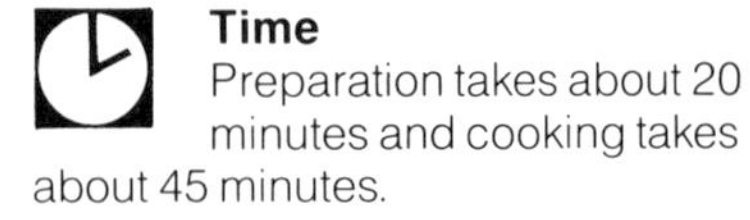

**Time**
Preparation takes about 20 minutes and cooking takes about 45 minutes.

**Variation**
Shellfish may be added with the fish, if desired. Substitute green peppers for red peppers.

**Serving Ideas**
The stew may also be served over rice. Accompany with a green salad.

SERVES 4

# BOILED MAINE LOBSTER

With today's lobster prices, it's hard to imagine that American colonists considered this delectable seafood humble and ordinary.

4 1lb lobsters
Water
Salt or seaweed
1 cup melted butter
Lemon wedges
Parsley sprigs

**Step 5** Once the claws are removed from the lobster by twisting off, crack each claw with a nutcracker, hammer or special lobster cracking tool.

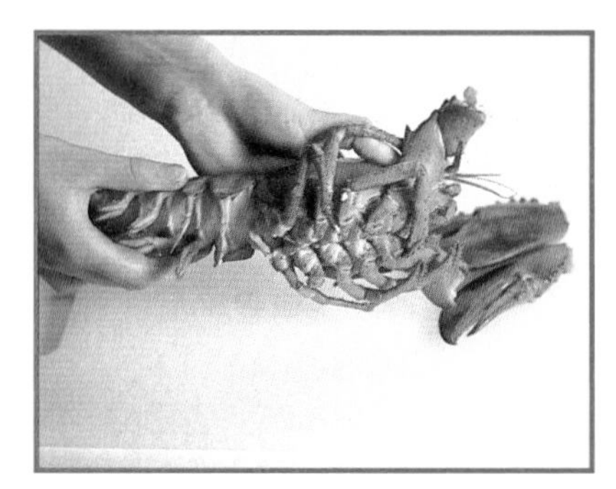

**Step 6** Separate body from tail by arching the lobster backwards. Break off the flipper and push the tail meat out with a fork.

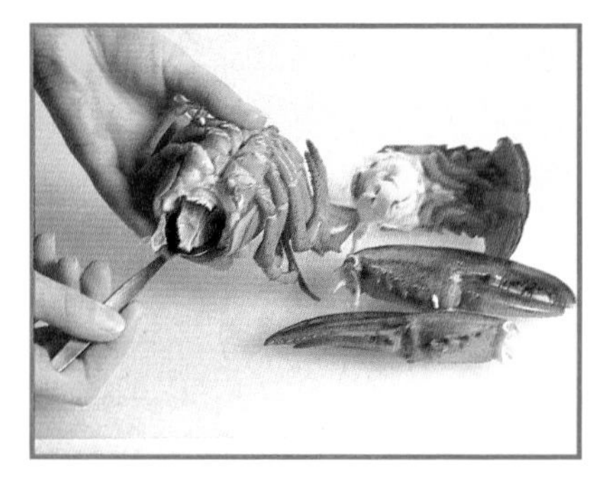

**Step 7** Remove the back from the body and discard the stomach sac and lungs. Retain the tomalley or liver to eat, if desired, and crack open the body to extract any remaining meat.

**1.** Fill a large stock pot full of water and add salt or a piece of seaweed. Bring the water to the boil and then turn off the heat.

**2.** Place the live lobsters into the pot, keeping your hand well away from the claws. Lower them in claws first.

**3.** Bring the water slowly back to the boil and cook the lobsters for about 15 minutes, or until they turn bright red.

**4.** Remove them from the water and drain briefly on paper towels. Place on a plate and garnish the plate with lemon wedges and parsley sprigs. Serve with individual dishes of melted butter for dipping.

## Cook's Notes

**Time**
Allow about 20 minutes for the water to boil, and 15 minutes for cooking the lobster.

**Preparation**
This method of cooking puts the lobster gently to sleep and makes the lobster flesh much more tender. Claws can be partially cracked before serving, if desired.

**Cook's Tip**
Lobster may be cooked in this way for a variety of recipes that are based on pre-cooked lobster.

SERVES 4-6

# MAPLE SYRUP MOUSSE

Pure maple syrup is a true delicacy. It isn't cheap, but the flavor it gives special recipes like this mousse makes it worth its price.

4 eggs, separated
2 extra egg whites
¾ cup maple syrup
1 cup heavy cream
Chopped pecans or walnuts to decorate

1. Place the syrup in a saucepan and bring to the boil. Continue boiling to reduce the syrup by one quarter.
2. Beat the egg yolks until thick and lemon colored.
3. Pour the maple syrup onto the egg yolks in a thin, steady stream, beating with an electric mixer. Continue beating until the mixture has cooled.
4. Beat the egg whites until stiff but not dry and whip the cream until soft peaks form.
5. Fold the cream and egg whites into the maple mixture and spoon into a serving bowl or individual glasses. Refrigerate until slightly set and top with chopped walnuts or pecans to serve.

**Step 3** Pour the hot syrup onto the beaten egg yolks in a thin, steady stream, beating constantly.

**Step 5** Fold the cream and the egg whites into the maple mixture using a rubber spatula or large metal spoon.

## Cook's Notes

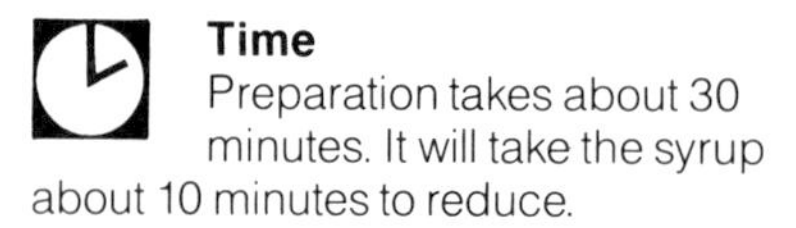

**Time**
Preparation takes about 30 minutes. It will take the syrup about 10 minutes to reduce.

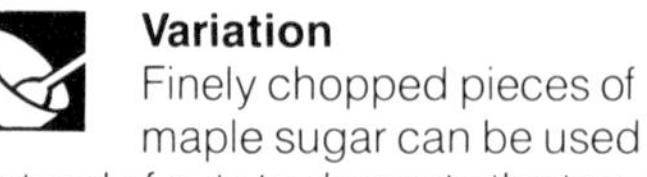

**Variation**
Finely chopped pieces of maple sugar can be used instead of nuts to decorate the top of the mousse.

**Watchpoint**
Be careful when boiling the syrup, since it can burn very easily.

MAKES 1 PIE

# Pumpkin Pie

American Indians taught the settlers about the pumpkin and it was one of the crops that helped to save their lives.

**Pastry**
1 cup all-purpose flour
Pinch salt
¼ cup butter, margarine or lard
Cold milk

**Pumpkin Filling**
1lb cooked and mashed pumpkin
2 eggs
1 cup evaporated milk
½ cup brown sugar
1 tsp ground cinnamon
¼ tsp ground allspice
Pinch nutmeg
Pecan halves for decoration

**Step 1** Rub the fat into the flour until the mixture resembles fine breadcrumbs.

**1.** To prepare the pastry, sift the flour and a pinch of salt into a mixing bowl. Rub in the fat until the mixture resembles fine breadcrumbs. Stir in enough cold milk to bring the mixture together into a firm ball. Cover and chill for about 30 minutes before use.

**2.** Roll out the pastry on a lightly-floured surface to a circle about 11 inches in diameter.

**Step 1** Add enough cold milk to bring the mixture together into a firm ball.

**Step 3** Roll the pastry around a lightly-floured rolling pin and then lower it into the dish.

**3.** Wrap the pastry around a lightly-floured rolling pin and lower it into a 10 inch round pie dish.

**4.** Press the pastry into the dish and flute the edge or crimp with a fork.

**5.** Prick the base lightly with the tines of a fork.

**6.** Combine all the filling ingredients in a mixing bowl and beat with an electric mixer until smooth. Alternatively, use a food processor. Pour into the pie crust and bake in a pre-heated 425°F oven. Bake for 10 minutes at this temperature and then lower the temperature to 350°F and bake for a further 40-50 minutes, or until the filling is set. Decorate with a circle of pecan halves.

## Cook's Notes

**Time**
Preparation takes about 30 minutes and cooking takes about 50-60 minutes.

**Cook's Tip**
Pricking the base of the pastry lightly will prevent it from rising up in an air bubble in the middle of the pie.

**Serving Ideas**
Serve warm or cold with whipped cream.

MAKES 1 PIE

# BLUEBERRY PIE

Americans love pie for dessert. In New England, where blueberries flourish, it's only natural to find them in a pie.

Double quantity pastry for Pumpkin Pie recipe

**Filling**

1lb blueberries
2 tbsps cornstarch
4 tbsps water
2 tbsps lemon juice
1 cup sugar
1 egg beaten with a pinch of salt

**1.** Prepare the pastry in the same way as for the Pumpkin Pie recipe.

**2.** Divide the pastry in half and roll out one half to form the base. Use a floured rolling pin to lower it into the dish, and press it against the sides. Chill the pastry in the dish and the remaining half of the pastry while preparing the filling.

**3.** Place the fruit in a bowl and mix the cornstarch with the water and lemon juice. Pour it over the fruit, add the sugar and mix together gently.

**4.** Spoon the fruit filling into the pastry base.

**5.** Roll out the remaining pastry on a lightly-floured surface and cut it into strips.

**6.** Use the strips to make a lattice pattern on top of the filling and press the edges to stick them to the pastry base. Cut off any excess pastry.

**7.** Using your fingers or a fork, crimp the edges to decorate.

**8.** Brush the crimped edge of the pastry and the lattice strips lightly with the beaten egg and bake in a pre-heated 425°F oven for about 10 minutes. Reduce the heat to 350°F and bake for a further 40-45 minutes. Serve warm or cold.

**Step 4** Spoon the blueberry filling into the pastry-lined pie dish.

**Step 6** Cut strips of pastry and use to make a lattice pattern on top of the pie.

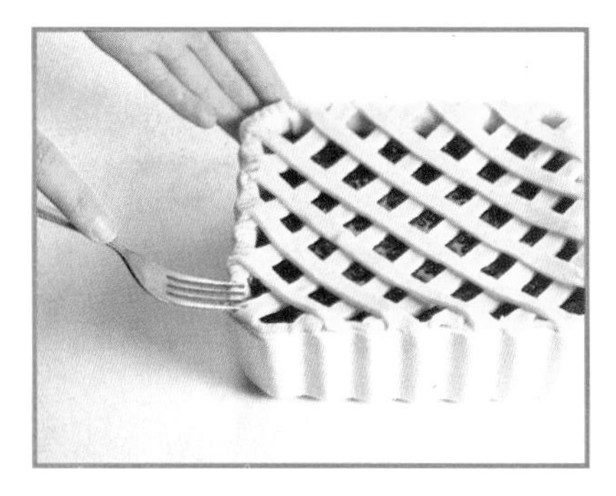

**Step 7** Crimp by hand, or use a fork to make a decorative edge.

## Cook's Notes

**Time**
Preparation takes about 30-40 minutes and cooking takes about 50-55 minutes.

**Cook's Tip**
Taste the blueberries before deciding how much sugar to add – it may not be necessary to add the full amount.

**Variation**
Other fruits such as raspberries or blackberries may be used in the pie instead of blueberries.

# Steamed Cranberry Pudding

Colonial women brought their favorite recipes with them and learned to adapt them to the local produce, hence an English steamed pudding with American cranberries.

1½ cups all-purpose flour
2 tsps baking powder
Pinch salt
1 cup chopped cranberries
1 small piece candied ginger, finely chopped
2 eggs, well beaten
½ cup honey
6 tbsps milk
Orange sauce
Grated juice and rind of 1 orange
Grated juice and rind of ½ lemon
½ cup sugar
1 tbsp cornstarch
¾ cup water
1 tbsp butter or margarine

**1.** Sift the dry ingredients together in a large bowl.

**2.** Toss in the cranberries and ginger.

**3.** Mix the eggs, honey and milk together and gradually stir into the dry ingredients and the cranberries. Do not over stir. The mixture should not be uniformly pink.

**4.** The mixture should be of thick dropping consistency. Add more milk if necessary.

**5.** Spoon the mixture into a well-buttered pudding basin or bowl, cover with buttered foil and tie the top securely.

**6.** Place the bowl on a rack in a pan of boiling water to come halfway up the sides. Cover the pan and steam the pudding for about 1½ hours, or until a skewer inserted into the center comes out clean. Leave to cool in the basin or bowl for about 10 minutes, loosen the edge with a knife and turn out onto a plate.

**7.** Meanwhile, place the sugar and cornstarch into a saucepan with the orange juice and rind and lemon juice and rind. Add the water, stirring to blend well. Bring to the boil and allow to simmer until clear. Beat in the butter at the end and serve with the pudding.

**Step 3** Stir the liquid ingredients into the dry until well blended and of thick dropping consistency.

**Step 5** Spoon into the prepared bowl or basin. Cover the top with foil and tie securely with string.

## Cook's Notes

**Time**
Preparation takes about 30-40 minutes and cooking takes about 1½ hours.

**Buying Guide**
Fresh cranberries are available in greengrocers and larger supermarkets. Frozen cranberries are also available and may be substituted for fresh.

**Variation**
If desired, use ground ginger instead of the candied ginger.

MAKES 1 LOAF

# Spiced Cranberry Nut Bread

Sassamanesh was the colorful Indian name for this equally colorful berry. Here, it brightens up a quickly prepared bread.

2 cups all-purpose flour
1 tsp baking powder
1 cup sugar
1 tsp baking soda
Pinch salt
¼ tsp ground nutmeg
¼ tsp ground ginger
½ cup orange juice
2 tbsps butter or margarine, melted
4 tbsps water
1 egg
1 cup fresh cranberries, roughly chopped
1 cup hazelnuts, roughly chopped

**Step 1** Sift the dry ingredients into a bowl and make a well in the center.

**1.** Sift the dry ingredients and spices into a large mixing bowl. Make a well in the center of the dry ingredients and pour in the orange juice, melted butter or margarine, water and egg. Using a wooden spoon, beat the liquid mixture, gradually drawing in the flour from the outside edge.

**2.** Add the cranberries and nuts and stir to mix completely.

**3.** Lightly grease a loaf pan about 9 x 5″. Press a strip of wax paper on the base and up the sides. Lightly grease the paper and flour the whole inside of the pan. Spoon or pour in the bread mixture and bake in a pre-heated 325°F oven for about 1 hour, or until a skewer inserted into the center of the loaf comes out clean.

**4.** Remove from the pan, carefully peel off the paper and cool on a wire rack. Lightly dust with confectioner's sugar, if desired, and cut into slices to serve.

**Step 1** Pour the liquid ingredients into the well and, using a wooden spoon, stir to gradually incorporate the flour from the outside edge.

**Step 2** Fold in the cranberries and the nuts.

## Cook's Notes

**Time**
Preparation takes about 25 minutes and cooking takes about 1 hour.

**Watchpoint**
Be sure to bake the bread mixture as soon as possible after the baking powder has been added or the bread will not rise the way it should.

**Serving Ideas**
Serve warm with butter or cream cheese with tea or coffee. May also be served cold.

# STEAMED BROWN BREAD

This is the classic accompaniment to one of Boston's famous dishes – baked beans. It's traditional to bake it in a can!

1½ cups fine cornmeal
2 cups wholewheat flour
1 cup all-purpose flour
Pinch salt
⅓ cup molasses mixed with 1 tsp bicarbonate of soda
1½ cups cold water
Butter or oil
Boiling water

**Step 3** Fill the cans with the bread mixture to about two thirds full.

**Step 3** Grease rinsed out cans generously with butter or margarine.

**Step 4** Cover the tops of the cans tightly with foil and place on a rack in boiling water to come halfway up the sides.

**1.** Sift the dry ingredients into a large bowl and return the bran to the bowl.

**2.** Mix the molasses, bicarbonate of soda and water together. Make a well in the center of the flour and pour in the mixture. Mix just until well blended.

**3.** Use a large can from canned tomatoes, coffee or canned fruit. Alternatively, use about 6 smaller cans. Wash them well and remove the labels. Grease generously with oil or butter. Spoon the bread mixture to come about two thirds of the way up the sides of the cans.

**4.** Cover the tops of the cans tightly with buttered or oiled foil. Place them on a rack in a deep saucepan. Pour enough boiling water around the cans to come about halfway up the sides. Allow water to bubble gently to steam the bread for 3-4 hours in the covered pan. Add more boiling water as necessary during cooking.

**5.** The bread is ready when a skewer inserted into the center of the bread comes out clean.

## Cook's Notes

**Time**
Preparation takes about 20 minutes and cooking takes about 3-4 hours. Cooking time may be slightly shorter for smaller cans.

**Variation**
Raisins, chopped dates or prunes may be added to the bread mixture if desired.

**Serving Ideas**
This bread is the traditional accompaniment to Boston Baked Beans. Alternatively, serve warm with butter or cream cheese.

# Southern Cooking

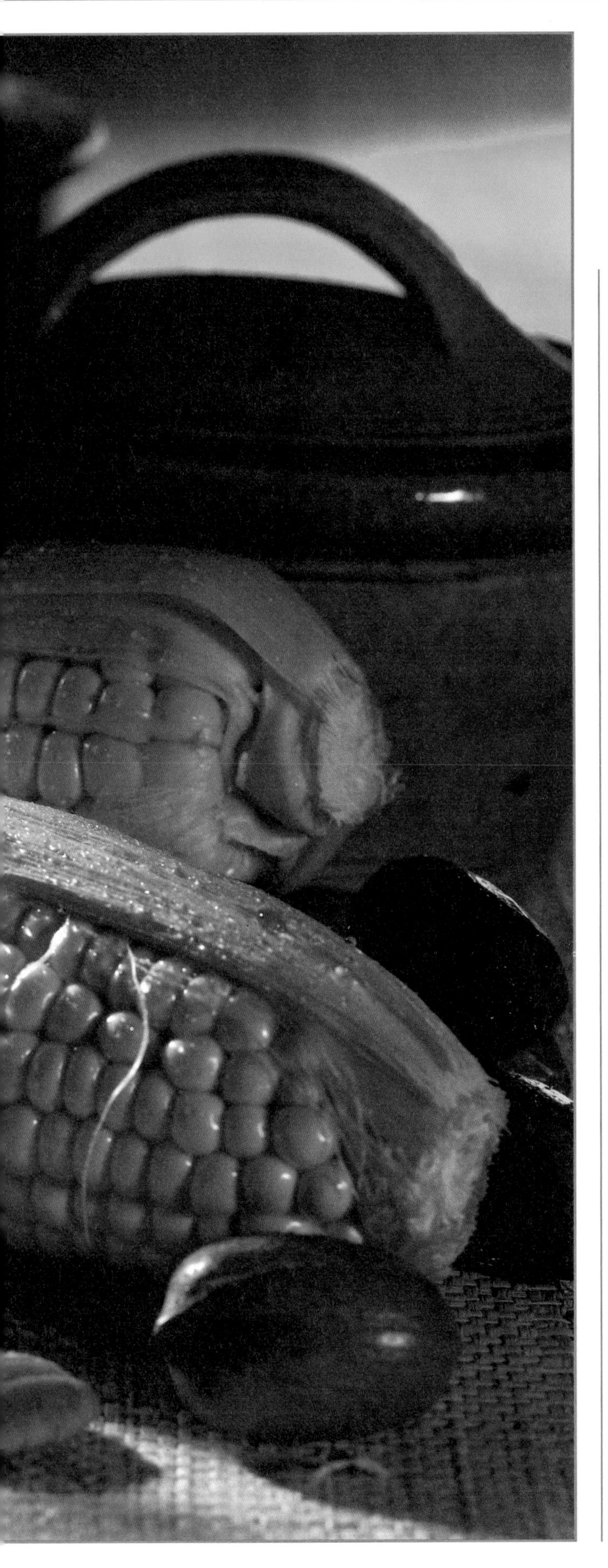

# INTRODUCTION

A thread of similarity runs through the cuisine of America in all its regional forms, modified slightly by the regions themselves, by the people who settled there, the crops they found or cultivated and the indigenous game of the forest or fish of rivers and sea. The South, of course, has its specialties, all with their own particular style and yet all particularly American.

Famous in history for its gracious living, elegant plantation houses and lavish entertaining, the South is also known for its farming heritage, with its hearty, unpretentious fare made up of whatever the cook had to hand, simmered slowly while the work of the day went on. These stews are every bit as satisfying as those of provincial France, and deserve to be better known.

The area of the United States that calls itself the South takes in a lot of territory down the Eastern Seaboard and around the Gulf of Mexico, along the Mississippi, through the mountains of Arkansas and Tennessee and into the rolling hills of Kentucky. But wherever you go in this region, there are familiar foods like biscuits or corn muffins that can't be surpassed anywhere, and that make you feel instantly at home.

SERVES 4-6

# CORN AND POTATO CHOWDER

Such a filling soup, this is really a complete meal in a bowl. Corn is a favorite ingredient in Southern cooking.

6 medium potatoes, peeled
Chicken or vegetable stock
1 onion, finely chopped
2 tbsps butter or margarine
1 tbsp flour
4oz cooked ham, chopped
4 ears fresh corn or about 4oz canned or frozen corn
3 cups milk
Salt and dash tabasco
Finely chopped parsley

**1.** Quarter the potatoes and place them in a deep saucepan. Add stock to cover and the onion, and bring the mixture to the boil. Lower the heat and simmer, partially covered, until the potatoes are soft, about 15-20 minutes.

**2.** Drain the potatoes, reserving ¾ pint of the cooking liquid. Mash the potatoes and combine with reserved liquid.

**3.** Melt the butter or margarine in a clean pan, add the ham and cook briefly. Stir in the flour and pour over the potato mixture, mixing well.

**4.** If using fresh corn, remove the husks and silk and, holding one end of the corn, stand the ear upright. Use a large, sharp knife and cut against the cob vertically from top to bottom just scraping off the kernels. Add the corn and milk to the potato mixture and bring almost to the boil. Do not boil the corn rapidly as this will toughen it. Add a pinch of salt and a dash of tabasco, and garnish with parsley before serving.

**Step 3** Pour the potato mixture onto the flour and ham gradually, stirring constantly until well blended.

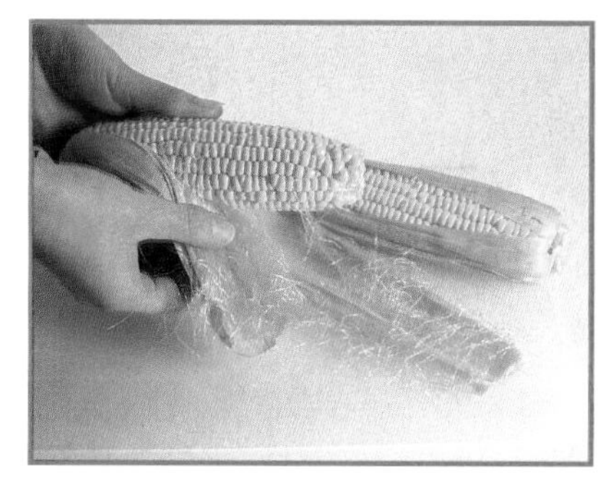

**Step 4** Remove the husks and silk from the ears of corn.

**Step 4** Use a sharp knife to cut the kernels off the cobs.

**Time**
Preparation takes about 25 minutes and cooking takes about 25-30 minutes.

**Preparation**
The soup may be prepared in advance up to adding the corn. Bring the mixture to a rapid boil, turn down the heat and then add the corn and continue with the recipe. This soup does not freeze well.

**Cook's Tip**
When cooking corn on its own or adding it to other ingredients, add the salt just before serving. Cooking corn with salt toughens it.

SERVES 4

# VIRGINIA PEANUT SOUP

Peanuts, popular all over the South, make a velvety rich soup that is easily made from ordinary store cupboard ingredients.

4 tbsps butter or margarine
2 tbsps flour
1 cup creamy peanut butter
¼ tsp celery seed
2½ cups chicken stock
½ cup dry sherry
½ cup coarsely chopped peanuts

**Step 2** Once the peanut butter and celery seed are added, gradually pour in the stock, stirring or whisking constantly.

**Step 4** Add the sherry to the soup before serving.

**1.** Melt the butter or margarine in a medium saucepan. Remove from the heat and stir in the flour.

**2.** Add the peanut butter and celery seed. Gradually pour on the stock, stirring constantly.

**3.** Return the pan to the heat and simmer gently for about 15 minutes. Do not allow to boil rapidly.

**4.** Stir in the sherry and ladle into a tureen or individual bowls. Sprinkle with the chopped peanuts.

## Cook's Notes

**Time**
Preparation takes about 15 minutes and cooking takes about 15 minutes.

**Variation**
For a crunchier texture, add 2 sticks of finely diced celery to the butter or margarine and cook until slightly softened before adding the flour.

**Preparation**
The soup is slightly difficult to reheat, so it is best prepared just before serving.

SERVES 4

# She Crab Soup

A female crab, with roe intact, is needed for a truly authentic soup. However, exceptions can be made with results just as delicious.

1 large crab, cooked
3 tbsps butter or margarine
1 onion, very finely chopped
2 tbsps flour
4 cups milk
6 tbsps sherry
Pinch salt, white pepper and ground mace
½ cup heavy cream, whipped
Red caviar

1. To dress the crab, take off all the legs and the large claws. Crack the large claws and legs and extract the meat.

2. Turn the crab shell over and press up with thumbs to push out the underbody. Cut this piece in quarters and use a skewer to pick out the meat. Discard the stomach sac and the lungs (dead man's fingers). Set the white meat aside with the claw meat.

3. Using a teaspoon, scrape out the brown meat from inside the shell and reserve it. If the roe is present reserve that, too.

4. Melt the butter or margarine in a medium saucepan and soften the onion for about 3 minutes. Do not allow to brown.

5. Stir in the flour and milk. Bring to the boil and then immediately turn down the heat to simmer. Add the brown meat from the crab and cook gently for about 20 minutes.

6. Add the sherry, salt, pepper, mace, white crab meat and roe. Cook a further 5 minutes.

7. Top each serving with a spoonful of whipped cream and red caviar.

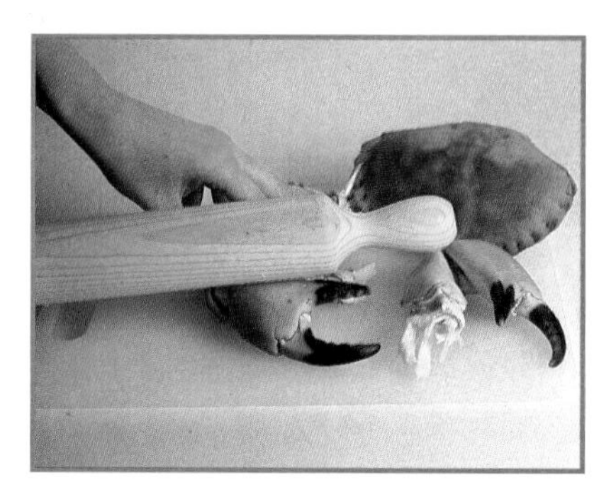

**Step 1** Remove the legs and large claws of the crab. Use a rolling pin or meat mallet to crack the large claws and legs to extract the meat.

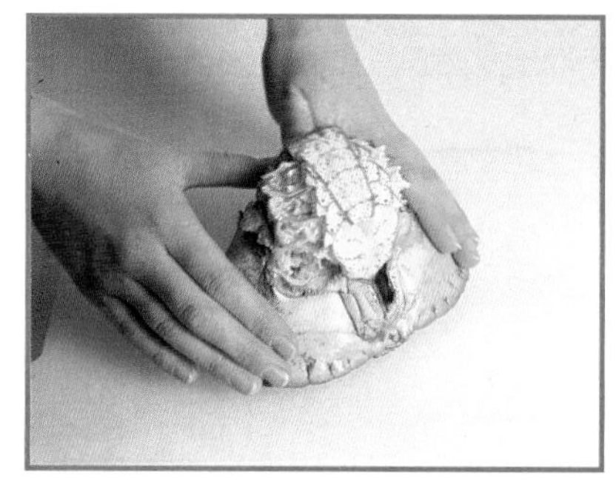

**Step 2** Turn the crab shell over and push out the underbody. Discard stomach sac and lungs.

**Step 3** Using a teaspoon, scrape out the brown meat from inside the shell.

## Cook's Notes

**Time**
Preparation takes about 35-40 minutes and cooking takes about 25 minutes.

**Variation**
Frozen crab meat may be substituted. Use about 4-6oz of white crab meat and omit the addition of the brown body meat. Do not use a dressed crab as the brown meat will usually have breadcrumbs added to it.

**Buying Guide**
Crabs are available freshly boiled from fishmongers. Buy a crab that is heavy for its size.

SERVES 2-4

# Sea Island Shrimp

Although this is a recipe from the Carolinas, it is popular everywhere succulent shrimp are available.

2 dozen raw large shrimp, unpeeled
4 tbsps butter or margarine
1 small red pepper, seeded and finely chopped
2 green onions, finely chopped
½ tsp dry mustard
2 tsps dry sherry
1 tsp Worcester sauce
4oz cooked crab meat
6 tbsps fresh breadcrumbs
1 tbsp chopped parsley
2 tbsps mayonnaise
Salt and pepper
1 small egg, beaten
Grated Parmesan cheese
Paprika

**1.** Remove all of the shrimp shells except for the very tail ends.

**2.** Remove the black veins on the rounded sides.

**3.** Cut the shrimp down the length of the curved side and press each one open.

**4.** Melt half of the butter or margarine in a small pan and cook the pepper to soften, about 3 minutes. Add the green onions and cook a further 2 minutes.

**5.** Combine the peppers with the mustard, sherry, Worcester sauce, crab meat, breadcrumbs, parsley and mayonnaise. Add seasoning and enough egg to bind together.

**6.** Spoon the stuffing onto the shrimp and sprinkle with the Parmesan cheese and paprika. Melt the remaining butter or margarine and drizzle over the shrimp.

**7.** Bake in a pre-heated 350°F oven for about 10 minutes. Serve immediately.

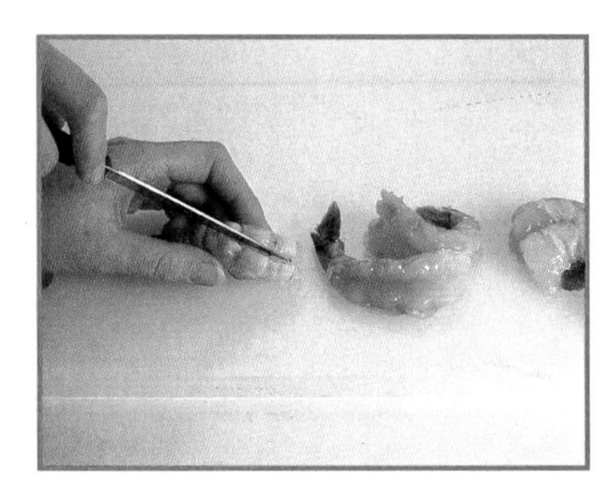

**Step 3** Cut the shrimp down the length of the curved side and press each one open.

**Step 6** Spoon the stuffing into the shrimp, pressing down lightly to spread shrimp open.

**Time**
Preparation takes about 30 minutes and cooking takes about 15 minutes.

**Variation**
Try chopped black or green olives in the stuffing for a change of flavor. Mushrooms may be cooked with the red pepper and green onions, if desired, and other herbs substituted for parsley.

**Serving Ideas**
Serve as an appetizer or as a main course for 2 people.

SERVES 2-4

# Jekyll Island Shrimp

Named for an island off the Georgia coast, this makes a rich appetizer or an elegant main course.

2lbs cooked shrimp
4 tbsps butter, softened
Pinch salt, white pepper and cayenne
1 clove garlic, crushed
6 tbsps fine dry breadcrumbs
2 tbsps chopped parsley
4 tbsps sherry
Lemon wedges or slices

**Step 1** Remove the heads and legs from the shrimp first. Remove any roe at this time.

1. To prepare the shrimp, remove the heads and legs first.
2. Peel off the shells, carefully removing the tail shells.
3. Remove the black vein running down the length of the rounded side with a wooden pick.
4. Arrange shrimp in a shallow casserole or individual dishes.

**Step 2** Pull off the tail shell and carefully remove the very end.

**Step 6** Spread the mixture to completely cover the shrimp.

5. Combine the remaining ingredients, except the lemon garnish, mixing well.
6. Spread the mixture to completely cover the shrimp and place in a pre-heated 375°F oven for about 20 minutes, or until the butter melts and the crumbs become crisp. Garnish with lemon wedges or slices.

## Cook's Notes

**Time**
Preparation takes about 35-40 minutes and cooking takes about 20 minutes.

**Buying Guide**
Freshly cooked shrimp are available from most fishmongers. Frozen shrimp will not be as good.

SERVES 4

# OREGANO OYSTERS

The combination of oregano and the anise taste of Pernod is an unusual but very complementary one, especially with fresh oysters.

1 tbsp butter or margarine
1 clove garlic, crushed
1 tbsp chopped parsley
1 tbsp chopped fresh oregano or 1½ tsps dried oregano
1 tbsp Pernod
¾ cup heavy cream
Salt and pepper
24 oysters on the half shell
12 strips bacon, cooked and crumbled
Coarse salt

**1.** Melt the butter or margarine in a saucepan. Add the garlic and cook to soften, but do not brown.

**2.** Add the parsley, oregano, Pernod and cream. Bring to the boil and lower the heat to simmering. Strain on any liquid from the oysters and then loosen them from their shells with a small, sharp knife.

**3.** Cook the mixture until reduced by about one quarter and slightly thickened. Test the seasoning and set the mixture aside.

**4.** Pour about 1 inch coarse salt into a baking pan.

**5.** Place the oysters on top of the salt and twist the shells into the salt so that they stand level.

**6.** Spoon some of the cream over each oyster and sprinkle with the crumbled bacon.

**7.** Bake in a pre-heated 400°F oven for 15-18 minutes. Serve immediately.

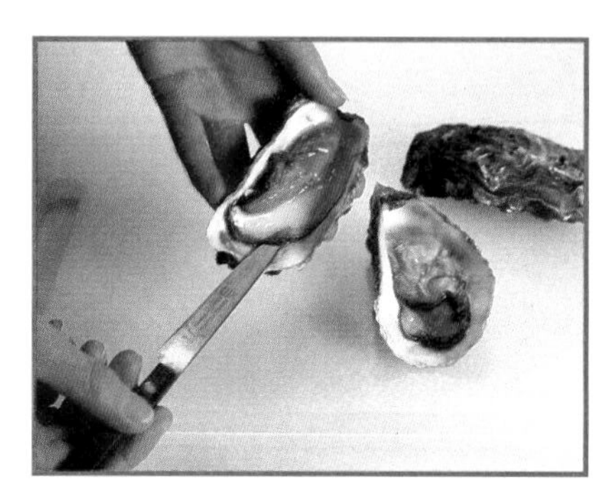

**Step 2** Using a small, sharp knife, loosen the oyster from its shell.

**Step 3** Cook mixture until reduced by a quarter.

**Step 5** Place the oysters in their shells into the coarse salt, twisting so that they stand level.

**Time**
Preparation takes about 25 minutes. Cooking takes about 20-25 minutes including time to cook the bacon.

**Buying Guide**
It is possible to purchase oysters already on the half shell. If you need to open them yourself, buy a special oyster knife with a short, strong blade. Insert the blade at the hinge and twist until shells separate.

**Variation**
If oysters are unavailable, use mussels or clams.

SERVES 4

# SNAPPER WITH FENNEL AND ORANGE SALAD

Red snapper brings Florida to mind. Combined with oranges, it makes a lovely summer meal.

Oil
4 even-sized red snapper, cleaned, heads and tails on
2 heads fennel
2 oranges
Juice of 1 lemon
3 tbsps light salad oil
Pinch sugar, salt and black pepper

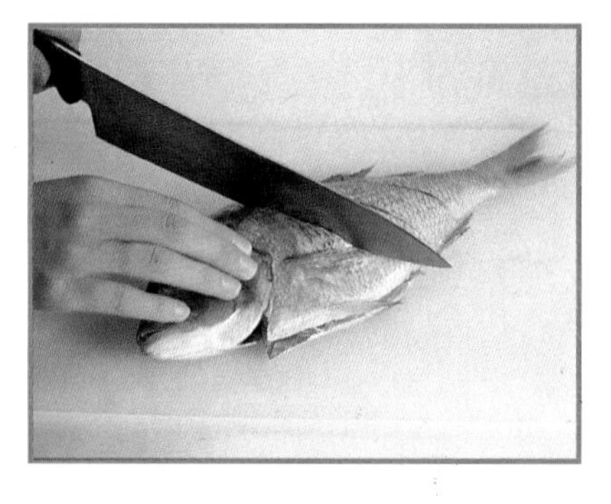

**Step 1** Make three cuts in the side of each fish for even cooking.

**1.** Brush both sides of the fish with oil and cut three slits in the sides of each. Sprinkle with a little of the lemon juice, reserving the rest.

**2.** Slice the fennel in half and remove the cores. Slice thinly. Also slice the green tops and chop the feathery herb to use in the dressing.

**3.** Peel the oranges, removing all the white pith.

**4.** Cut the oranges into segments. Peel and segment over a bowl to catch the juice.

**5.** Add lemon juice to any orange juice collected in the bowl. Add the oil, salt, pepper and a pinch of sugar, if necessary. Mix well and add the fennel, green herb tops and orange segments, stirring carefully. Broil the fish 3-5 minutes per side, depending on thickness. Serve the fish with the heads and tails on, accompanied by the salad.

**Step 2** Slice the fennel in half and remove the cores.

**Step 4** Peel and segment the oranges over a bowl to catch the juice.

## Cook's Notes

**Time**
Preparation takes about 30 minutes and cooking takes about 6-10 minutes.

**Variation**
Other fish may be used in the recipe if snapper is not available. Substitute red mullet or any of the exotic fish from the Seychelles Islands or Hawaii.

**Cook's Tip**
When broiling whole fish, making several cuts on the side of each fish will help to cook it quickly and evenly throughout.

SERVES 4

# BROILED FLOUNDER

A mayonnaise-like topping puffs to a golden brown to give this mild-flavored fish a piquant taste.

4 double fillets of flounder
2 eggs, separated
Pinch salt, pepper and dry mustard
1 cup peanut oil
4 tbsps pickle relish
1 tbsp chopped parsley
1 tbsp lemon juice
Dash tabasco

**1.** Place the egg yolks in a blender, food processor or deep bowl.

**2.** Blend in the salt, pepper and mustard. If blending by hand, use a small whisk.

**3.** If using the machine, pour the oil through the funnel in a thin, steady stream with the machine running. If mixing by hand, add oil a few drops at a time, beating well in between each addition.

**4.** When half the oil has been added, the rest may be added in a thin steady stream while beating constantly with a small whisk.

**5.** Mix in the relish, parsley, lemon juice and tabasco. Beat the egg whites until stiff but not dry and fold into the mayonnaise.

**6.** Broil the fish about 2 inches from the heat source for about 6-10 minutes, depending on the thickness of the fillets.

**7.** Spread the sauce over each fillet and broil for 3-5 minutes longer, or until the sauce puffs and browns lightly.

**Step 4** Add the oil to the egg yolk mixture in a thin, steady stream while beating constantly.

**Step 5** Fold stiffly-beaten egg whites thoroughly into the mayonnaise.

**Step 7** Spread or spoon the sauce over each fish fillet before broiling.

**Time**
Preparation takes about 20 minutes. If preparing the mayonnaise by hand this will take about 15-20 minutes. The fish takes 9-15 minutes to cook.

**Watchpoint**
When preparing the mayonnaise either by machine or by hand, do not add the oil too quickly or the mayonnaise will curdle. If it does curdle, beat another egg yolk in a bowl and gradually beat in the curdled mixture. This should bring it back together again.

**Variation**
This same topping may be used on other fish besides flounder.

**Serving Ideas**
Serve with broiled tomatoes.

SERVES 4

# River Inn Quail

Definitely a dish for special occasions, this is deceptively simple, impressive and perfect for entertaining.

12 dressed quail
6 tbsps butter
3 tbsps oil
1 clove garlic, crushed
4oz mushrooms, sliced
4 tbsps chopped pecans or walnuts
4 tbsps raisins
1 cup chicken stock
Salt and pepper
3 tbsps sherry
1 tbsp cornstarch
1 tsp tomato paste (optional)
1 bunch watercress

**1.** Rub each quail inside and out with butter.

**2.** Pour the oil into a baking pan large enough to hold the quail comfortably. Cook in a pre-heated 350°F oven for about 25 minutes, uncovered.

**3.** Remove the pan from the oven and place under a pre-heated broiler to brown the quail.

**4.** Add garlic, mushrooms, pecans, raisins and stock to the quail.

**5.** Replace in the oven and continue to cook, uncovered, until the quail are tender – a further 20 minutes.

**6.** Remove the quail and other ingredients to a serving dish, leaving the pan juices behind.

**7.** Mix the cornstarch and sherry and add it to the pan, stirring constantly.

**8.** Place the pan over medium heat and cook until the cornstarch thickens and clears. If the baking pan isn't flameproof, transfer the ingredients to a saucepan before thickening the sauce. Add tomato paste, if necessary, for color.

**9.** Pour the sauce over the quail and garnish with watercress to serve.

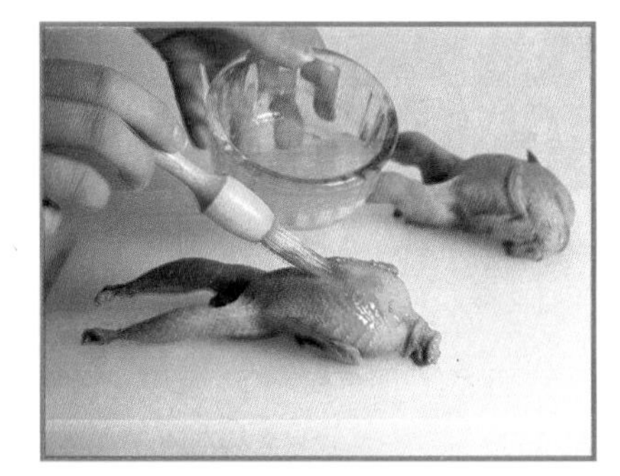

**Step 1** Rub the inside and outside of each quail with some of the softened butter.

**Step 3** Remove the precooked quail from the oven and place under a pre-heated broiler for about 3-4 minutes until golden brown.

## Cook's Notes

**Time**
Preparation takes about 25 minutes and cooking takes about 45-50 minutes.

**Serving Ideas**
Serve the quail with rice or potatoes and a vegetable accompaniment such as Quick Fried Herbed Vegetables or Minted Mixed Vegetables.

**Watchpoint**
Quail are very tender birds and can dry out easily. Do not prepare the dish in advance and reheat.

SERVES 6

# Cornish Hens with Southern Stuffing

Cornbread makes a delicious stuffing and a change from the usual breadcrumb variations.

Full quantity Corn Muffin recipe
2 tbsps butter or margarine
2 sticks celery, finely chopped
2 green onions, chopped
2oz chopped country or Smithfield ham
2oz chopped pecans
2 tbsps bourbon
Salt and pepper
1 egg, beaten
6 Cornish game hens
12 strips bacon

**1.** Prepare the Corn Muffins according to the recipe, allow to cool completely and crumble finely.

**2.** Melt the butter or margarine and soften the celery and onions for about 5 minutes over very low heat.

**3.** Add the ham, pecans, cornbread crumbs and seasoning. Add bourbon and just enough egg to make a stuffing that holds together but is not too wet.

**4.** Remove the giblets from the hens, if included, and fill each bird with stuffing. Sew up the cavity with fine string or close with small skewers.

**5.** Criss-cross 2 strips of bacon over the breasts of each bird and tie or skewer the ends of the bacon together.

**6.** Roast in a pre-heated 400°F oven for 45 minutes – 1 hour, or until tender. Baste the hens with the pan juices as they cook.

**7.** Remove the bacon, if desired, during the last 15 minutes to brown the breasts, or serve with the bacon after removing the string or skewers.

**Step 3** Add just enough egg to the stuffing mixture to hold it together.

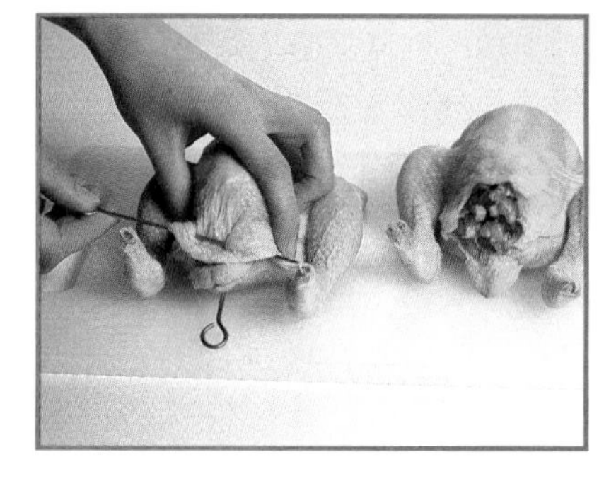

**Step 4** Sew up the cavity of the stuffed birds with fine string, or close with small skewers.

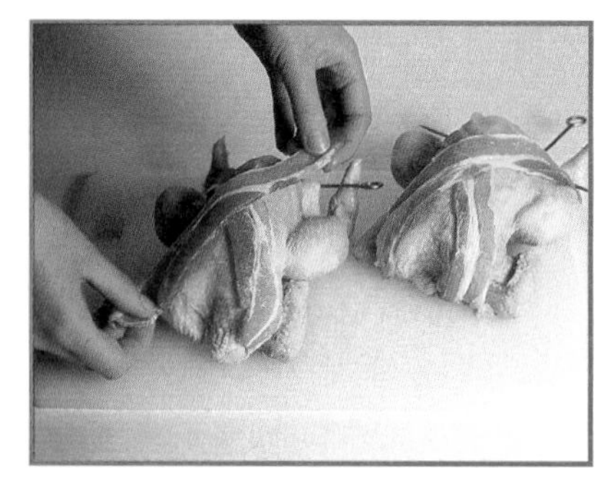

**Step 5** Criss-cross two strips of bacon over the breast of each bird and tie or skewer the ends together.

## Cook's Notes

**Time**
Preparation takes about 45-50 minutes and cooking takes about 14 minutes for the cornbread and 45 minutes – 1 hour for the hens.

**Variation**
The stuffing may also be used to stuff a whole chicken or prepared in double or triple quantities for a turkey.

SERVES 4

# FRIED CHICKEN

No discussion of Southern cooking is complete without mentioning fried chicken. Eating it is even better than talking about it!

3lb frying chicken portions
2 eggs
2 cups flour
1 tsp each salt, paprika and sage
½ tsp black pepper
Pinch cayenne pepper (optional)
Oil for frying
Parsley or watercress

**Step 2** Dip the chicken pieces in the egg to coat them well.

**Step 4** Coat the chicken on all sides with flour, shaking off the excess.

**Step 6** Fry the chicken skin side first for 12 minutes, turn over and fry a further 12 minutes.

**1.** Rinse chicken and pat dry.

**2.** Beat the eggs in a large bowl and add the chicken one piece at a time, turning to coat.

**3.** Mix flour and seasonings in a large paper or plastic bag.

**4.** Place chicken pieces coated with egg into the bag one at a time, close bag tightly and shake to coat each piece of chicken. Alternatively, dip each coated chicken piece in a bowl of seasoned flour, shaking off the excess.

**5.** Heat oil in a large frying pan to the depth of about ½ inch.

**6.** When the oil is hot, add the chicken skin side down first. Fry about 12 minutes and then turn over. Fry a further 12 minutes or until the juices run clear.

**7.** Drain the chicken on paper towels and serve immediately. Garnish serving plate with parsley or watercress.

## Cook's Notes

**Time**
Preparation takes about 20 minutes and cooking takes about 24 minutes.

**Preparation**
The chicken should not be crowded in the frying pan. If your pan is small, fry the chicken in several batches.

**Cook's Tip**
When coating anything for frying, be sure to coat it just before cooking. If left to stand, coating will usually become very soggy.

SERVES 6

# COUNTRY CAPTAIN CHICKEN

A flavorful dish named for a sea captain with a taste for the spicy cuisine of India.

3lbs chicken portions
Seasoned flour
6 tbsps oil
1 medium onion, chopped
1 medium green pepper, seeded and chopped
1 clove garlic, crushed
Pinch salt and pepper
2 tsps curry powder
2 14oz cans tomatoes
2 tsps chopped parsley
1 tsp chopped marjoram
4 tbsps currants or raisins
4oz blanched almond halves

**1.** Remove skin from the chicken and dredge with flour, shaking off the excess.

**2.** Heat the oil and brown the chicken on all sides until golden. Remove to an ovenproof casserole.

**3.** Pour off all but 2 tbsps of the oil. Add the onion, pepper and garlic and cook slowly to soften.

**4.** Add the seasonings and curry powder and cook, stirring frequently, for 2 minutes. Add the tomatoes, parsley, marjoram and bring to the boil. Pour the sauce over the chicken, cover and cook in a pre-heated 350°F oven for 45 minutes. Add the currants or raisins during the last 15 minutes.

**5.** Meanwhile, toast the almonds in the oven on a baking sheet along with the chicken. Stir them frequently and watch carefully. Sprinkle over the chicken just before serving.

**Step 4** Add the curry powder to the vegetables in the frying pan and cook for two minutes over low heat, stirring frequently.

**Step 4** Cook the remaining sauce ingredients and pour over the chicken.

**Step 5** Toast the almonds on a baking sheet in the oven until light golden brown.

## Cook's Notes

**Time**
Preparation takes about 30 minutes and cooking takes about 50 minutes.

**Preparation**
Country Captain Chicken can be prepared completely ahead of time and reheated for about 20 minutes in a moderate oven.

**Serving Ideas**
If desired, serve the chicken with an accompaniment of rice.

SERVES 6-8

# BRUNSWICK STEW

Peppers, potatoes, corn, tomatoes, onions and lima beans are staple ingredients in this recipe, which often includes squirrel in its really authentic version.

3lbs chicken portions
6 tbsps flour
3 tbsps butter or margarine
8oz salt pork, rinded and cut into ¼ inch dice
3 medium onions, finely chopped
3 pints water
3 14oz cans tomatoes
3 tbsps tomato paste
4oz fresh or frozen lima beans
4oz corn
2 large red peppers, seeded and cut into small dice
3 medium potatoes, peeled and cut into ½ inch cubes
Salt and pepper
1-2 tsps cayenne pepper or tabasco, or to taste
2 tsps Worcester sauce
1 cup red wine

**1.** Shake the pieces of chicken in the flour in a plastic bag as for Fried Chicken. In a large, deep sauté pan, melt the butter until foaming. Place in the chicken without crowding the pieces and brown over moderately high heat for about 10-12 minutes. Remove the chicken and set it aside.

**2.** In the same pan, fry the salt pork until the fat is rendered and the dice are crisp.

**3.** Add the onions and cook over moderate heat for about 10 minutes, or until softened but not browned.

**4.** Pour the water into a large stock pot or saucepan and spoon in the onions, pork and any meat juices from the pan. Add the chicken, tomatoes and tomato paste. Bring to the boil, reduce the heat and simmer for about 1-1½ hours.

**5.** Add the lima beans, corn, peppers and potatoes. Add cayenne pepper or tabasco to taste. Add the Worcester sauce and red wine.

**6.** Cook for a further 30 minutes or until the chicken is tender. Add salt and pepper to taste.

**7.** The stew should be rather thick, so if there is too much liquid, remove the chicken and vegetables and boil down the liquid to reduce it. If there is not enough liquid, add more water or chicken stock.

**Step 3** Add the onions and cook slowly until tender but not browned.

**Step 4** Scrape the contents of the sauté pan into a large stock pot or saucepan of water.

**Time**
Preparation takes about 1 hour and cooking takes about 2 hours.

**Preparation**
If desired, prepare the stew ahead of time, leaving out the last half hour of cooking. Bring slowly to the boil and then simmer for about 30 minutes more before serving.

**Freezing**
The stew may be frozen for up to 2 months in rigid containers. Bring the stew to room temperature before freezing.

SERVES 2

# SAVE-YOUR-MARRIAGE SUPPER

To foster domestic peace anytime, use this quick and easy recipe to make a whole meal in one convenient parcel.

2 lamb steaks or 4 rib chops
Oil
1 large potato, scrubbed
4 baby carrots, scraped
1 medium onion, peeled and sliced
1 medium green pepper, seeded and sliced
1 tbsp chopped fresh dill
Salt and pepper

**Step 1** Quickly seal and brown the lamb chops in a small amount of oil over high heat.

**1.** Heat a frying pan and add a small amount of oil. Quickly fry the lamb on both sides to sear and brown.

**2.** Cut 2 pieces of foil about 12 x 18″. Lightly oil the foil.

**3.** Cut the potatoes in half and place half on each piece of foil, cut side up.

**4.** Top with the lamb and place the carrots on either side.

**5.** Place the onion slices on the lamb and the pepper slices on top of the onions.

**6.** Sprinkle with dill, salt and pepper, and seal into parcels.

**7.** Bake at 400°F for about 45 minutes-1 hour, or until the potatoes are tender and the meat is cooked. Open the parcels at the table.

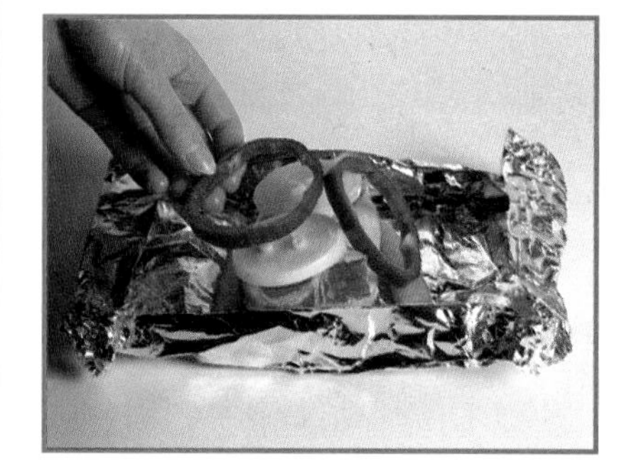

**Step 3** Place half a potato on each piece of lightly-oiled foil, cut side up, and place on remaining ingredients.

**Step 6** Sprinkle with salt, pepper and dill and seal into parcels.

## Cook's Notes

**Time**
Preparation takes about 30 minutes and cooking takes about 45 minutes-1 hour.

**Variation**
Other vegetables may be added or substituted. Use sliced parsnips in place of or in addition to the carrots. Substitute a red pepper for the green pepper. Pork chops may also be used, and the cooking time increased by about 15 minutes.

**Serving Ideas**
This dish is really a complete meal in itself, but add a tomato or green salad for an accompaniment, if desired.

SERVES 8-10

# ALABAMA COLA GLAZED HAM

Don't be afraid to try this somewhat unusual approach to roast ham. Cola gives it a marvelous taste and color.

10lb joint country or Smithfield ham
4 cups cola soft drink
Whole cloves
1 cup packed dark brown sugar

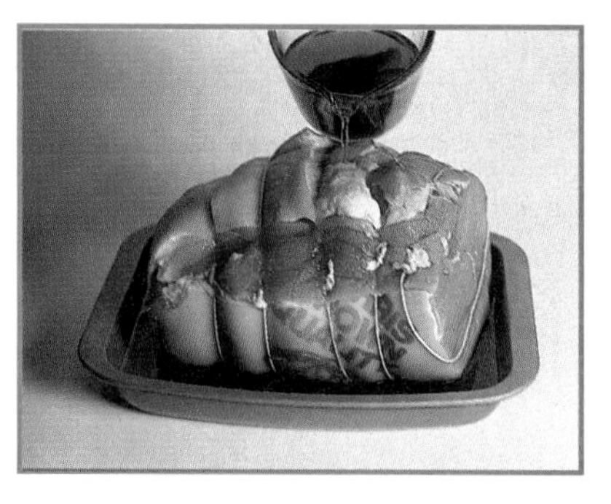

**Step 2** Place the ham rind side down in a roasting pan, pour over the cola and bake.

**1.** Soak the ham overnight.

**2.** Preheat oven to 350°F. Place the ham rind side down in a roasting pan. Pour over all but 6 tbsps of the cola and bake, uncovered, 1½ hours or until the internal temperature registers 140°F.

**3.** Baste the ham every 20 minutes with pan juices using a large spoon or a bulb baster.

**4.** Remove the ham from the oven and allow it to cool for 10-15 minutes. Remove the rind from the ham with a small, sharp knife and score the fat to a depth of ¼ inch. Stick 1 clove in the center of every other diamond.

**5.** Mix sugar and the remaining cola together and pour or spread over the ham. Raise the oven temperature to 375°F.

**6.** Return the ham to the oven and bake for 45 minutes, basting every 15 minutes. Cover loosely with foil if the ham begins to brown too much.

**7.** Allow to stand 15 minutes before slicing.

**Step 4** Remove the rind from the ham with a small, sharp knife. Stick one clove in the center of every other diamond after scoring the fat.

**Step 5** Pour or spread the glaze over the ham before continuing to bake.

## Cook's Notes

**Time**
Preparation takes about 30 minutes, with overnight soaking for the ham. Cooking takes about 2 hours 15 minutes.

**Serving Ideas**
Glazed ham is especially nice served with the Sweet Potato Pudding or Fried Okra. Southern Biscuits or Corn Bread often accompany ham as well.

**Preparation**
Gammon ham requires overnight soaking to remove saltiness.

SERVES 4 or 8

# COUNTRY HAM WITH BOURBON RAISIN SAUCE

The tart and sweet flavor of this sauce has long been the choice to complement savory country ham.

8 slices country or Smithfield ham, cut about ¼ inch thick
Milk
Oil or margarine for frying

**Sauce**
1½ tbsps cornstarch
1 cup apple cider
½ tsp ginger or allspice
2 tsps lemon juice
2 tbsps bourbon
2oz raisins
Pinch salt

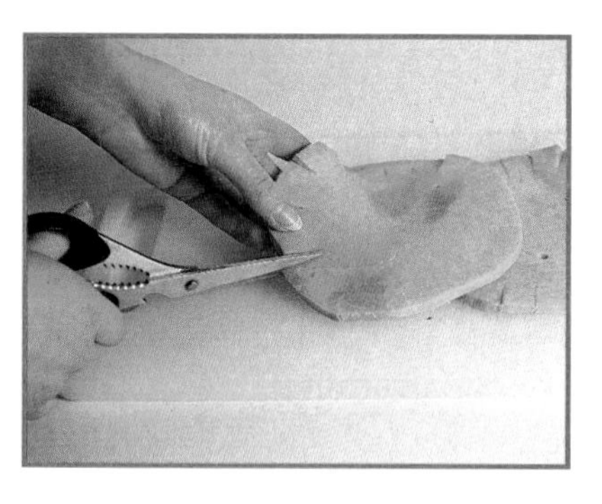

**Step 2** Before frying the ham, snip the edges at intervals of ½ inch with kitchen scissors. This will prevent the ham slices from curling.

**1.** Soak the ham slices in enough milk to barely cover for at least 30 minutes. Rinse and pat dry. Trim off the rind and discard it.

**2.** Heat a small amount of oil or margarine in a large frying pan and brown the ham slices about 2 minutes per side over medium-high heat.

**3.** Mix the cornstarch with about 6 tbsps of the apple cider and deglaze the frying pan with the remaining cider. Stir in the ginger or allspice and the lemon juice.

**4.** Stirring constantly, pour in the cornstarch mixture and bring the liquid to the boil. Cook and stir constantly until thickened. Add the bourbon and raisins and cook a further 5 minutes. Add salt to taste. Reheat the ham quickly, if necessary, and pour over the sauce to serve.

**Step 3** Pour the apple cider into the hot pan and scrape to remove any browned meat juices.

**Step 4** When the raisins are added to the sauce, cook a further five minutes, or until the raisins are plumped and softened.

**Time**
Preparation takes about 20 minutes, with at least 30 minutes soaking in milk for the ham. Cooking takes about 2 minutes per side for the ham and about 10 minutes for the sauce.

**Variation**
If desired, cooked ham slices or steaks may be used in place of the country or Smithfield ham. In this case, omit the soaking procedure and simply fry to brown lightly about 1-2 minutes per side. The apple cider you use may be dry or sweet. If using hard or sweet cider, a pinch of sugar will add to the flavor.

**Cook's Tip**
Soaking country or Smithfield ham in milk will help to remove the saltiness, giving it an improved, milder flavor.

SERVES 4-6

# JELLIED AVOCADO SALAD

Salads set with gelatine are cooling treats in summer or perfect do-ahead dishes anytime.

Juice of 1 small lemon
1½ tbsps unflavored gelatine
2 ripe avocados
3oz cream cheese or low fat soft cheese
½ cup sour cream or natural yogurt
2 tbsps mayonnaise
3 oranges, peeled and segmented
Flat Italian parsley or coriander to garnish

**Step 6** Pour the avocado mixture into oiled custard cups with a piece of wax paper in the bottom.

**1.** Reserve about 2 tsps of the lemon juice. Pour the rest into a small dish, sprinkle the gelatine on top and allow to stand until spongy.

**2.** Cut the avocados in half and twist to separate. Reserve half of one avocado with the stone attached and brush the cut surface with lemon juice, wrap in plastic wrap and keep in the refrigerator.

**3.** Remove the stone from the other half and scrape the pulp from the three halves into a food processor.

**4.** Add the cheese, sour cream or yogurt and mayonnaise and process until smooth.

**5.** Melt the gelatine and add it to the avocado mixture with the machine running.

**6.** Place a small disc of wax paper in custard cups, oil the sides of the cups and the paper and pour in the mixture. Tap the cups lightly on a flat surface to smooth the top and eliminate any air bubbles, cover with plastic wrap and chill until set.

**7.** Loosen the set mixture carefully from the sides of the cups and invert each onto a serving plate to unmold. Peel and slice the remaining avocado half and use to decorate the plate along with the orange segments. Place parsley or coriander leaves on top of each avocado mold to serve.

**Step 7** Make sure the mixture pulls away completely from the sides of the dishes before inverting and shaking to unmold.

## Cook's Notes

**Time**
Preparation takes about 25 minutes. The salads will take about 2 hours to set completely.

**Cook's Tip**
Adding lemon juice to the mixture and brushing the avocado slices with lemon juice will help to keep them from turning brown. The salad will discolor slightly even with the addition of lemon juice if kept in the refrigerator more than one day.

**Preparation**
The avocado salad may be kept in the refrigerator overnight and turned out the next day. Do not keep longer than a day in the refrigerator.

SERVES 6

# CABBAGE AND PEANUT SLAW

Boiled dressings are old favorites in the South. This one gives a lively sweet-sour taste to basic coleslaw.

1 small head white cabbage, finely shredded
2 carrots, shredded
2 tsps celery seed
1 cup dry-roasted peanuts
1 egg
½ cup white wine vinegar
½ cup water
½ tsp dry mustard
2 tbsps sugar

**1.** Combine the vegetables, celery seed and peanuts in a large bowl.

**2.** Beat the egg in a small bowl.

**3.** Add vinegar, water, mustard and sugar and blend thoroughly.

**4.** Place the bowl in a pan of very hot water and whisk until thickened. Cool and pour over the vegetables.

**Step 3** Add the vinegar, water, mustard and sugar to the egg and blend thorougly.

**Step 4** Place in a pan of very hot water and whisk until thickened.

**Time**
Preparation takes about 30 minutes.

**Variation**
Shredded red cabbage and finely chopped onion may be added to the salad, if desired.

**Preparation**
The salad may be prepared ahead of time and kept in the refrigerator overnight.

SERVES 6

# QUICK FRIED VEGETABLES WITH HERBS

Crisply cooked vegetables with plenty of chives make a perfect side dish, hot or cold.

4 sticks celery
4 medium zucchini
2 red peppers, seeded
3-4 tbsps oil
Pinch salt and pepper
1 tsp chopped fresh oregano or marjoram
4 tbsps snipped fresh chives

**Step 1** Cut the celery sticks into ½ inch slices using a large, sharp knife.

**1.** Slice the celery on the diagonal into pieces about 1½ inch thick.

**2.** Cut the zucchini in half lengthwise and then cut into ½ inch thick slices.

**3.** Remove all the seeds and the white pith from the peppers and cut them into diagonal pieces about 1 inch.

**4.** Heat the oil in a heavy frying pan over medium high heat. Add the celery and stir-fry until barely tender.

**5.** Add zucchini and peppers and stir-fry until all the vegetables are tender crisp.

**6.** Add the salt, pepper and oregano or marjoram and cook for 30 seconds more. Stir in chives and serve immediately.

**Step 3** Seed the peppers and cut them into strips. Cut the strips into 1 inch diagonal pieces.

**Step 6** Stir-fry all the vegetables, seasonings and herbs until the vegetables are tender crisp.

## Cook's Notes

**Time**
Preparation takes about 25 minutes and cooking takes about 5 minutes.

**Preparation**
The cooking time for this dish is short, so have everything prepared before actual cooking begins.

**Serving Ideas**
Serve hot as an accompaniment to Southern Fried Chicken, Cola Glazed Ham or with Cornish Hens with Southern Cornbread Stuffing. Vegetables may also be served cold as a salad with a dash of lemon or lime juice added.

SERVES 4-6

# MINTED MIXED VEGETABLES

Carrots, cucumber and zucchini are all complemented by the taste of fresh mint. In fact,most vegetables are, so experiment.

3 medium carrots
1 cucumber
2 zucchini
½ cup water
1 tsp sugar
Pinch salt
1½ tbsps butter, cut into small pieces
1 tbsp coarsely chopped fresh mint leaves

**Step 2** Peel the cucumber, quarter it and remove the seed before cutting into sticks.

**Step 5** Combine all the vegetables and cook until liquid is almost evaporated.

**Step 5** Add the butter, cut in small pieces and stir while the liquid evaporates.

**1.** Peel the carrots and cut them into sticks about ½ inch thick and 2½ inches long.

**2.** Peel the cucumber and cut it into quarters. Remove the centers and cut into sticks the same size as the carrots.

**3.** Cut the zucchini into sticks the same size as the other vegetables.

**4.** Combine the carrots, water, sugar and salt in a medium saucepan. Cover the pan and bring to the boil over high heat. Reduce the heat to medium and cook for about 3 minutes. Uncover the pan and cook a further 3 minutes.

**5.** Increase the heat and add the cucumber and zucchini and boil until the vegetables are tender crisp. Add the butter and stir over heat until melted and the liquid has completely evaporated, glazing the vegetables. Remove from the heat, add the mint and toss well.

## Cook's Notes

**Time**
Preparation takes about 25-30 minutes and cooking takes about 6-10 minutes.

**Variation**
Other root vegetables such as parsnips or rutabagas may be used instead of or in addition to the carrots.

**Preparation**
If the vegetables are cooking faster than the liquid is evaporating, pour off some of the liquid and continue to cook until completely evaporated.

SERVES 4-6

# FRIED OKRA

Cornmeal and okra, two Southern specialties, combine in a classic vegetable dish that's delicious with meat, poultry, game or fish.

1 cup yellow cornmeal
1 tsp salt
2 eggs, beaten
1½lbs fresh okra, washed, stemmed and cut crosswise into ½ inch thick slices
2 cups oil for frying

**Step 1** Dredge the egg-coated, sliced okra in the cornmeal and salt mixture.

**Step 4** Remove the okra from the oil with a draining spoon and place on paper towels.

**1.** Combine the cornmeal and salt on a plate. Coat okra pieces in the beaten egg. Dredge the okra in the mixture.

**2.** Place the oil in a large, deep sauté pan and place over moderate heat.

**3.** When the temperature reaches 375°F add the okra in batches and fry until golden brown.

**4.** Drain thoroughly on paper towels and serve immediately.

## Cook's Notes

**Time**
Preparation takes about 15-20 minutes and cooking takes about 3 minutes per batch.

**Preparation**
Do not coat the okra in the cornmeal too soon before cooking. If allowed to stand, cornmeal will become soggy.

**Variation**
Small okra can be coated and fried whole.

SERVES 6

# Sweet Potato Pudding

All puddings are not necessarily desserts. This one goes with meat or poultry for an unusual side dish.

2 medium-size sweet potatoes
2 cups milk
2 eggs
¾ cup sugar
1 tsp cinnamon
¼ cup pecans, roughly chopped
2 tbsps butter
6 tbsps bourbon

**Step 2** When the egg and sugar mixture is light and fluffy, combine it with cinnamon and pecans and add to the potato and milk mixture.

**1.** Peel the potatoes and grate them coarsely. Combine with the milk.

**2.** Beat the eggs and gradually add the sugar, continuing until light and fluffy. Combine with the cinnamon and the pecans.

**3.** Stir into the potatoes and milk and pour the mixture into a lightly buttered shallow baking dish. Dot with the remaining butter.

**4.** Bake about 45 minutes to 1 hour in a pre-heated 350°F oven. Bake until the pudding is set and then pour over the bourbon just before serving.

**Step 3** Pour the mixture into a lightly-buttered shallow baking dish and dot with the remaining butter.

**Step 4** Pour the bourbon over the baked pudding just before serving.

## Cook's Notes

**Time**
Preparation takes about 25 minutes and cooking takes 45 minutes to 1 hour.

**Buying Guide**
The sweet potatoes to buy for this recipe are the ones with pale orange or yellow pulp. These are also known as yams in the Southern United States.

**Serving Ideas**
While this pudding is usually served as a savoury accompaniment to poultry or ham, it can also be served as a sweet pudding with whipped cream or ice cream.

SERVES 6-8

# STAINED GLASS DESSERT

Named for the effect of the cubes of colorful gelatine in the filling, this pretty and light pudding can be made well in advance of serving.

3oz each of three fruit-flavored gelatine (assorted)
2 cups Graham crackers, crushed
6 tbsps sugar
½ cup butter or margarine
3 tbsps unflavored gelatine
4 tbsps cold water
3 eggs, separated
6 tbsps sugar
4oz cream cheese
Juice and rind of 1 large lemon
½ cup whipping cream

**1.** Prepare the flavored gelatines according to package directions.

**2.** Pour into 3 shallow pans and refrigerate until firm.

**3.** Mix the crushed Graham cracker with the sugar in a food processor and pour melted butter through the funnel with the machine running to blend thorougly.

**4.** Press half the mixture into an 8 inch springform pan lined with wax paper. Refrigerate until firm. Reserve half the mixture for topping.

**5.** Sprinkle the gelatine onto the water in a small saucepan and allow to stand until spongy. Heat gently until the gelatine dissolves and the liquid is clear. Combine the egg yolks, lemon juice and sugar and beat until slightly thickened. Beat in the cream cheese a bit at a time. Pour in the gelatine in a thin, steady stream, beating constantly. Allow to stand, stirring occasionally until beginning to thicken. Place in a bowl of ice water to speed up the setting process.

**6.** Whip the cream until soft. Whip the egg whites until stiff peaks form and fold both the cream and the egg whites into the lemon-cream cheese mixture when the gelatine has begun to thicken.

**7.** Cut the flavored gelatines into cubes and fold carefully into the cream cheese mixture.

**8.** Pour onto the prepared crust. Sprinkle the remaining crust mixture on top, pressing down very carefully.

**9.** Chill overnight in the refrigerator. Loosen the mixture carefully from the sides of the pan, open the pan and unmold. Slice or spoon out to serve.

**Step 7** Fold the cubes of unflavored gelatine carefully into the lemon-cheese mixture using a rubber spatula.

**Step 8** Sprinkle reserved crumb topping carefully over the mixture and press down lightly.

## Cook's Notes

**Time**
Preparation takes about 35-40 minutes. Flavored gelatines will take about 1-1½ hours to set, and the finished cake must be refrigerated overnight.

**Preparation**
Cake may be prepared a day or two in advance and kept in the refrigerator. Do not keep longer than 2 days.

**Variation**
Use orange juice or lime juice instead of lemon. Alternatively soak the gelatine in water and use vanilla extract to flavor the cream cheese mixture.

SERVES 6

# Lemon Chess Pie

No one is really sure how this zesty lemon and cornmeal pie came to be so named, but it's delicious nonetheless.

1½ cups all-purpose flour
Pinch salt and sugar
6 tbsps butter or margarine
2 tbsps plus 1 tsp vegetable shortening
4-5 tbsps cold water

**Filling**

4 tbsps softened butter
1 cup sugar
3-4 eggs, depending on size
1 tbsp yellow cornmeal
Rind and juice of 1 lemon

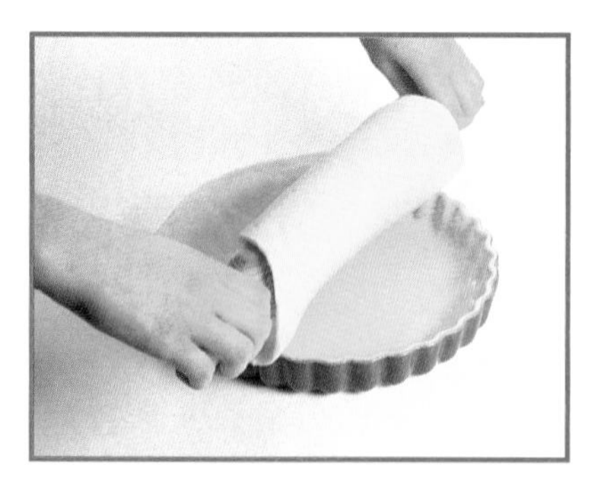

**Step 9** Lift the pastry around the rolling pin and carefully unroll to lower it into the dish.

**1.** Sift the flour, salt and sugar into a bowl or process once or twice in a food processor.

**2.** Add the butter or margarine and shortening and rub into the flour until the mixture resembles fine breadcrumbs, or use the food processor.

**3.** Add enough water to bring the mixture together in a firm dough. Knead lightly to eliminate cracks, wrap and chili for 30 minutes while preparing the filling.

**4.** Cream the butter with the sugar until the sugar dissolves.

**5.** Add the eggs, one at a time, beating well in between each addition.

**6.** Stir in the cornmeal, rind and juice of the lemon.

**7.** Roll out the pastry in a circle on a well-floured surface.

**8.** Roll the pastry carefully onto the rolling pin and transfer to a 9 inch pie or flan dish.

**9.** Lower the pastry carefully into the dish and press against the sides and base. Trim the edges with a sharp knife if using a pie dish, or roll over the rim of the flan dish with the rolling pin to cut off the excess.

**10.** Pour in the filling and bake at 350°F for about 45 minutes. Lower the temperature to 325°F if the pie begins to brown too quickly. Cook until the filling sets. Allow to cool completely before serving. Sprinkle lightly with powdered sugar before cutting, if desired.

**Step 10** Pour the filling evenly over the base of the unbaked pastry.

**Time**
Preparation takes about 30 minutes and cooking takes about 45 minutes.

**Freezing**
The pie may be frozen uncooked. Open freeze in the dish and when firm, wrap well and freeze for up to 3 months. Defrost at room temperature and then bake according to the recipe directions.

**Serving Ideas**
Chess Pie may be served with whipped cream. Decorate the edge of the pie with twisted lemon slices, if desired.

SERVES 6

# STRAWBERRY SHORTCAKE

Summer wouldn't be the same without strawberry shortcake. Add a liqueur to the fruit for a slightly sophisticated touch.

2 cups all-purpose flour
1 tbsp baking powder
Pinch salt
3 tbsps sugar
6 tbsps cream cheese, softened
3 tbsps butter or margarine
1 egg, beaten
⅓-½ cup milk
Melted butter
1lb fresh or frozen strawberries
Powdered sugar
Juice of half an orange
4 tbsps Eau de Fraises or orange liqueur
1 cup whipped cream

**1.** Sift the flour, baking powder, salt and sugar into a large bowl.

**2.** Using 2 knives, forks or a pastry blender, cut in the cheese and butter or margarine. A food processor can also be used.

**3.** Blend in the egg and enough milk to make a firm dough.

**4.** Knead lightly on a floured surface and then roll out to a thickness of ½ inch.

**5.** Cut the dough into an even number of 3 inch circles. Re-roll the trimmings and cut as before. Brush half of the circles with the melted butter and place the other halves on top, pressing down lightly. Bake on an ungreased baking sheet for about 15 minutes in a pre-heated 425°F oven. Allow to cool slightly and then transfer to a wire rack.

**6.** Hull the strawberries and wash well. Purée half of them in a food processor with the orange juice and liqueur. Add powdered sugar to taste if desired. Cut the remaining strawberries in half and combine with the purée.

**7.** Separate the shortcakes in half and place the bottoms on serving plates. Spoon over the strawberries and sauce and pipe or spoon on the cream.

**8.** Sprinkle the tops of the shortcake with powdered sugar and place on top of the cream. Serve slightly warm or at room temperature.

**Step 5** Brush one half of the dough circles with butter and place the other halves on top, pressing down lightly.

**Step 7** The shortcakes should separate in half easily with the help of a fork.

## Cook's Notes

**Time**
Preparation takes about 30-35 minutes and cooking takes about 15 minutes.

**Variation**
Other fruit may be used to fill the shortcakes. Substitute peaches, apricots or other berries. Use orange liqueur or substitute brandy.

MAKES 24

# PECAN TASSIES

Like miniature pecan pies, these small pastries are popular throughout the Southern states, especially at Christmas.

**Pastry**
½ cup butter or margarine
6 tbsps cream cheese
1 cup all-purpose flour

**Filling**
¾ cup chopped pecans
1 egg
¾ cup packed light brown sugar
1 tbsp softened butter
1 tsp vanilla extract
Powdered sugar

**1.** Beat the butter or margarine and cheese together to soften.

**2.** Stir in the flour, adding more if necessary to make the dough easy to handle, although it will still be soft. If possible, roll the dough into 1 inch balls. Chill thoroughly on a plate.

**3.** Mix all the filling ingredients together thorougly, omitting powdered sugar.

**4.** Place a ball of chilled dough into a small tart pan and, with floured fingers, press up the sides and over the base of the pans. Repeat with all the balls of dough.

**5.** Spoon in the filling and bake for about 20-25 minutes at 350°F.

**6.** Allow to cool about 5 minutes and remove carefully from the pans. Cool completely on a wire rack before sprinkling with powdered sugar.

**Step 2** Roll the dough into 1 inch balls and chill until firm.

**Step 4** Place a ball of dough in a small tart pan and, with floured fingers, press up the sides and over the base.

**Step 5** Use a teaspoon to fill the tart pans, taking care not to get filling over the edge of the pastry.

**Time**
Preparation takes about 25 minutes. The dough will take at least 1 hour to chill thoroughly. Cooking takes about 20-25 minutes.

**Preparation**
If the dough is too soft to handle after mixing, chill for about 30 minutes or until easier to handle.

**Variation**
If pecans are unavailable, substitute walnuts or hazelnuts.

**Serving Ideas**
Serve with coffee or tea or as petit fours after a formal dinner. The Tassies can be made in a larger size and served as a dessert with whipped cream.

MAKES 6-8

# Southern Biscuits

Hot biscuits with butter and sometimes honey are almost a symbol of Southern cooking, for breakfast, lunch, dinner or all three!

1¾ cups all-purpose flour
½ tsp salt
2 tsps baking powder
1 tsp sugar
½ tsp baking soda
5 tbsps margarine or 4 tbsps shortening
¾ cup buttermilk

**Step 2** Rub the fat into the flour until the mixture resembles coarse crumbs. Mix in enough milk to form a soft dough that can be handled.

**1.** Sift the flour, salt, baking powder, sugar and baking soda into a large bowl.

**2.** Rub in the fat until the mixture resembles coarse crumbs.

**Step 5** Cut the dough into thick rounds with a plain pastry cutter.

**3.** Mix in enough buttermilk to form a soft dough. It may not be necessary to use all the milk.

**4.** Turn the dough out onto a floured surface and knead lightly until smooth.

**5.** Roll the dough out on a floured surface to a thickness of ½-¾ inch. Cut into rounds with a 2½ inch cookie cutter.

**6.** Place the circles of dough on a lightly-greased baking sheet about 1 inch apart. Bake in a pre-heated 450°F oven for 10-12 minutes. Serve hot.

## Cook's Notes

**Time**
Preparation takes about 20 minutes and cooking takes about 10-12 minutes.

**Serving Ideas**
Serve biscuits with Southern Fried Chicken, Brunswick Stew, and Cola Glazed Ham. Biscuits are often served hot for breakfast and can be substituted for the shortcake in the Strawberry Shortcake recipe.

**Freezing**
Biscuits freeze and reheat well. Freeze for up to 3 months and thaw at room temperature. To reheat, wrap in foil and place in a moderate oven for about 5 minutes.

MAKES 12

# Corn Muffins

A cross between cake and bread, these muffins are slightly sweet and crumbly. Originally an Indian recipe, they've become typically Southern.

1 cup all-purpose flour
4 tbsps sugar
2 tsps baking powder
½ tsp salt
1 cup yellow cornmeal
1 egg, slightly beaten
4 tbsps oil
1⅓ cups milk

**Step 2** Sift the dry ingredients into a large bowl, leaving a well in the center.

**Step 4** Beat the liquid ingredients in the well with a wooden spoon, gradually incorporating the dry ingredients.

**Step 5** Spoon the batter into the prepared pans. It may be slightly lumpy.

**1.** Pre-heat the oven to 450°F. Grease a 12-space muffin tin liberally with oil. Heat the pans for 5 minutes in the oven.

**2.** Sift the flour, sugar, baking powder and salt into a large bowl. Add the cornmeal and stir to blend, leaving a well in the center.

**3.** Combine the egg, oil and milk and pour into the well.

**4.** Beat with a wooden spoon, gradually incorporating the dry ingredients into the liquid. Do not overbeat the mixture. It can be slightly lumpy.

**5.** Spoon the batter into the pans and bake for about 14 minutes.

**6.** Cool briefly in the pans and then remove to a wire rack to cool further. Serve warm.

## Cook's Notes

**Time**
Preparation takes about 20 minutes and cooking takes about 14 minutes.

**Variation**
If you have a cast iron pan, coat liberally with oil and place in the oven to pre-heat. Pour the batter into the pan and then bake. Cut into wedges and serve directly from the pan. The corn muffin recipe may also be used with a corn stick pan. Cut the baking time down to 10-12 minutes.

**Freezing**
Corn muffins may be baked and frozen well wrapped for up to 2 months. Defrost at room temperature and reheat wrapped in foil for about 5 minutes in a moderate oven. Do not overheat as the muffins can dry out easily. Store well wrapped.

MAKES 5 CUPS

# CITRONADE

Nothing surpasses a cold glass of lemonade in the summer. This is the essential beverage for picnics and barbecues.

1 lemon
¾ cup sugar
4½ cups water
Maraschino cherries
Lemon slices

**Step 2** Blend with water and sugar in a blender or food processor until smooth.

**Step 3** Pour into glasses or a pitcher with the cherries and lemon slices.

**1.** Wash the lemon well and cut into small pieces, removing the seeds. Place in a blender or food processor with the sugar and 1 cup water.

**2.** Blend until smooth, add remaining water and mix well.

**3.** Pour into ice-filled glasses or into a pitcher filled with ice and garnish with the cherries and lemon slices.

## Cook's Notes

**Time**
Preparation takes about 20 minutes.

**Preparation**
Citronade may be prepared well in advance and kept in a refrigerator for several days. If storing for any length of time, do not add the cherries or lemon slices until ready to serve.

**Variation**
1 small orange may be substituted for the lemon. Cut down the sugar quantity by 4 tbsps. If using limes, substitute 2 limes for the lemon.

MAKES 1 DRINK

# Mint Juleps

The official drink of the Kentucky Derby, it's mint and bourbon with a splash of soda – delicious but potent.

2 shots bourbon
3 sprigs of fresh mint
1 tsp sugar
Soda or carbonated mineral water

**Step 1** Crush the mint and sugar together in a bowl, glass or jug.

1. Place 1 sprig of mint into a bowl, glass or jug and crush thoroughly with the sugar.

2. Add 1/3-1/4 cup of soda or mineral water, mash again and add the bourbon.

3. Pour the mixture through a strainer into a tall glass filled with crushed ice. Stir until the glass frosts, or leave in the refrigerator about 5 minutes. Decorate the glass with the remaining sprigs of mint.

**Step 3** Pour through a strainer into a tall glass filled with ice.

**Preparation**
Mint Juleps are best prepared just before serving. If you wish to partially prepare them in advance, change the order slightly. Crush the required amount of sugar and mint together and then add the bourbon. Crush again and then leave in the refrigerator until ready to add the soda and pour over ice. Mint Juleps can be made in larger quantities.

**Time**
Preparation takes about 10 minutes.

**Variation**
While not traditional, some recipes for Mint Juleps add a dash of Creme de Menthe.

CAJUN
COOKING

# INTRODUCTION

Driven from their lands in Canada by the British in the late 18th century, the people from the French colony of Acadia moved south to settle in the fertile bayou country of southern Louisiana. They made a home for themselves in the swampy, mysterious marshland around New Orleans, and a colorful Cajun culture, part French and part American, evolved.

The food was based on French country cooking, but adapted to the local ingredients. Cajun cooks exchanged ideas with Creole cooks, and some of the Spanish, West Indian and African influence of the latter crept into the Cajun repertoire.

Both Cajun and Creole cooking rely on seafood, rice, herbs, peppers and green onions as staple ingredients, and both are frequently spicy and hot in character. Whatever the similarities or differences, one thing is certain, Cajun food is among the most spirited in America today.

SERVES 6

# Shrimp Bisque

This classic Cajun recipe makes a first course or a full meal. It isn't a smooth purée like its French counterpart.

3 tbsps butter or margarine
1 onion, finely chopped
1 red pepper, seeded and finely chopped
2 sticks celery, finely chopped
1 clove garlic, minced
Pinch dry mustard and cayenne pepper
2 tsps paprika
3 tbsps flour
4 cups fish stock
1 sprig thyme and bay leaf
8oz raw, peeled shrimp
Salt and pepper
Snipped chives

**Step 2** Cook the mustard, cayenne, paprika and flour briefly until the mixture darkens in color.

**1.** Melt the butter or margarine and add the onion, pepper, celery and garlic. Cook gently to soften.

**2.** Stir in the mustard, cayenne, paprika and flour. Cook about 3 minutes over gentle heat, stirring occasionally.

**3.** Pour on the stock gradually, stirring until well blended. Add the thyme and bay leaf and bring to the boil. Reduce the heat and simmer about 5 minutes or until thickened, stirring occasionally.

**4.** Add the shrimp and cook until pink and curled, about 5 minutes. Season with salt and pepper to taste and top with snipped chives before serving.

**Step 3** Pour on the stock gradually and stir or whisk until well blended.

**Step 4** Use kitchen scissors to snip the chives finely over the top of the soup before serving.

**Time**
Preparation takes about 20 minutes and cooking takes about 8-10 minutes.

**Variation**
If using peeled, cooked shrimp add just before serving and heat through for about 2 minutes only.

**Cook's Tip**

Cook spices such as paprika briefly before adding any liquid to develop their flavor and eliminate harsh taste.

SERVES 4-6

# Hot Pepper Egg Salad

Cajun cooks excel at using what is to hand, and this salad is made with just those kinds of ingredients.

4 eggs
Half a bunch of green onions, chopped
Half a small red pepper, chopped
Half a small green pepper, chopped
4oz cooked, peeled shrimp
1 small jar artichoke hearts, drained and quartered

**Dressing**

6 tbsps oil
2 tbsps white wine vinegar
1 clove garlic, finely chopped
1 tsp dry mustard
1-2 tsps hot red pepper flakes, or 1 small fresh chili, seeded and finely chopped
Salt

**1.** Prick the large end of the eggs with an egg pricker or a needle.

**2.** Lower each egg carefully into boiling, salted water. Bring the water back to the boil, rolling the eggs in the water with the bowl of a spoon.

**3.** Cook the eggs for 9 minutes once the water comes back to the boil. Drain and rinse under cold water until completely cool. Peel and quarter. Combine the eggs with the other ingredients in a large bowl.

**4.** Mix the dressing ingredients together using a whisk to get a thick emulsion.

**5.** Pour the dressing over the salad and mix carefully so that the eggs do not break up.

**6.** Serve on beds of shredded lettuce, if desired.

**Step 2** Lower each egg carefully into the water and roll around with the bowl of a spoon to set the yolk.

**Step 4** Mix the dressing ingredients together using a whisk to get a thick emulsion.

## Cook's Notes

**Time**
Preparation takes about 25 minutes and cooking takes about 9 minutes to boil the eggs.

**Preparation**
If preparing the eggs in advance, leave in the shells and in cold water. This will prevent a gray ring forming around the yolks.

**Cook's Tip**
Rolling the eggs around in the hot water helps to set the yolk in the center of the white and makes sliced or quartered eggs more attractive.

SERVES 6

# GUMBO Z'HERBES

Gumbo is an African word for okra, which helps to thicken this soup-stew. Z'Herbes refers to all the greens that go into it.

1lb spring greens, collard, mustard, beet or turnip greens
8oz spinach, well washed
4oz chicory (Belgian endive)
8oz green cabbage leaves
1 large bunch watercress, well washed
1 large bunch parsley, well washed
6 carrot and radish tops (if available)
4 cups water
Salt, pepper and a pinch cayenne
2 tbsps butter or margarine
1 large red pepper, seeded and coarsely chopped
Half a bunch green onions, coarsely chopped
8oz okra, trimmed and sliced
1 bay leaf
1 tsp thyme
Pinch cinnamon and nutmeg

**Step 1** Using a small, sharp knife, trim down any coarse stalks from the greens, spinach or cabbage.

**Step 3** Purée the vegetables in a food processor or a food mill until very smooth.

**1.** Trim any coarse stalks on the cabbage and spinach and wash both well. Wash greens, chicory, watercress, parsley and carrot and radish tops.

**2.** Bring water to the boil in a large stock pot and add the greens, spinach, cabbage, chicory, watercress, parsley and carrot and radish tops. Return the mixture to the boil, reduce the heat and simmer, partially covered, for about 2 hours.

**3.** Strain and reserve the liquid. Purée the vegetables in a food processor until smooth, and return to the rinsed out pot. Measure the liquid and make up to 3 cups with water, if necessary.

**4.** Melt the butter or margarine, cook the peppers, onions and okra briefly and add to the gumbo. Add the bay leaf, thyme and spices and cook a further 30 minutes over gentle heat. Remove the bay leaf, adjust the seasoning and serve.

## Cook's Notes

**Time**
Preparation takes about 25 minutes and cooking takes 2 hours and 30 minutes.

**Preparation**
Fresh spinach is often very sandy, so wash at least 3 times before cooking, changing the water every time.

**Cook's Tip**
Okra will help to thicken the soup. If the soup is still too thin, add 1 tbsp cornstarch dissolved in 2 tbsps cold water. Bring to the boil, stirring until the cornstarch thickens and clears.

SERVES 6-8

# Crab Meat Balls

Delicious as a first course or a cocktail snack, crab meat balls can be made ahead, then coated and fried at the last minute.

1lb fresh or frozen crab meat, chopped finely
4 slices white bread, crusts removed and made into crumbs
1 tbsp butter or margarine
1 tbsp flour
½ cup milk
½ red or green chili, seeded and finely chopped
1 green onion, finely chopped
1 tbsp chopped parsley
Salt
Flour
2 eggs, beaten
Dry breadcrumbs
Oil for frying

**1.** Combine the crab meat with the fresh breadcrumbs and set aside.

**2.** Melt the butter and add the flour off the heat. Stir in the milk and return to moderate heat. Bring to the boil, stirring constantly.

**3.** Stir the white sauce into the crab meat and breadcrumbs, adding the chili, onion and parsley. Season with salt to taste, cover and allow to cool completely.

**4.** Shape the cold mixture into 1 inch balls with floured hands.

**5.** Coat with beaten egg using a fork to turn balls in the mixture or use a pastry brush to coat with egg.

**Step 4** Flour hands well and shape cold crab mixture into balls.

**Step 5** Brush on beaten egg or dip into egg to coat.

**6.** Coat with the dry breadcrumbs.

**7.** Fry in oil in a deep sauté pan, saucepan or deep-fat fryer at 350°F until golden brown and crisp, about 3 minutes per batch of 6. Turn occasionally while frying.

**8.** Drain on paper towels and sprinkle lightly with salt.

## Cook's Notes

**Time**
Preparation takes about 40-50 minutes, including time for the mixture to cool. A batch of 6 balls takes about 3 minutes to cook.

**Variation**
Use finely chopped shrimp instead of crab meat. Omit chili if desired, or use a quarter red or green pepper.

**Economy**
Cooked whitefish such as haddock or whiting can be substituted for half of the crab meat. Crab sticks can also be used.

SERVES 8-10

# RED BEAN AND RED PEPPER SOUP

Red beans are very popular in southern Louisiana, and here they make a hearty soup combined with red peppers and red wine.

1lb dried red kidney beans
Water to cover
2 onions, coarsely chopped
3 sticks celery, coarsely chopped
2 bay leaves
Salt and pepper
3 large red peppers, seeded and finely chopped
4 tbsps red wine
10 cups chicken stock
Lemon wedges and 4 chopped hard-boiled eggs to garnish

**Step 1** Soak the beans overnight in enough water to cover, or boil for two minutes and leave to soak for an hour. The beans will swell in size.

**1.** Soak the beans in the water overnight. Alternatively, bring them to the boil and boil rapidly for 2 minutes. Leave to stand for 1 hour.

**2.** Drain off the liquid and add the onions, celery, bay leaves, salt and pepper, red peppers, red wine and stock.

**3.** Bring to the boil over high heat, stirring occasionally. Reduce the heat and allow to simmer, partially covered, for about 3 hours, or until the beans are completely tender.

**4.** Remove the bay leaves and purée the soup in a food processor or blender.

**5.** Serve garnished with the chopped hard-boiled egg. Serve lemon wedges on the side.

**Step 2** Combine the beans with the other ingredients in a large stock pot and pour on enough chicken stock to cover.

**Step 3** When the beans are soft enough to mash easily, remove bay leaves and purée the soup.

## Cook's Notes

**Time**
Preparation takes about 25 minutes, with overnight soaking for the beans. Cooking takes about 3 hours.

**Watchpoint**
It is dangerous to eat dried pulses that are not thoroughly cooked. Make sure the beans are very soft before puréeing.

**Freezing**
The soup may be prepared and puréed in advance and frozen for up to 3 months. Freeze in small containers so that the soup will defrost faster. Defrost at room temperature, breaking the mixture up with a fork as the soup defrosts.

SERVES 6

# GREEN RICE

Fresh herbs are a must for this rice dish, but use whatever mixture suits your taste or complements the main course.

2 tbsps oil
2 tbsps butter
¾ cup uncooked long-grain rice
2 cups boiling water
Pinch salt and pepper
3oz mixed chopped fresh herbs (parsley, thyme, marjoram, basil)
1 small bunch green onions, finely chopped

**Step 1** Cook the rice in the oil and butter until it begins to turn opaque.

**Step 3** Cook very gently for about 20 minutes, or until all the liquid has been absorbed by the rice and the grains are tender.

**Step 4** Stir the onions and herbs into the rice and fluff up the grains with a fork.

**1.** Heat the oil in a large, heavy-based saucepan and add the butter. When foaming, add the rice and cook over moderate heat for about 2 minutes, stirring constantly.

**2.** When the rice begins to look opaque, add the water, salt and pepper and bring to the boil, stirring occasionally.

**3.** Cover the pan and reduce the heat. Simmer very gently, without stirring, for about 20 minutes or until all the liquid has been absorbed and the rice is tender.

**4.** Chop the herbs very finely and stir into the rice along with the chopped green onions. Cover the pan and leave to stand for about 5 minutes before serving.

## Cook's Notes

**Time**
Preparation takes about 20 minutes and cooking takes about 20-25 minutes.

**Serving Ideas**
Serve as a side dish to any meat, poultry or game recipe.

**Cook's Tip**
The rice must simmer very slowly if it is to absorb all the water without overcooking. Add extra water or pour some off as necessary during cooking, depending on how much liquid the rice has absorbed.

SERVES 6

# MAQUE CHOUX

Sweetcorn is essential to this recipe, but other vegetables can be added, too. In true Cajun style, use what you have to hand.

4 tbsps oil
2 tbsps butter or margarine
2 medium-size onions, peeled and finely chopped
1 clove garlic, crushed
1 medium-size green pepper, seeded and cut into small dice
6 tomatoes, peeled, seeded and diced
8oz fresh corn kernels or frozen corn
1 cup chicken or vegetable stock
Pinch salt
½ tsp cayenne pepper
4 tbsps heavy cream

**Step 1** Cook the onions and garlic until soft and transparent but not browned.

**1.** Heat the oil in a large casserole and add the butter. When foaming, add the onions and garlic and cook, stirring frequently, for about 5 minutes or until both are soft and transparent but not browned.

**2.** Add the green pepper, tomatoes, corn and stock. Bring to the boil over high heat.

**3.** Reduce the heat, partially cover the casserole and allow to cook slowly for about 10 minutes, or until the corn is tender. Add the cayenne pepper and salt and stir in the cream. Heat through and serve immediately.

**Step 2** Add the vegetables and liquid to the onions and cook until the corn is tender.

**Step 3** Stir in the cream and return to the heat to warm through. Serve immediately.

## Cook's Notes

**Time**
Preparation takes about 25 minutes. Cooking takes about 10 minutes for frozen corn and slightly longer for fresh corn.

**Variation**
Use canned tomatoes, coarsely chopped. Make up the tomato liquid to the required measurement with water. If desired, fresh chili peppers may be used in place of the cayenne pepper. Use half to one whole chili pepper according to taste. Cream may be omitted, if desired.

**Cook's Tip**
Sweetcorn toughens if cooked at too high a temperature for too long, or if boiled too rapidly.

SERVES 6

# Sweet Potato and Sausage Casserole

This close relative of the French soufflé is easier to make, and includes two Southern favorites – sweet potatoes and sausage.

2lbs sweet potatoes
2 tbsps oil
8oz sausage meat
1 small onion, finely chopped
2 sticks celery, finely chopped
½ green pepper, finely chopped
Pinch sage and thyme
Pinch salt and pepper
2 eggs, separated

**1.** Peel the sweet potatoes and cut them into 2 inch pieces. Place in boiling water to cover and add a pinch of salt. Cook quickly, uncovered, for about 20 minutes or until the sweet potatoes are tender to the point of a knife. Drain them well and leave them to dry.

**2.** Purée the potatoes using a potato masher.

**3.** While the potatoes are cooking, heat the oil in a large frying pan and add the sausage meat. Cook briskly, breaking up with a fork until the meat is golden brown. Add the onion, celery and green pepper, and cook for a further 5 minutes. Add the sage, thyme and a pinch of seasoning.

**4.** Beat the egg yolks into the mashed sweet potatoes and, using an electric mixer or a hand whisk, beat the egg whites until stiff but not dry.

**5.** Drain any excess fat from the sausage meat and combine it with the sweet potatoes. Fold in the whisked egg whites until thoroughly incorporated. Spoon the mixture into a well-buttered casserole dish or soufflé dish and bake in a preheated 375°F oven until well risen and brown on the top, about 25-30 minutes. Serve immediately.

**Step 3** Brown the sausage meat in oil, mashing with a fork to break up lumps as the meat cooks.

**Step 4** Add the egg yolks to the potato mixture, beating well with a wooden spoon.

**Step 4** Whisk the egg whites until stiff but not dry.

**Time**
Preparation takes about 35 minutes and cooking takes a total of 45 minutes.

**Serving Ideas**
Serve as a side dish with poultry, or on its own as a light main course.

**Cook's Tip**
Since this mixture is heavier than a normal soufflé mixture, do not expect it to rise as high.

MAKES 8

# CAJUN PIES

We've baked this traditional meat pie in individual portions. It's spicy hot, so add cayenne gradually to taste.

**Pastry**

3 tbsps butter or margarine
2 eggs
4-6 tbsps milk or water
2½-3½ cups all-purpose flour
Pinch sugar and salt

**Filling**

2 tbsps butter or margarine
½ small onion, finely chopped
½ small green pepper, finely chopped
1 stick celery, finely chopped
1 clove garlic, crushed
¾lb ground pork
1 bay leaf, finely crushed
1 tsp cayenne pepper
Pinch salt
2 tbsps flour
1 cup beef stock
1 tbsp tomato paste
1 tsp dried thyme

**1.** To prepare the pastry, soften the butter or margarine in a food processor or with an electric mixer until creamy. Beat in the eggs one at a time and add the milk or water.

**2.** Sift in 2½ cups flour, sugar and salt and mix until blended. If necessary, add the remaining flour gradually until the mixture forms a ball. Wrap well and refrigerate about 30 minutes.

**3.** Melt the butter or margarine in a large frying pan and cook the onion, pepper, celery, garlic and pork over moderate heat. Break up the meat with a fork as it cooks.

**4.** Add the bay leaf, cayenne pepper, salt and flour and cook, scraping the bottom of the pan often, until the flour browns.

**5.** Pour on the stock and stir in the tomato paste and thyme. Bring to the boil and cook, stirring occasionally, until thickened. Chill thoroughly and remove the bay leaf.

**6.** Divide the pastry into 8 pieces and roll each out to a circle about ⅛ inch thick.

**7.** Spread the chilled filling on half of each circle to within ½ inch of the edge. Brush the edge with water.

**8.** Fold over and seal the edges together firmly. Crimp the edges with a fork.

**9.** Heat oil in a deep sauté pan or a deep fat fryer to about 350°F. Fry 2 or 3 pies at a time for about 2 minutes, holding them under the surface of the oil with a metal spoon to brown evenly. Remove from the oil with a draining spoon and drain on paper towels. Serve immediately.

**Step 7** Spread the filling on half of each pastry circle and brush the edges with water.

**Step 8** Fold over and seal the edges together, pressing them firmly. Crimp with a fork.

## Cook's Notes

**Time**
Preparation takes about 30-40 minutes, and cooking takes about 15 minutes for the filling and 2 minutes for each batch of 2 pies.

**Cook's Tip**
The dough may be prepared in advance and kept in a refrigerator for about 2 days.

**Variation**
Ground beef may be substituted for the pork. Double the quantity of vegetables for a vegetarian filling.

SERVES 6

# SEAFOOD GUMBO FILÉ

Either filé powder, made from sassafras leaves, or okra gives a Cajun gumbo its characteristic texture. Gumbos are good without filé, too.

1lb cooked, unpeeled shrimp
Half quantity spice mixture (see Shellfish Boil)
5 cups water
4 tbsps butter or margarine
1 onion, peeled and sliced
1 green pepper, seeded and sliced
2 cloves garlic, finely chopped
3 tbsps flour
½ tsp thyme
1 bay leaf
2 tbsps chopped parsley
Dash Worcester sauce
12 oysters, shelled
8oz tomatoes, peeled and chopped
2 tbsps filé powder (optional)
Salt and pepper
Cooked rice

**1.** Peel the shrimp and reserve the shells. Mix shells with the spice mixture and water and bring to the boil in a large stock pot. Reduce the heat and allow to simmer for about 20 minutes.

**2.** Melt the butter or margarine and, when foaming, add the onion, green pepper, garlic and flour. Cook slowly, stirring constantly until the flour is a pale golden brown. Gradually strain on the stock, discarding the shells and spice mixture. Add the thyme and bay leaf and stir well. Bring to the boil and then simmer until thick.

**Step 1** Peel the shrimp adding the heads, tail shell, legs and roe, if present, to the spice mixture in a large stock pot.

**Step 3** Loosen the oysters from their shells and add to the hot gumbo. If desired, strain the oyster liquid through a very fine mesh strainer.

**3.** Add the parsley and the Worcester sauce to taste. Add the oysters, peeled shrimp and tomatoes and heat through gently to cook the oysters.

**4.** Stir in the filé powder and leave to stand to thicken. Adjust the seasoning and serve over rice.

## Cook's Notes

**Time**
Preparation takes about 25-30 minutes and cooking takes about 20-25 minutes.

**Variation**
If they are available, use raw, unpeeled shrimp and cook with the water and the spice mixture until they turn pink and curl up. Drain them, reserving the liquid. Peel and return the shells to the stock. Re-boil the stock and allow to simmer for about 15 minutes.

**Cook's Tip**
If filé powder is not available, use equal portions of butter or margarine and flour mixed together to a paste. Add a bit of the paste at a time to the gumbo, and boil in between additions until the desired thickness is reached.

SERVES 4-6

# SHELLFISH BOIL

This is the Cajun way to cook seafood. Drained seafood is piled onto newspaper-covered tables for everyone to dig in.

3 quarts water
1 lemon, quartered
1 onion, cut in half but not peeled
1 celery stick, cut in 3 pieces
2 cloves garlic, left whole
Pinch salt
4 bay leaves, finely crumbled
4 dried red chili peppers, crumbled
1 tbsp each whole cloves, whole allspice, coriander seed and mustard seed
1 tbsp dill weed, fresh or dry
2 tsps celery seed
1lb raw, unpeeled shrimp
2lbs mussels, well scrubbed

**Step 2** Add the shrimp to the boiling liquid and cook them until pink and curled.

**Step 3** Remove the seaweed beards and any barnacles from the mussel shells.

**1.** Place the water, lemon, onion, celery, garlic, salt, bay leaves and spices together in a large pot and cover. Bring to the boil, reduce the heat and cook slowly for 20 minutes.

**2.** Add the shrimp in two batches and cook until pink and curled. Remove with a draining spoon.

**3.** Remove the seaweed beards from the mussels, and discard any that do not close when tapped.

**4.** Add mussels to the pot and cook, stirring frequently, for about 5 minutes or until shells have opened. Discard any that do not open.

**5.** Spoon shrimp and mussels into serving bowls and serve immediately.

## Cook's Notes

**Time**
Preparation takes about 30 minutes, cooking takes about 20 minutes to boil the stock and about 5 minutes for each batch of shrimp and mussels.

**Serving Ideas**
Serve as an appetizer, or double the quantity for a main course.

**Variation**
Usually crawfish are cooked in this way. Crabs are also used.

SERVES 4

# BLACKENED FISH

Cajun cooks all have their own special recipes for the spice mixture, but all agree that the food should have a *very* brown crust when properly blackened.

4 fish fillets, about 8oz each
1 cup unsalted butter
1 tbsp paprika
1 tsp garlic powder
1 tsp cayenne pepper
½ tsp ground white pepper
1 tsp finely ground black pepper
2 tsps salt
1 tsp dried thyme

**1.** Melt the butter and pour about half into each of four custard cups and set aside.

**2.** Brush each fish fillet liberally with the remaining butter on both sides.

**3.** Mix together the spices and thyme and sprinkle generously on each side of the fillets, patting it on by hand.

**4.** Heat a large frying pan and add about 1 tbsp butter per fish fillet. When the butter is hot, add the fish, skin side down first.

**5.** Turn the fish over when the underside is very brown and repeat with the remaining side. Add more butter as necessary during cooking.

**6.** When the top side of the fish is very dark brown, repeat with the remaining fish fillets, keeping them warm while cooking the rest.

**7.** Serve the fish immediately with the cups of butter for dipping.

**Step 2** Use a pastry brush to coat the fish well on both sides with the melted butter. Alternatively, spoon the butter over or dip the fish in the butter.

**Step 3** Mix the seasoning ingredients together well and press firmly onto both sides of the fish to coat.

**Step 5** Cook the underside and topside of the fish until very dark brown.

## Cook's Notes

**Time**
Preparation takes about 20 minutes and cooking takes about 2 minutes per side for each fillet.

**Variation**
Red fish or pompano is the usual choice. If these fish are not available, substitute other varieties of fish fillets or steaks that are approximately ¾ inch thick.

**Preparation**
The fish must be very dark brown on the top and the bottom before serving. Leave at least 2 minutes before attempting to turn the fish over.

SERVES 4

# Trout with Oyster Stuffing

Oysters are used freely in Cajun cooking since they're plentiful in this part of the world. They make a luxurious stuffing for whole fish.

4 whole trout, about 8oz each
½ cup butter or margarine
1 onion, finely chopped
2 sticks celery, finely chopped
1 small red pepper, seeded and finely chopped
4 green onions, finely chopped
1 clove garlic, crushed
12 oysters on the half shell
2 tsps chopped parsley
1 tsp chopped fresh dill
¼ tsp white pepper
¼ tsp cayenne pepper
¼ tsp black pepper
Pinch salt
1 cup dry breadcrumbs
2 small eggs, lightly beaten

**1.** Wash the trout well inside and pat dry.

**2.** Melt half the butter or margarine in a medium saucepan. Add onions, celery, red pepper, green onions and garlic. Cook over a moderate heat for about 3 minutes to soften the vegetables.

**3.** Remove the oysters from the shells with a sharp knife and add them to the vegetables. Strain and reserve any oyster liquid. Cook the oysters about 2 minutes, breaking them up into large pieces while they cook. Stir in the white pepper, cayenne pepper and black pepper, dill and parsley.

**4.** Remove from the heat, add the breadcrumbs and gradually beat in the egg, adding just enough to hold the stuffing ingredients together. Season with salt.

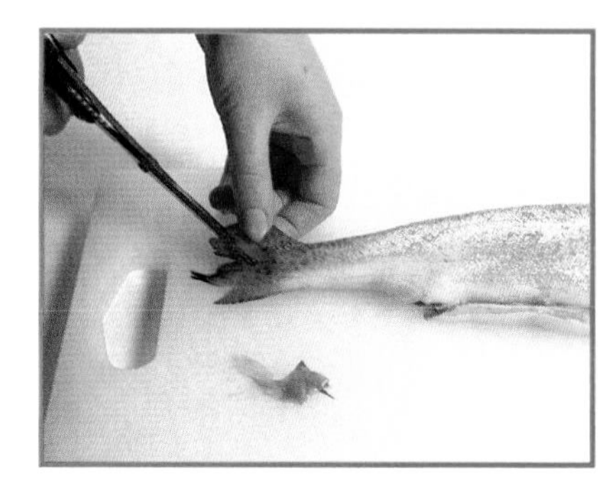

**Step 1** Trim the fins, neaten the tail of the trout and rinse well. Pat dry.

**Step 5** Spoon some of the stuffing into the cavity of each fish.

**5.** Stuff the cavity of each trout with an equal amount of the stuffing and place the trout in a baking dish.

**6.** Spoon over the remaining butter and bake, uncovered, in a pre-heated 350°F oven for about 25 minutes. Brown under a pre-heated broiler before serving, if desired.

## Cook's Notes

**Time**
Preparation takes about 30 minutes and cooking takes about 30 minutes.

**Variation**
Other varieties of fish, such as sea bass, gray mullet or red snapper, can also be used.

**Economy**
Since oysters are expensive, they may be omitted from the recipe or may be replaced with mussels, if desired. Canned oysters, which are somewhat cheaper, may also be used.

SERVES 2

# BARBECUED SHRIMP

It's the sauce rather than the cooking method that gives this dish its name. It's spicy, zippy and *hot*.

- 1lb large shrimp, cooked and unpeeled
- ½ cup unsalted butter
- 1 tsp each white, black and cayenne pepper
- Pinch salt
- 1 tsp each chopped fresh thyme, rosemary and marjoram
- 1 clove garlic, crushed
- 1 tsp Worcester sauce
- ½ cup fish stock
- 4 tbsps dry white wine
- Cooked rice

**Step 1** Remove the legs and eyes from the shrimp. Leave on the long antennae, if desired.

**1.** Remove the eyes and the legs from the shrimp.

**2.** Melt the butter in a large frying pan and add the white pepper, black pepper, cayenne pepper, herbs and garlic. Add the shrimp and toss over heat for a few minutes. Remove the shrimp and set them aside.

**3.** Add the Worcester sauce, stock and wine to the ingredients in the pan. Bring to the boil and cook for about 3 minutes to reduce. Add salt to taste.

**4.** Arrange the shrimp on a bed of rice and pour over the sauce to serve.

**Step 2** Melt the butter and add the spices and herbs and shrimp, and cook briefly.

**Step 3** Add the Worcester sauce, wine and stock to the pan and boil rapidly to reduce.

## Cook's Notes

**Time**
Preparation takes about 15 minutes and cooking takes about 5 minutes.

**Preparation**
Because the shrimp are pre-cooked, cook them very briefly again, just to heat through. Use uncooked, unpeeled shrimp if possible. Cook these until they curl and turn pink.

**Serving Ideas**
Serve with the recipe for Green Rice or use plain boiled rice. The shrimp may also be served cold. If serving cold, prepare the sauce with 6 tbsps oil instead of the butter.

SERVES 4

# CRAWFISH PIE

This seafood, plentiful in southern Louisiana, is used in many delicious ways. The boiling mixture adds spice, and the browned flour a nutty taste and good color.

**Pastry**

2 cups all-purpose flour, sifted
Pinch salt
½-¾ cup butter or margarine
Cold water

1lb raw crawfish or shrimp
½ quantity spice mixture for Shellfish Boil (see recipe)

**Filling**

3 tbsps oil
3 tbsps flour
½ green pepper, seeded and finely diced
2 green onions, finely chopped
1 stick celery, finely chopped
1 cup light cream
Salt and pepper

**Step 6** Roll the pastry out thinly and use a rolling pin to transfer it to the baking dish.

**1.** Sift the flour into a bowl with a pinch of salt and rub in the butter or margarine until the mixture resembles fine breadcrumbs. Add enough cold water to bring the mixture together. Knead into a ball, wrap well and chill for about 30 minutes before use.

**2.** Combine the spice mixture with about 2½ cups water. Bring to the boil and add the crawfish or shrimp. Cook for about 5 minutes, stirring occasionally until the shellfish curl up. Remove from the liquid and leave to drain.

**3.** Heat the oil in a small saucepan for the filling and add the flour. Cook slowly, stirring constantly until the flour turns a rich dark brown.

**4.** Add the remaining filling ingredients, stirring constantly while adding the cream. Bring to the boil, reduce the heat and cook for about 5 minutes. Add the crawfish or shrimp to the sauce.

**5.** Divide the pastry into 4 and roll out each portion on a lightly-floured surface to about ¼ inch thick.

**6.** Line individual flan or pie dishes with the pastry, pushing it carefully onto the base and down the sides, taking care not to stretch it. Trim off excess pastry and reserve.

**7.** Place a sheet of wax paper or foil on the pastry and pour on rice, pasta or baking beans to come halfway up the sides. Bake the pastry blind for about 10 minutes in a preheated 400°F oven.

**8.** Remove the paper and beans and bake for an additional 5 minutes to cook the base.

**9.** Spoon in the filling and roll out any trimmings to make a lattice pattern on top. Bake a further 10 minutes to brown the lattice and heat the filling. Cool slightly before serving.

## Cook's Notes

**Time**
Preparation takes about 30 minutes and cooking takes about 10 minutes for the filling and 25 minutes to finish the dish.

**Cook's Tip**
Baking the pastry blind helps it to crisp on the base and brown evenly without overcooking the filling.

**Serving Ideas**
Serve as a light main course with a salad, or make smaller pies to serve as a first course.

SERVES 4

# CRAWFISH ETOUFÉE

This is a thick stew usually made with the local seafood.

⅓ cup butter or margarine
1 small onion, chopped
1lb crawfish or shrimp
6 tbsps flour
1 cup water or fish stock
1 tbsp tomato paste
2 tbsps chopped parsley
2 tsps chopped dill
Salt and pepper
2 tsps tabasco or to taste
Cooked rice

**Step 1** Cook the onion and crawfish or shrimp quickly until it curls up.

**1.** Melt half the butter or margarine, add the onion and cook to soften slightly. Add scampi and cook quickly until it curls. Remove to a plate.

**2.** Add the flour to the pan and cook slowly until golden brown, stirring frequently.

**3.** Pour on the water and stir vigorously to blend. Add tomato paste and bring to the boil. Add parsley, dill, tabasco and seasoning to taste and return the onions and the scampi to the sauce. Heat through for 5 minutes and serve over rice.

**Step 3** Add the water gradually, stirring vigorously. The mixture should be very thick.

**Step 3** Return the crawfish or shrimp and onions to the sauce to heat through. Juices from both will thin down the sauce.

## Cook's Notes

**Time**
Preparation takes about 20 minutes and cooking takes about 15 minutes.

**Watchpoint**
Shrimp, scampi and other types of seafood become very tough if cooked too quickly or over heat that is too high.

**Preparation**
The sauce must be very thick, so add the water gradually, reserving some to add once the sauce comes to the boil.

SERVES 4

# Seafood Pan Roast

This mixture of oysters and crab is a descendant of French gratin recipes. It's quick to make, and other seafood may be added.

24 small oysters on the half shell
1 cup fish stock
1 cup light cream
⅓ cup butter or margarine
6 tbsps flour
1 bunch green onions, chopped
2oz parsley, chopped
2 tbsps Worcester sauce
½ tsp tabasco
Pinch salt
1 large or 2 small cooked crabs
4 slices bread, crusts trimmed and made into crumbs

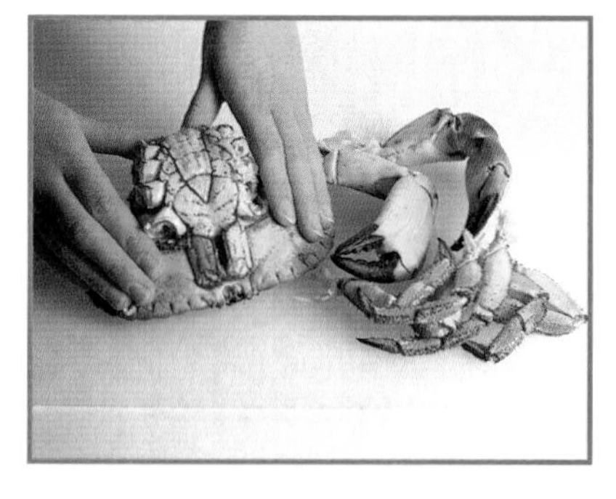

**Step 3** Turn the crabs over and push out the body with your thumbs.

**1.** Remove the oysters from their shells with a small, sharp knife. Place the oysters in a saucepan and strain over any oyster liquid. Add the fish stock and cook gently until the oysters curl around the edges. Remove the oysters, keep them warm and strain the liquid into a clean pan.

**2.** Add the cream to the oyster liquid and bring to the boil. Allow to boil rapidly for about 5 minutes.

**3.** Remove crab claws and legs. Turn the crabs over and push out the body with your thumbs.

**4.** Remove the stomach sac and lungs (dead man's fingers) and discard.

**5.** Cut the body in four sections with a large, sharp knife and pick out the meat with a skewer.

**6.** Crack claws and legs to extract the meat. Leave the small legs whole for garnish, if desired.

**7.** Scrape out the brown meat from inside the shell and combine it with the breadcrumbs and white meat from the body and claws.

**8.** Melt the butter or margarine in a medium-size saucepan and stir in the flour. Cook gently for 5 minutes. Add the onions and parsley and cook a further 5 minutes. Pour over the cream and fish stock mixture, stirring constantly. Add the Worcester sauce, tabasco and salt, and cook about 15-20 minutes over low heat, stirring occasionally. Fold in the crab meat and breadcrumb mixture.

**9.** Place the oysters in the bottom of a buttered casserole or in individual dishes and spoon the crab meat mixture on top. Broil to brown, if desired, and serve immediately.

## Cook's Notes

**Time**
Preparation takes about 40 minutes and cooking takes about 30 minutes.

**Buying Guide**
If fresh oysters on the half shell and freshly cooked crabs are not available, substitute canned oysters and use their liquid for part of the fish stock measurement. Canned oysters will not need as long to cook. Canned or frozen crab meat may be used in place of the fresh crabs, substituting about 8oz for the fresh crab meat.

**Serving Ideas**
If serving as a first course, this recipe will serve 6. Add French bread and a salad for a light main course.

SERVES 8

# BACKBONE STEW

A mixture of three kinds of pepper is typically Cajun. Normally made with pork, this stew is also good with inexpensive cuts of lamb.

3lb middle neck or other neck cut of lamb
$\frac{1}{4}$ tsp each cayenne, white and black pepper
Pinch salt
6 tbsps oil
2 onions, sliced
1 large red pepper, seeded and sliced
2 sticks celery, sliced
6 tbsps flour
2 cloves garlic, crushed
5 cups stock or water
2 tbsps chopped parsley

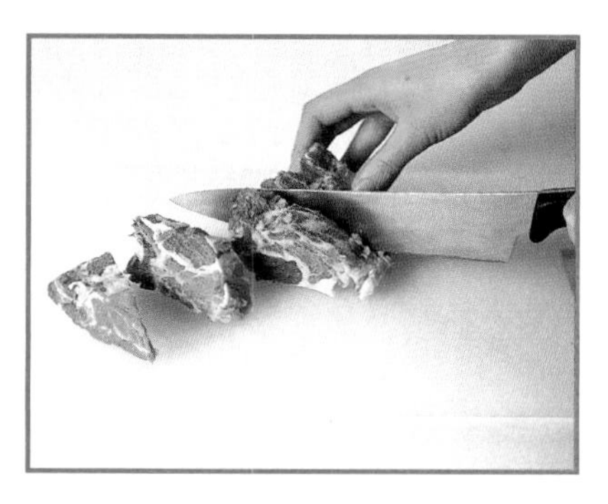

**Step 1** Cut in between the bones to divide the meat into even-size pieces.

**1.** Cut the lamb between the bones into individual pieces. Sprinkle a mixture of red, white and black pepper and salt over the surface of the chops, patting it in well.

**2.** Heat the oil in a large stock pot or casserole and when hot add the meat, a few pieces at a time, and brown on both sides.

**3.** When all the meat is brown, remove to a plate and add the onions, pepper and celery to the oil. Lower the heat and cook to soften. Remove and set aside with the meat.

**4.** Add the flour to the remaining oil in the pan and stir well. Cook slowly until a dark golden brown. Add the garlic and stir in the stock or water. Return the meat and vegetables to the pan or casserole and bring to the boil. Cover and cook slowly for 1½-2 hours, or until the lamb is very tender. Sprinkle with parsley and serve immediately.

**Step 1** Mix the peppers together and sprinkle over the surface of the meat, patting in well.

**Step 2** Brown the meat, a few pieces at a time, over very high heat.

## Cook's Notes

**Time**
Preparation takes about 25 minutes and cooking takes about 2 hours.

**Variation**
The stew may be prepared with pork chops, sliced pork loin or with an inexpensive cut of beef.

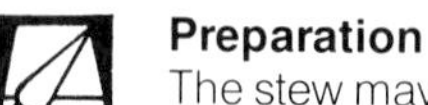

**Preparation**
The stew may be prepared in advance and kept in the refrigerator for up to 2 or 3 days. Reheat slowly. Flavors will intensify.

SERVES 4-6

# DIRTY RICE

The name comes from the mixture of finely chopped chicken livers, celery, green pepper and onions that colours the rice.

1 cup long-grain rice
2 cups water
1lb chicken livers
1 stick celery, roughly chopped
1 green pepper, seeded and roughly chopped
2 medium onions, roughly chopped
2 tbsps oil
Salt and pepper
Chopped parsley to garnish

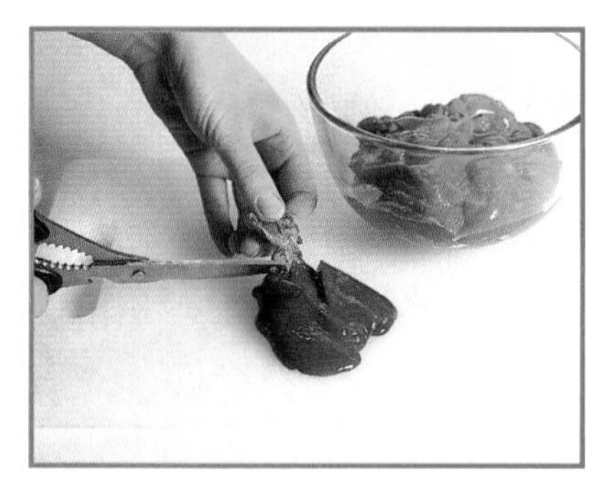

**Step 2** Pick over chicken livers to remove fat and any discolored portions.

**1.** Cook the rice in the water with a pinch of salt. When cooked, leave to stand while preparing the liver.

**2.** Pick over the chicken livers to remove any fat and discolored portions.

**3.** Place the livers, celery, pepper and onions in a food processor and process to finely chop the ingredients. The mixture will look soupy.

**4.** Heat the oil in a large frying pan and add the liver mixture. Cook over moderate heat, stirring gently.

**5.** Once the mixture has set, turn down the heat to very low, cover the pan and cook about 30-40 minutes, or until rich golden brown in color.

**6.** Stir in the cooked rice, fluffing up the mixture with a fork. Heat through, season to taste and serve garnished with chopped parsley.

**Step 4** Cook the liver mixture, stirring gently, in oil in a large frying pan.

**Step 6** When the liver mixture has browned, stir in the cooked rice using a fork to fluff the mixture up.

## Cook's Notes

**Time**
Preparation takes about 20 minutes and cooking takes about 30-40 minutes.

**Serving Ideas**
The rice may be served as a main dish, in which case this recipe serves 2-3. The rice is often served cold as an appetizer. Also use the recipe as a side dish.

**Cook's Tip**
Removing the yellowish or greenish portions from the chicken liver will eliminate bitter taste.

SERVES 4

# GINGERSNAP PORK CHOPS

Ginger-flavored cookies give a spicy lift to pork chop gravy, thickening it at the same time.

4 even-sized pork chops, loin or shoulder
1 tsp ground black pepper
Pinch salt
1 tsp ground ginger
¼ tsp each rubbed sage, cayenne pepper, ground coriander and paprika
Pinch dried thyme
2 tbsps oil
2 tbsps butter
1 small onion, finely chopped
1 stick celery, finely chopped
½ clove garlic, crushed
1½ cups chicken stock
12-14 gingersnap cookies

**Step 2** Brown the chops on both sides in the hot oil until golden.

**1.** Trim the chops if they have excess fat. Mix together the herbs and spices and press the mixture onto the chops firmly on both sides.

**2.** Heat the oil in a large frying pan and, when hot, add the chops. Brown on both sides and remove to a plate.

**3.** Add the butter to the frying pan and, when foaming, add the onions, celery and garlic. Cook to soften and pour on the stock.

**4.** Return the chops to the pan, cover and cook for about 30-40 minutes, or until tender.

**5.** When the chops are cooked, remove them to a serving dish and keep them warm. Crush the gingersnaps in a food processor. Alternatively, place the gingersnaps in a plastic bag and use a rolling pin to crush them. Stir the crushed gingersnaps into the pan liquid and bring to the boil.

**6.** Stir constantly to allow the gingersnaps to soften and thicken the liquid. Boil rapidly for about 3 minutes to reduce, and pour over the chops to serve.

**Step 5** Use the crushed gingersnaps to thicken the pan liquid. Cook slowly until dissolved.

## Cook's Notes

**Time**
Preparation takes about 20 minutes and cooking takes about 50 minutes.

**Variation**
Chicken or rabbit may be used in place of the pork.

**Cook's Tip**
The gingersnaps should thicken the cooking liquid sufficiently. If not, combine 2 tsps cornstarch with 1 tbsp water and some of the hot cooking liquid. Return to the pan and bring to the boil, stirring constantly until thickened and cleared.

SERVES 4

# Pigeons in Wine

Pigeons are country fare and these are treated in a provincial French manner with the Cajun touch of white, black and red pepper.

4 pigeons
½ tsp each cayenne, white and black pepper
2 tbsps oil
2 tbsps butter or margarine
12oz button onions
2 sticks celery, sliced
4 carrots, peeled and sliced
4 tbsps flour
1½ cups chicken stock
½ cup dry red wine
4oz button mushrooms, quartered or left whole if small
3oz fresh or frozen lima beans
2 tsps tomato paste (optional)
2 tbsps chopped parsley
Pinch salt

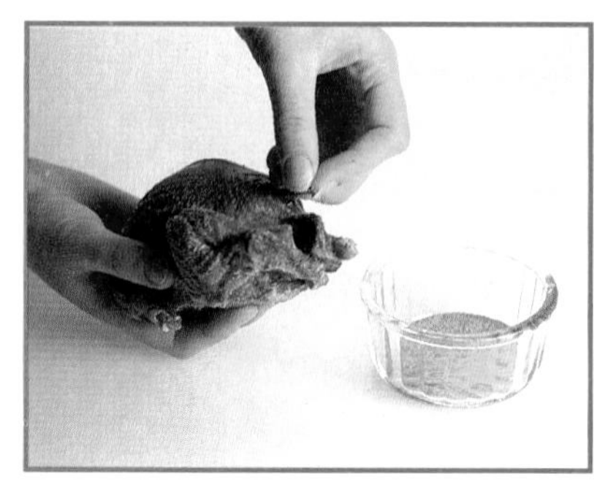

**Step 1** Season the pigeons inside their cavities with the three kinds of pepper.

**1.** Wipe the pigeons with a damp cloth and season them inside the cavities with the three kinds of pepper and a pinch of salt.

**2.** Heat the oil in a heavy-based casserole and add the butter or margarine. Once it is foaming, place in the pigeons, two at a time if necessary, and brown them on all sides, turning them frequently. Remove from the casserole and set them aside.

**3.** To peel the button onions quickly, trim the root ends slightly and drop the onions into rapidly boiling water. Allow it to come back to the boil for about 1 minute. Transfer to cold water and leave to cool completely. The skins should come off easily. Trim roots completely.

**4.** Add the onions, celery and carrots to the fat in the casserole and cook for about 5 minutes to brown slightly. Add the flour and cook until golden brown, stirring constantly.

**5.** Pour in the stock and the wine and stir well. Bring to the boil over high heat until thickened.

**6.** Stir in the tomato paste, if using, and return the pigeons to the casserole along with any liquid that has accumulated. Partially cover the casserole and simmer gently for about 40-45 minutes, or until the pigeons are tender. Add the mushrooms and lima beans halfway through the cooking time. To serve, skim any excess fat from the surface of the sauce and sprinkle over the chopped parsley.

## Cook's Notes

**Time**
Preparation takes about 30 minutes and cooking takes about 50 minutes-1 hour.

**Variation**
The casserole may be prepared with Cornish hens quail or pheasant. The quail will take only half the cooking time.

**Serving Ideas**
This casserole is generally served from the dish in which it was cooked. Alternatively, arrange on individual plates, coat with some of the sauce and serve the rest separately. Accompany with rice.

SERVES 4-6

# CHICKEN WITH EGGPLANT AND SMOKED HAM STUFFING

Eggplants and smoked ham are favorite Cajun ingredients.
They add interest to roast chicken in this rich stuffing.

3lb roasting chicken
1 small eggplant
2 tbsps butter or margarine
2 shallots, finely chopped
4oz smoked ham, chopped
1½ cups fresh breadcrumbs
1 tsp chopped fresh thyme
1 tsp chopped fresh oregano
2 tsps chopped parsley
Salt and pepper
Pinch cayenne pepper
1-2 eggs, beaten
2 tbsps additional butter, softened

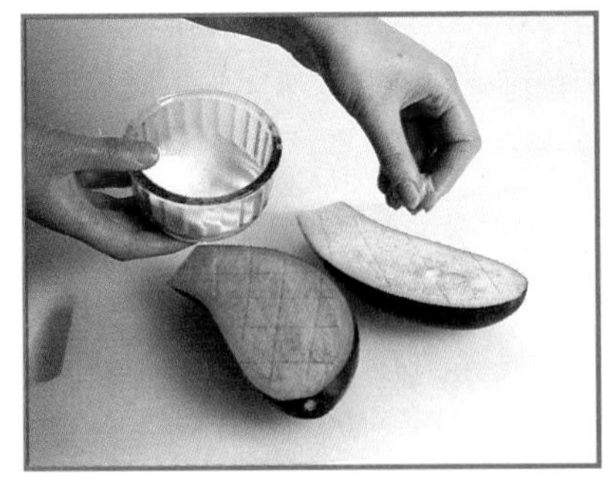

**Step 1** Sprinkle the cut surface of the eggplant lightly with salt and leave to stand.

**1.** Cut the eggplant in half lengthwise and remove stem. Lightly score the surface with a sharp knife and sprinkle with salt. Leave to stand for about 30 minutes for the salt to draw out any bitter juices.

**2.** Melt 2 tbsps butter in a medium saucepan and when foaming, add the shallots. Cook slowly to soften slightly.

**3.** Rinse the eggplant and pat dry. Cut into ½ inch cubes. Cook with the shallot until fairly soft. Add the remaining stuffing ingredients, beating in the egg gradually until the mixture just holds together. Add salt and pepper to taste.

**4.** Remove the fat from just inside the chicken cavity and fill with the stuffing. Tuck the wing tips under the chicken to hold the neck flap down. Stitch up the cavity opening on the chicken or secure with skewers. Tie the legs together and place the chicken in a roasting pan. Spread over the remaining softened butter and roast in a pre-heated 350°F oven for about 1 hour, or until the juices from the chicken run clear when the thickest part of the thigh is pierced with a sharp knife. Leave the chicken to stand for 10 minutes before carving. If desired, make a gravy with the pan juices.

**Step 4** Before stuffing the chicken, remove the fat from just inside the cavity opening.

## Cook's Notes

**Time**
Preparation takes about 30 minutes and cooking takes about 5-6 minutes for the stuffing and about 1 hour for the chicken.

**Variation**
Other ingredients, such as chopped red or green peppers, celery or green onions, may be added to the stuffing.

**Watchpoint**
Do not stuff the chicken until ready to cook.

SERVES 4

# Braised Rabbit with Peppers

Rabbit was a staple in the diets of the early Cajun settlers, who used local ingredients to vary this classic French game stew.

2¼lb rabbit joints
1 lemon slice
Flour for dredging
Pinch salt and pepper
1 tsp dry mustard
1 tsp paprika
¼ tsp each cayenne, white and black pepper
1 tsp garlic powder
¼ tsp dried dill
Oil for frying
1 onion, thinly sliced
1 small green pepper, seeded and thinly sliced
1 small red pepper, seeded and thinly sliced
14oz canned tomatoes
1 cup chicken stock
4 tbsps dry white wine
1 bay leaf

**1.** Soak the rabbit overnight with the lemon slice in cold water to cover.

**2.** Drain the rabbit and pat dry with paper towels.

**3.** Combine flour, spices, herbs and seasoning and dredge the rabbit with the mixture.

**4.** Heat the oil and fry the rabbit on all sides until golden brown. Remove to a plate.

**5.** Cook the onion and peppers for about 1 minute. Add the tomatoes, stock and bay leaf and bring to the boil. Return the rabbit to the pan and spoon over the sauce. Partially cover and cook over gentle heat until tender, about 45-50 minutes.

**6.** Add the wine during the last 10 minutes of cooking. Remove the bay leaf before serving.

**Step 3** Dredge the rabbit in the seasoned flour mixture and shake off the excess.

**Step 4** Heat the oil and fry the rabbit on both sides until golden brown.

**Step 5** Cook the rabbit in the sauce with the peppers and onions until tender to the point of a knife.

## Cook's Notes

**Time**
Preparation takes about 25 minutes, with overnight soaking for the rabbit. Cooking takes about 50 minutes-1 hour.

**Variation**
If yellow peppers are available, use the three colors for an attractive dish.

**Cook's Tip**
Soaking the rabbit with lemon overnight helps to whiten the meat and to remove any strong taste.

P
S

SERVES 4-6

# Chicken and Sausage Jambalaya

A jambalaya varies according to what the cook has to hand.
It could contain seafood, ham, poultry, sausage or a tasty mixture.

3lbs chicken portions, skinned, boned, and cut into cubes
3 tbsps butter or margarine
1 large onion, roughly chopped
3 sticks celery, roughly chopped
1 large green pepper, seeded and roughly chopped
1 clove garlic, crushed
1 tsp each cayenne, white and black pepper
1 cup uncooked rice
14oz canned tomatoes
6 oz smoked sausage, cut into ½ inch dice
3 cups chicken stock
Salt
Chopped parsley

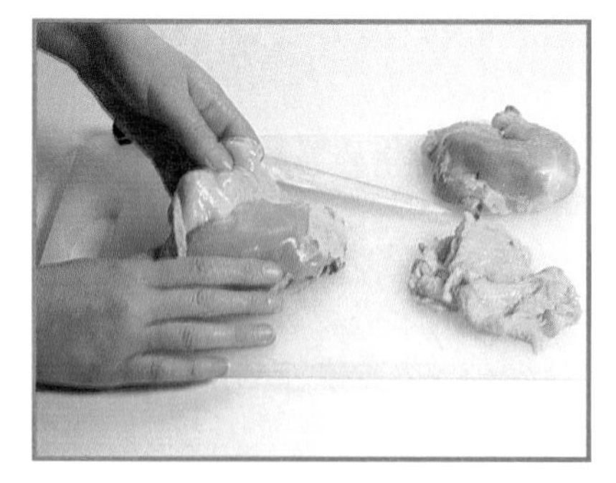

Remove the skin from the chicken and set aside.

**1.** Use the chicken bones, skins, onion and celery trimmings to make stock. Cover the ingredients with water, bring to the boil and then simmer slowly for 1 hour. Strain and reserve.

**2.** Melt the butter or margarine in a large saucepan and add the onion. Cook slowly to brown and then add the celery, green pepper and garlic and cook briefly.

**3.** Add the three kinds of pepper and the rice, stirring to mix well.

**4.** Add the chicken; tomatoes, sausage and stock and mix well. Bring to the boil, then reduce the heat to simmering and cook about 20-25 minutes, stirring occasionally until the chicken is done and the rice is tender. The rice should have absorbed most of the liquid by the time it has cooked.

**Step 1** Put the skin and bones in a large stock pot with the onion and celery trimmings to make the stock. Add water to cover.

## Cook's Notes

**Time**
Preparation takes about 35-40 minutes and cooking takes about 20-25 minutes.

**Preparation**
Check the level of liquid occasionally as the rice is cooking and add more water or stock as necessary. If there is a lot of liquid left and the rice is nearly cooked, uncover the pan and boil rapidly.

**Serving Ideas**
Jambalaya is often served as a first course, in which case this recipe serves 8. It can aslo be used as a side dish to serve 6 people.

SERVES 4-6

# COUSH-COUSH (FRIED CORNMEAL)

Cornmeal is a favorite in the South, as a bread, a coating for frying or a warming breakfast meal.

1½ cups yellow cornmeal
4 tbsps all-purpose flour
1 tbsp baking powder
2 tsps sugar
Pinch salt
2½ cups water
⅓ cup butter or margarine

**Step 1** Combine the dry ingredients in a bowl and mix in the water gradually, stirring well to form a smooth paste.

**1.** Mix the cornmeal and the other dry ingredients in a large bowl and add the water gradually, mixing until smooth.

**2.** Melt the butter in a medium frying pan and, when foaming, add the cornmeal mixture, spreading it out smoothly in the pan.

**3.** Turn up the heat and fry until brown and crisp on the bottom.

**4.** Stir the mixture to distribute the brown crust.

**5.** Reduce the heat and cover the pan tightly.

**6.** Cook the mixture for about 10-15 minutes, stirring occasionally.

**7.** Spoon into serving bowls and serve hot.

**Step 4** Stir the mixture to distribute the brown crust throughout it.

## Cook's Notes

**Time**
Preparation takes about 15 minutes and cooking takes approximately 20-25 minutes.

**Preparation**
If necessary, add more water if the mixture seems too dry.

**Serving Ideas**
Serve for breakfast with fruit, jam, milk and sugar or syrups. Use a fruit syrup, maple syrup, cane sugar or golden syrup.

MAKES 12

# OREILLES DE COCHON

These light, delicate pastries have a rather unusual name – Pig's Ears! It refers strictly to the shape the dough takes when deep-fried.

1 cup all-purpose flour
1 tsp baking powder
¼ tsp salt
4 tbsps cold water
Oil for frying
1½ cups cane syrup mixed with ¾ cup molasses
3oz finely chopped pecans

**Step 1** Sift the dry ingredients into a bowl and make a well in the center.

**1.** Sift the flour, baking powder and salt together in a large bowl. Make a well in the center and pour in the cold water.

**2.** Using a wooden spoon, mix until a stiff dough forms, and then knead by hand until smooth.

**3.** Divide the dough into 12 portions, each about the size of a walnut. Roll out each portion of dough on a floured surface until very thin.

**4.** Heat the oil in a deep fat fryer to 350°F. Drop each piece of pastry into the hot fat using two forks. Twist the pastry just as it hits the oil. Cook one at a time until light brown.

**5.** In a large saucepan, boil the syrup until it forms a soft ball when dropped into cold water.

**6.** Drain the pastries on paper towels after frying and dip carefully into the hot syrup. Sprinkle with pecans before the syrup sets and allow to cool before serving.

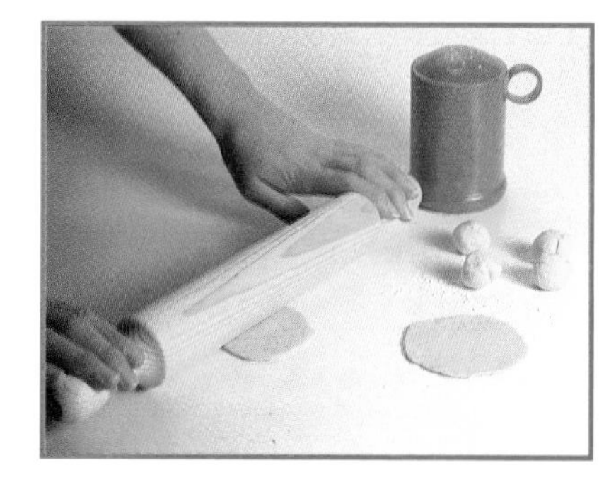

**Step 3** On a floured surface, roll out each piece until very thin.

## Cook's Notes

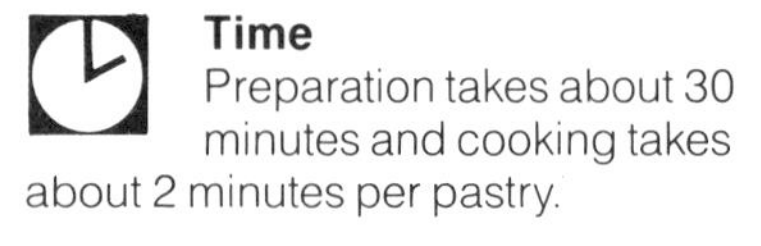

**Time**
Preparation takes about 30 minutes and cooking takes about 2 minutes per pastry.

**Economy**
When pecans are expensive, substitute less expensive nuts or omit entirely.

**Cook's Tip**
The pastries must be served on the day they are made because they do not keep well.

MAKES 1 CAKE

# SYRUP CAKE

Rather like gingerbread, but with a spicy taste of cinnamon, nutmeg and cloves instead, this cake can be served cool with coffee or tea or warm with cream.

1 cup vegetable shortening
1 cup molasses
3 eggs, beaten
3 cups all-purpose flour
1 tbsp baking powder
Pinch salt
1 tsp cinnamon
¼ tsp ground nutmeg
Pinch ground cloves
4 tbsps chopped pecans
4 tbsps raisins

**Step 1** Cream the shortening until light and fluffy. Beat in the molasses with an electric mixer.

**1.** Cream the shortening until light and fluffy. Add the molasses and beat with an electric mixer. Add the eggs one at a time, beating well in between each addition.

**2.** Sift the flour together with a pinch of salt and baking powder. Combine with the molasses mixture and add the spices.

**3.** Stir in the nuts and raisins and pour the mixture into a lightly greased 9 x 13″ baking pan.

**4.** Bake for about 45 minutes in a pre-heated 375°F oven.

**5.** To test for doneness, insert a skewer into the center of the cake. If it comes out clean, the cake is done. Allow to cool and cut into squares to serve.

**Step 2** Sift in the dry ingredients and combine by hand.

**Step 5** Insert a skewer into the center of the cake. If it comes out clean the cake is done.

## Cook's Notes

**Time**
Preparation takes about 20 minutes and cooking takes about 45 minutes.

**Variation**
The cake may be prepared without the nuts and raisins, if desired. Add vanilla extract or lemon rind, if desired, for extra flavor.

**Cook's Tip**
Lightly oil the inside of the measuring cup when measuring syrups like molasses. The syrup will not stick to the cup but will pour right out.

MAKES ABOUT 36

# Brown Sugar Cookies

This rather thick dough bakes to a crisp golden brown cookie, perfect as an accompaniment to ice cream or fruit salad.

1¼ cups packed light brown sugar
3 tbsps light corn syrup
4 tbsps water
1 egg
2⅓ cups all-purpose flour
1 tbsp ground ginger
1 tbsp bicarbonate of soda
Pinch salt
1 cup finely chopped pecans

**Step 1** Combine the sugar, syrup, water and egg with an electric mixer until light.

**1.** Mix the brown sugar, syrup, water and egg together in a large bowl. Beat with an electric mixer until light.

**2.** Sift flour with the ginger, baking soda and salt into the brown sugar mixture and add the pecans. Stir by hand until thoroughly mixed.

**3.** Lightly oil three baking sheets and drop the mixture by spoonfuls about 2 inches apart.

**4.** Bake in a pre-heated 375°F oven until lightly browned around the edges, about 10-12 minutes. Leave on the baking sheet for 1-2 minutes before removing with a palette knife to a wire rack to cool completely.

**Step 3** Use a spoon to drop the batter about 2 inches apart onto a greased baking sheet.

**Step 4** Bake until browned around the edges. Cool slightly and remove with a palette knife.

## Cook's Notes

**Time**
Preparation takes about 20 minutes and cooking takes about 10-12 minutes per batch.

**Variation**
Add raisins to the dough, or use other nuts instead of pecans.

**Preparation**
The dough will keep in the refrigerator for several days. Allow to stand at room temperature for at least 15 minutes before using.

MAKES 12-16

# PRALINES

A sugary, crunchy and thoroughly delectable confection with pecans. These are a favorite treat in the Bayou country and all over the South.

1½ cups unsalted butter
1 cup sugar
1 cup packed light brown sugar
1 cup milk
½ cup heavy cream
1 cup chopped pecans
2 tbsps vanilla or rum extract
1 tbsp water
Butter or oil

**Step 2** Simmer the sugar mixture until it is a deep golden brown.

**Step 3** When pecans and liquid are added the mixture will foam. Stir until foam subsides.

**Step 3** Drop the mixture by spoonfuls onto greased baking sheets.

**1.** Melt the butter in a large, heavy-based pan. Add the sugars, milk and cream and bring mixture to the boil, stirring constantly.

**2.** Reduce the heat to simmering and cook to a deep golden brown syrup. Stir continuously. After about 20 minutes, drop a small amount of the mixture into ice water. If it forms a hard ball, the syrup is ready. The hardball stage registers 250°F on a sugar thermometer.

**3.** Add the pecans, flavoring and water. Stir until the mixture stops foaming. Grease baking sheets with butter or oil and drop on the mixture by spoonfuls into mounds about 2 inches in diameter. The pralines will spread out as they cool. Allow to cool completely before serving.

## Cook's Notes

**Time**
Preparation takes about 25 minutes, and cooking takes about 20 minutes.

**Watchpoint**
When adding the flavorings and water, the mixture may spatter and can burn the skin. Add liquid with a long-handled spoon or wear oven gloves.

**Variation**
Pralines are popular when made with sesame seeds, too. Add them in place of pecans.

CREOLE
COOKING

# INTRODUCTION

What is Creole cooking? It's American cooking, but with a difference. It's Southern cooking, but with further refinement. Its home is New Orleans, where cooking has always been considered an art. This reverence for culinary matters is no doubt traceable to the strong French influence in Southern Louisiana. But there were other influences at work on the local cuisine, too.

To be considered a Creole in the strictest sense, you would have to be descended from a French or Spanish family who came to the area before 1803. Other groups, including West Indians, had also settled here, all with their individual ideas about what to eat and how to cook it.

Instead of the formality of the food favored by the aristocracy, the French settlers relied mostly on peasant-type dishes, although as the area became more civilized grand dining was revived for special occasions. The recipes were altered to suit the local ingredients. Rice became a mainstay because it grew easily in the warm, humid climate. Fish and shellfish were abundant. Vegetables like tomatoes and red and green peppers flourished in the long growing season. The French used herbs to add flavor, the West Indians spices and the Spanish a dash of hot pepper. Africans brought in new vegetables like okra. Thus was born Creole cuisine, definitely American, definitely Southern and definitely different from any other cuisine in the world.

SERVES 4

# CREOLE TOMATOES

A perfect side dish for grilled chicken or fish, this is especially good for summer, when tomatoes are at their best.

4 large ripe tomatoes
1 small green pepper, seeded and thinly sliced
4 green onions, sliced
1 clove garlic, crushed
4 tbsps white wine
Pinch cayenne pepper
Salt
1 tbsp butter or margarine
4 tbsps heavy cream

**Step 1** Place tomatoes in a pan of boiling water.

**Step 3** Remove the peel in strips, starting at the stem end.

**Step 4** Cut in half through the stem end. Scoop out seeds with a small spoon.

**1.** Remove the tomato stems and place tomatoes in a pan of boiling water.

**2.** Leave for 30 seconds and remove with a draining spoon. Place immediately in a bowl of ice cold water.

**3.** Use a small, sharp knife to remove the peel, beginning at the stem end.

**4.** Cut the tomatoes in half and scoop out the seeds. Strain the juice and reserve it, discarding the seeds.

**5.** Place tomatoes cut side down in a baking dish and sprinkle over the reserved juice. Add the sliced pepper, onions, garlic, wine, cayenne pepper and salt. Dot with butter or margarine.

**6.** Place in a preheated 350°F oven for about 15-20 minutes, or until tomatoes are heated through and tender, but not falling apart. Strain juices into a small saucepan.

**7.** Bring juices to the boil to reduce slightly. Stir in the cream and reboil. Spoon over the tomatoes to serve.

## Cook's Notes

**Time**
Preparation takes about 30 minutes and cooking takes 15-20 minutes.

**Preparation**
Once the cream is added to the tomato liquid, allow the mixture to come just to the boil. Boiling rapidly at this stage can cause curdling.

**Cook's Tip**
Placing tomatoes into boiling water for 30 seconds and then into cold loosens the peel. This process works well with peaches, too.

SERVES 4

# CREOLE EGGPLANT

Stuffed eggplants are a good suggestion for either appetizers or light meals. Shrimp are the customary filling, but other ingredients substitute well.

2 eggplants
⅓ cup butter or margarine
1 onion, finely chopped
1 stick celery, finely chopped
1 small red pepper, seeded and chopped
1 clove garlic, crushed
Salt and pepper
4oz cooked, peeled shrimp
Dry breadcrumbs

**Step 1** Cut the eggplants in half lengthwise, score the surface lightly with a sharp knife and sprinkle with salt.

**1.** Cut the eggplants in half lengthwise and remove the stems. Score the cut surface lightly and sprinkle with salt. Leave the eggplants to stand on paper towels for 30 minutes. Rinse, pat dry and wrap in foil. Bake for 15 minutes in a preheated 350°F oven.

**2.** Scoop out the center of the baked eggplants, leaving a margin of ¼ inch flesh inside the skins to form a shell. Chop the scooped out flesh roughly. Melt the butter and add the chopped eggplant, onion, celery, pepper and garlic. Cook slowly to soften the vegetables.

**3.** Season with salt and pepper and add the shrimp. Spoon the mixture into the shells, sprinkle with breadcrumbs and bake in an ovenproof dish for an additional 20 minutes. Serve hot.

**Step 2** Using a small knife or teaspoon, scoop out the center of the eggplant, leaving a thin border to form a shell.

**Step 3** Spoon the filling carefully into the eggplant shells, mounding it slightly on top.

## Cook's Notes

**Time**
Preparation takes 30 minutes and cooking takes about 35 minutes.

**Cook's Tip**
Sprinkling eggplants with salt and leaving them to stand draws out the bitter juices, making them easier to digest and better tasting.

**Serving Ideas**
Serve as a first course or as a vegetable side dish.

SERVES 6

# CHICKEN AND SHRIMP PEPPERS

Peppers feature prominently in Creole cooking, either as a colorful addition or a major part of a recipe like this one.

3 large green or red peppers
¼ cup butter or margarine
1 small onion, finely chopped
1 stick celery, finely chopped
1 clove garlic, crushed
2 chicken breasts, skinned, boned and finely diced
4oz cooked, peeled shrimp
2 tsps chopped parsley
½ loaf of stale French bread, made into crumbs
1-2 eggs, beaten
Salt, pepper and a pinch cayenne pepper
6 tsps dry breadcrumbs

**1.** Cut the pepper in half lengthwise and remove the cores and seeds. Leave the stems attached, if desired.

**2.** Melt the butter in a frying pan and add the onion, celery, garlic and chicken. Cook over moderate heat until the vegetables are softened and the chicken is cooked. Add the shrimp and parsley. Season with salt, pepper and cayenne.

**3.** Stir in the French breadcrumbs and add enough beaten egg to make the mixture hold together.

**4.** Spoon filling into each pepper half, mounding the top slightly. Place the peppers in a baking dish that holds them closely.

**5.** Pour enough water down the side of the dish to come about ½ inch up the sides of the peppers. Cover and bake in a pre-heated 350°F oven for about 45 minutes, or until the peppers are just tender.

**6.** Sprinkle each with the dried breadcrumbs and place under a preheated broiler until golden brown. Serve hot or cold.

**Step 1** Cut peppers in half and remove seeds and white core.

**Step 4** Spoon filling into the pepper halves, mounding the top and smoothing out.

**Step 5** Place peppers close together in a baking dish and carefully pour in about ½ inch water.

## Cook's Notes

**Time**
Preparation takes about 30 minutes and cooking takes about 45-50 minutes.

**Variation**
Use green onions in place of the small onion. Add chopped nuts or black olives to the filling, if desired.

**Serving Ideas**
Serve as a first course, either hot or cold, or as a light lunch or supper with a salad.

SERVES 4

# Eggs Sardou

A traditional New Orleans brunch dish, this can double as an appetizer or light supper dish, too.

1½lbs fresh spinach
1½ tbsps butter or margarine
1 tbsp flour
1 cup milk
Salt, pepper and nutmeg
4 artichoke hearts, quartered
4 eggs

**Hollandaise Sauce**

3 egg yolks
⅔ cup unsalted butter
1 tbsp lemon juice
Pinch salt and pepper
1 large piece canned pimento, drained and cut into thin strips

**1.** Strip the spinach leaves from the stalks and wash the leaves well. Place the leaves in a large saucepan and add a pinch of salt. Cover the pan and cook the spinach over moderate heat in only the water that clings to the leaves. When the spinach is just wilted, take off the heat and drain well. Chop roughly and set aside.

**2.** Melt the butter or margarine in a medium-sized saucepan and stir in the flour. Gradually add the milk, whisking constantly, and place the sauce over low heat. Whisk the sauce as it comes to the boil and allow it to boil rapidly for about one minute to thicken. Stir in the spinach and season the sauce with salt, pepper and nutmeg. Add the artichoke hearts and set the sauce aside.

**3.** Fill a large sauté pan with water and bring to the boil. Turn down the heat and, when the water is just barely simmering, break an egg into a cup or onto a saucer. Gently lower the egg into the water to poach. Repeat with the remaining eggs. Poach over gentle heat, never allowing the water to boil. Alternatively, cook in a special poaching pan. Cook until the whites have set but the yolks are still soft. Remove the eggs from the pan with a draining spoon and place in cold water until ready to use.

**4.** Place the egg yolks in a food processor or blender with the lemon juice and seasoning. Process once or twice to mix. Place the butter in a small saucepan and melt over gentle heat. Turn up the heat and when the butter is bubbling, take off the heat. With the machine running, gradually pour the butter onto the eggs in a very thin but steady stream.

**5.** To assemble the dish, reheat the spinach sauce and place an equal amount of it on each plate. Make a well in center. Place the eggs back into hot water briefly to reheat, and drain well. Place an egg in the hollow of the spinach sauce on each plate. Spoon over some of the Hollandaise sauce to coat each egg completely. Make a cross with two strips of pimento on top of each egg and serve immediately.

**Step 5** To reheat eggs, place briefly in hot water, remove with a draining spoon and hold over a towel to drain and dry completely.

## Cook's Notes

**Time**
Preparation takes about 45 minutes and cooking takes about 5 minutes for the spinach, 5-10 minutes for the sauce and about 5-6 minutes for the eggs.

**Cook's Tip**
If eggs should curdle when making a Hollandaise sauce, 1 tbsp iced water worked into the sauce quickly can sometimes bring it together again.

**Variation**
Artichoke hearts may be omitted and mushrooms used instead. Omit the pimento cross on top and sprinkle lightly with paprika before serving.

SERVES 4

# Oeufs Marchand de Vin

This is a classic egg dish from New Orleans served for brunch – the meal that's too late for breakfast but too early for lunch!

Full quantity Hollandaise sauce from the recipe for Eggs Sardou
4 eggs
4 slices smoked bacon
1 beefsteak tomato
4 slices bread
Oil for frying

**Marchand de Vin Sauce**

3 tbsps oil
½ small onion, finely chopped
1½ tbsps flour
1 clove garlic
6 mushrooms, finely chopped
¾ cup brown stock
6 tbsps red wine
Salt and pepper

**1.** Heat the oil for the Marchand de Vin sauce. Add the onion and cook until softened. Add the flour and cook slowly stirring frequently, until golden brown. Add the garlic and mushrooms and pour on the stock, stirring to blend well. Add the wine and bring the sauce to the boil. Lower the heat and simmer for about 15-20 minutes, stirring occasionally. Season to taste.

**2.** Prepare the Hollandaise sauce and poach the eggs according to the recipe for Eggs Sardou.

**3.** Fry the bacon in a small amount of oil, or broil until crisp. Drain, crumble and set aside.

**4.** Cut the bread with a pastry cutter into 3 inch diameter circles. Fry in enough oil to just cover until golden brown and crisp. Drain on paper towels and place on a serving plate. Spoon some of the Marchand de Vin sauce on top and keep warm in the oven.

**5.** Slice the tomatoes thickly and place one slice on top of the sauce on each bread croûte and continue to keep warm.

**6.** Reheat the eggs and drain well. Place one egg on top of each tomato slice. Spoon over some of the Hollandaise sauce and sprinkle with the bacon to serve.

**Step 1** Add the flour and cook slowly until a golden brown, stirring frequently.

**Step 4** To fry the bread, cut into circles and place in the oil, holding the bread under the oil with a spatula to brown both sides quickly. Drain on paper towels.

## Cook's Notes

**Time**
Preparation takes about 45 minutes and cooking takes about 15 minutes for the Marchand de Vin sauce and about 30 minutes total time.

**Cook's Tip**
Hollandaise sauce may be reheated by pouring the sauce into a bowl and placing the bowl in a pan of hot water. Stir the sauce frequently until evenly heated through. Never reheat over direct heat.

**Preparation**
The Marchand de Vin sauce may be prepared several days in advance and kept in the refrigerator. Reheat gently until boiling.

MAKES $2\frac{1}{2}$ CUPS

# Horseradish Pecan Sauce

This creamy, piquant sauce has a variety of uses. The recipe makes a lot, but a sauce this good won't go to waste.

1 cup sour cream or natural yogurt
4 tbsps prepared horeseradish
2 tbsps white wine vinegar
1 tbsp Creole-style mustard or other whole grain mustard
Pinch salt, white pepper and sugar
1 cup whipping cream
6 tbsps finely chopped pecans

**Step 1** Combine sour cream, horseradish, vinegar, mustard, sugar and seasoning. Stir carefully to mix.

**1.** Combine sour cream or yogurt and horseradish in a small bowl. Add the vinegar, mustard, sugar, salt and pepper, and stir into the sour cream. Do not over-stir. Chill in the refrigerator for at least 2 hours.

**2.** Whip the cream until soft peaks form.

**3.** Mix the chopped pecans into the sour cream sauce and stir in a spoonful of cream to lighten the mixture. Fold in the remaining cream and serve chilled.

**Step 3** Fold in pecans and cream using a large spoon or spatula.

## Cook's Notes

**Time**
Preparation takes about 15 minutes, with 2 hours chilling time.

**Cook's Tip**
Cream that has been refrigerated for at least 2 hours is easier to whip.

**Serving Ideas**
The sauce is good with cold poached salmon, seafood, cold roast beef or hot baked potatoes.

SERVES 6-8

# RED BEANS AND RICE

Served every Monday in New Orleans, this is a delicious way of making a small amount of meat go a long way.

8oz dried red kidney beans
1 bay leaf
1 sprig thyme
8oz ham or bacon
¼ cup butter or margarine
1 onion, finely chopped
1 green pepper, seeded and cut into small dice
3 sticks celery, finely chopped
2 cloves garlic, crushed
1 tsp cayenne pepper
Salt
8oz rice, cooked
4 green onions, finely chopped

**Step 1** Soak the kidney beans in water overnight, until they swell in size.

**1.** Pick over the beans and place them in a large stockpot or bowl. Cover with water and leave to soak overnight. Drain them and place in a pot of fresh water with the sprig of thyme, bay leaf and a pinch of salt. Add the piece of ham or bacon and bring to the boil. Partially cover the pan and leave to boil rapidly for 10 minutes. Reduce the heat and then simmer for 2½-3 hours, adding more water if necessary.

**2.** When the beans have been cooking for about half the required length of time, melt the butter in a small frying pan and cook the onion, pepper, garlic and celery until the onions look translucent. Add this mixture to the beans and continue cooking them.

**3.** Once the beans are soft, mash some of them against the side of the pot with a large spoon. Alternatively, remove about ¾ cup of the mixture and blend to a smooth purée in a food processor or blender. Pour back into the pot to thicken the rest of the beans.

**4.** Remove the piece of ham or bacon, trim off excess fat and cut the meat into ½ inch pieces. Return to the beans and add cayenne pepper. Stir well and continue to cook the beans. Remove thyme and bayleaf before serving.

**5.** To serve, place rice on serving plates and spoon over some of the beans. Sprinkle the top with the chopped green onion.

**Step 3** Once the beans are completely softened, mash some of them against the side of the pot with a large spoon.

## Cook's Notes

**Time**
Preparation takes about 25 minutes, with overnight soaking for the beans. Cooking takes about 2½-3 hours.

**Watchpoint**
The beans must boil vigorously for the first 10 minutes of cooking time. Make sure that the beans are completely cooked – it can be dangerous to eat dried pulses that are insufficiently cooked.

**Variation**
Smoked sausage or garlic sausage may be used instead of the ham or bacon.

SERVES 4-6

# CHICKEN GUMBO

The African influence on Creole cuisine includes this soup-stew, which takes its name from the African word for okra.

3lb chicken, cut into 6-8 pieces
½ cup oil
1 cup flour
2-3 dried red chili peppers or 1-2 fresh chili peppers
1 large onion, finely chopped
1 large green pepper, roughly chopped
3 sticks celery, finely chopped
2 cloves garlic, crushed
8oz andouille sausage or garlic sausage, diced
4 cups chicken stock
1 bay leaf
Dash tabasco
Salt and pepper
4oz fresh okra
Cooked rice

**1.** Heat the oil in a large sauté pan or frying pan and brown the chicken on both sides, 3-4 pieces at a time. Transfer the chicken to a plate and set it aside.

**2.** Lower the heat under the pan and add the flour. Cook over a very low heat for about 30 minutes, stirring constantly until the flour turns a rich, dark brown. Take the pan off the heat occasionally, so that the flour does not burn.

**3.** Add the chili peppers, onion, green pepper, celery, garlic and sausage to the roux and cook for about 5 minutes over very low heat, stirring continuously.

**4.** Pour on the stock and stir well. Add the bay leaf and a dash of tabasco, if desired, and return the chicken to the pan. Cover and cook for about 30 minutes or until the chicken is tender.

**5.** Top and tail the okra and cut each part into 2-3 pieces. If okra is small, leave whole. Add to the chicken and cook for a further 10-15 minutes. Remove the bay leaf and serve the Gumbo over rice.

**Step 2** Continue cooking over low heat, stirring constantly as the flour begins to brown.

**Step 3** When the flour is a rich dark brown, add the remaining sauce ingredients. Cook over a very low heat for 5 minutes, then add the stock slowly.

## Cook's Notes

**Time**
Preparation takes about 30 minutes and cooking takes about 1 hour 25 minutes.

**Cook's Tip**
Brown rouxs are frequently used in Creole cooking. A roux may be made ahead of time and kept in the refrigerator to use whenever needed. If the roux is cold, heat the liquid before adding.

**Variation**
Gumbo may also be made with shrimp, pork or pigeon.

SERVES 6

# FRIED CHICKEN CREOLE

Not the usual crisp Southern-style fried chicken, this is cooked in a tomato sauce flavored with garlic, herbs and wine.

3lb frying chicken, cut into serving pieces
Flour for dredging
Salt and pepper
6 tbsps oil
5 tbsps butter or margarine
1 small onion, finely chopped
1 clove garlic, crushed
4oz bacon or uncooked ham, diced
6 tomatoes, peeled and chopped
2 tsps fresh thyme or 1 tsp dried thyme
Salt and pepper
½ cup white wine
2 tbsps chopped parsley

**1.** Mix the flour with salt and pepper and dredge the chicken lightly, shaking the pieces to remove any excess flour. Heat the oil in a large sauté pan or frying pan and, when hot, add the butter.

**Step 1** Dredge the chicken very lightly with flour and shake to remove the excess.

**2.** Add the chicken drumstick and thigh pieces skin side down and allow to brown. Turn the pieces over and brown on the other side. Brown over moderately low heat so that the chicken cooks as well as browns. Push the chicken to one side of the pan, add the breast meat, and brown in the same way.

**3.** Add the garlic, onion and bacon or ham to the pan and lower the heat. Cook slowly for about 10 minutes, or until the bacon browns slightly. Add the tomatoes and thyme and lower the heat. Cook until the chicken is just tender and the tomatoes are softened.

**4.** Using a draining spoon, transfer the chicken and other ingredients to a serving dish and keep warm. Remove all but about 4 tbsps of the fat from the pan and deglaze with the wine, scraping up the browned bits from the bottom. Bring to the boil and allow to reduce slightly. Pour over the chicken to serve, and sprinkle with chopped parsley.

**Step 2** Brown all the chicken on both sides slowly, until golden.

## Cook's Notes

**Preparation**
Brown the chicken slowly so that it cooks at the same time as it browns. This will cut down on the length of cooking time needed once all the ingredients are added.

**Time**
Preparation takes about 25 minutes and cooking takes about 30-40 minutes.

**Variation**
Add finely chopped green or red pepper along with the onion and garlic. Celery may also be added at the same time. If more sauce is desired, use one 14 oz can of tomatoes and juice.

SERVES 4

# PECAN CHICKEN

Pecans are often used in the South in both sweet and savory dishes. Here, their rich, sweet taste complements a stuffing for chicken.

4 boned chicken breasts
3 tbsps butter or margarine
1 small onion, finely chopped
3oz pork sausage meat
3oz fresh breadcrumbs
1 tsp chopped thyme
1 tsp chopped parsley
1 small egg, lightly beaten
1 cup pecan halves
1 cup chicken stock
1 tbsp flour
2 tbsps sherry
Salt and pepper
Chopped parsley or 1 bunch watercress to garnish

**1.** Cut a small pocket in the thick side of each chicken breast using a small knife.

**2.** Melt 1 tbsp butter in a small saucepan and add the onion. Cook a few minutes over gentle heat to soften. Add the sausage meat and turn up the heat to brown. Break up the sausage meat with a fork as it cooks.

**3.** Drain any excess fat and add the breadcrumbs, herbs and a pinch of salt and pepper. Allow to cool slightly and add enough egg to hold the mixture together. Chop pecans, reserving 8, and add to the stuffing.

**4.** Using a small teaspoon, fill the pocket in each chicken breast with some of the stuffing.

**5.** Melt 1 tbsp butter in a casserole and place in the chicken breasts, skin side down first. Brown over moderate heat and turn over. Brown the other side quickly to seal.

**6.** Pour in the stock, cover the casserole and cook for about 25-30 minutes in a preheated 350°F oven until tender.

**7.** When chicken is cooked, remove it to a serving plate to keep warm. Reserve cooking liquid.

**8.** Melt remaining butter in a small saucepan and stir in the flour. Cook to a pale straw color. Strain on the cooking liquid and add the sherry. Bring to the boil and stir constantly until thickened. Add the pecans and seasoning.

**9.** Spoon some of the sauce over the chicken. Garnish with chopped parsley or a bouquet of watercress.

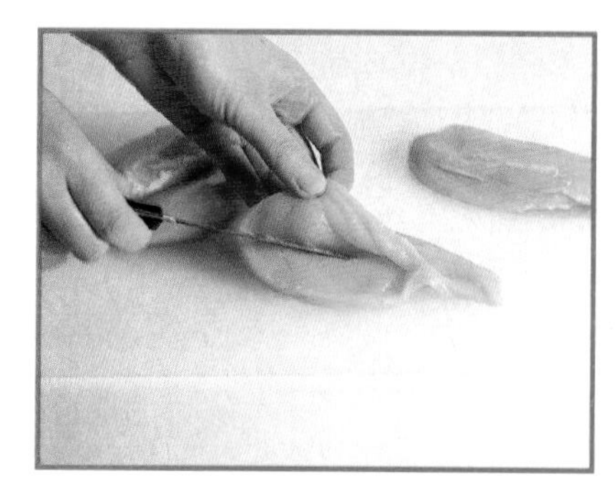

**Step 1** Use a small, sharp knife to cut a pocket in each chicken breast.

**Step 4** Open each pocket in the chicken and spoon in the stuffing.

## Cook's Notes

**Time**
Preparation takes about 30 minutes and cooking takes about 40 minutes.

**Variation**
If pecans are unavailable, use hazelnuts. Crush the hazelnuts roughly for the garnish and brown lightly in the butter before adding flour for the sauce.

**Serving Ideas**
Serve with a combination of white and wild rice.

SERVES 4-6

# CHICKEN ST. PIERRE

A French name for a very Southern combination of chicken, lima beans, peppers and onions made into a spicy, aromatic stew.

3lb chicken, cut in 8 pieces
⅓ cup butter or margarine
3 tbsps flour
1 large red pepper, diced
1 large green pepper, diced
6 green onions, chopped
½ cup dry white wine
1 cup chicken stock
6oz lima beans
1 tsp chopped thyme
Salt, pepper and pinch nutmeg
Dash tabasco (optional)

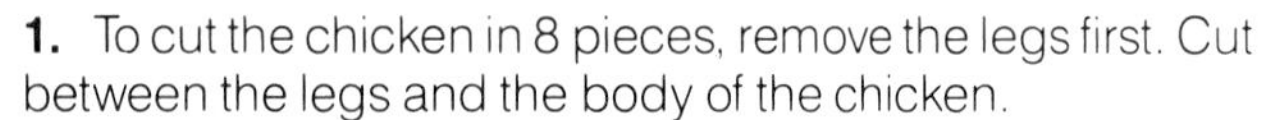

**1.** To cut the chicken in 8 pieces, remove the legs first. Cut between the legs and the body of the chicken.

**2.** Bend the legs backwards to break the joint and cut away from the body.

**3.** Cut the drumstick and thigh joints in half.

**4.** Cut down the breastbone with a sharp knife and then use poultry shears to cut through the bone and ribcage to remove the breast joints from the back.

**5.** Cut both breast joints in half, leaving some white meat attached to the wing joint. Cut through bones with poultry shears.

**6.** Heat the butter in a large saute pan and when foaming add the chicken, skin side down. Brown on one side, turn over and brown other side. Remove the chicken and add the flour to the pan. Cook to a pale straw color. Add the peppers and onions and cook briefly.

**7.** Pour on the wine and chicken stock and bring to the boil. Stir constantly until thickened. Add the chicken, lima beans, thyme, seasoning and nutmeg. Cover the pan and cook about 25 minutes, or until the chicken is tender. Add tabasco to taste, if desired, before serving.

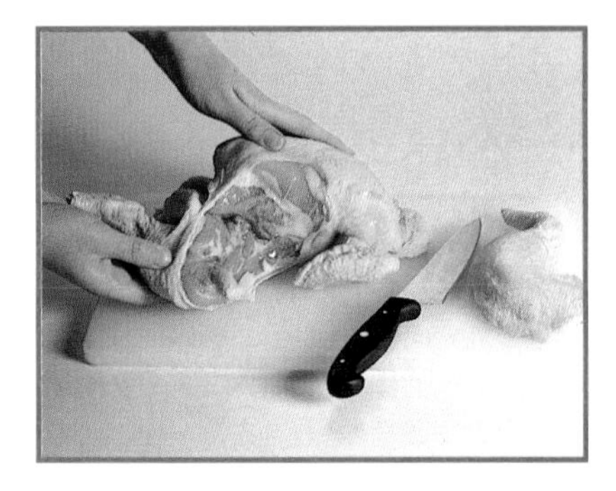

**Step 2** Bend chicken legs back to break the joint, then cut between leg and body of chicken.

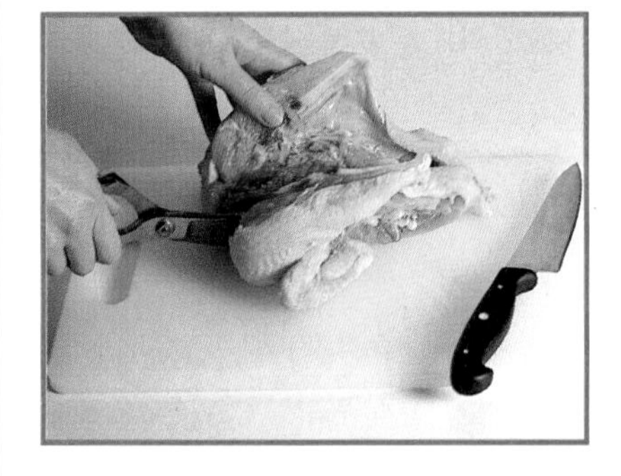

**Step 4** Cut through the breastbone and rib cage with poultry shears.

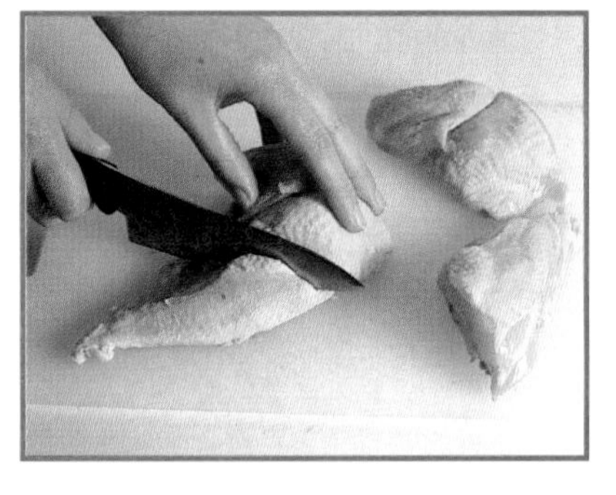

**Step 5** Cut the breast joint in two, leaving white meat attached to the wing.

**Time**
Preparation takes about 35 minutes and cooking takes about 40 minutes.

**Preparation**
For crisper vegetables, add them after the chicken and sauce have cooked for about 15 minutes.

**Freezing**
Chicken can be prepared in advance and reheated or frozen for up to three months. Thaw completely before reheating.

SERVES 8-10

# CREOLE OXTAILS

Oxtails are very economical, but rich in flavor. As they cook, they thicken their own sauce, so very little flour is needed.

4½lbs oxtails
Flour for dredging
Salt and pepper
2 onions, coarsely chopped
1 large green pepper, coarsely chopped
3 sticks celery, coarsely chopped
4 cloves garlic, crushed
2lbs canned tomatoes
2 cups beef stock
2 tbsps red wine vinegar
2 tbsps dark brown sugar
Pinch dried thyme
1 bay leaf
Pinch cayenne pepper
Oil for frying
1 tbsp Dijon or Creole mustard
Dash tabasco
Chopped parsley

**1.** Trim excess fat from the oxtails and cut them into 2 inch pieces.

**2.** Place a few pieces in a sieve and sprinkle over flour, salt and pepper. Shake the sieve to dredge the pieces of meat lightly in flour and repeat until all pieces are coated.

**3.** Heat the oil in a large casserole or saucepan and brown the meat in several batches.

**4.** When all the oxtails are browned, remove them to a plate and add the onion, green pepper, celery and garlic to the pan or casserole. Cook over moderately high heat, stirring until the vegetables have softened but not browned. Return the oxtails to the pan and add the tomatoes, stock, vinegar, brown sugar, thyme, bay leaf and cayenne pepper.

**5.** Bring to the boil and then reduce the heat. Cover and cook gently on top of the stove or in a preheated 350°F oven for about 3½ hours, or until the meat is very tender.

**6.** When the oxtails are cooked, transfer them to a serving dish and remove the bay leaf from the sauce. Skim the fat and purée the vegetables and the sauce in a food processor until smooth. Add the mustard, dash tabasco and a pinch of salt, if necessary. Spoon over the oxtails and sprinkle with chopped parsley, if desired.

**Step 3** Brown a few pieces of oxtail at a time in hot oil in a casserole or saucepan.

**Step 4** Return the oxtails to the pan and add tomatoes, stock, vinegar, brown sugar, thyme, bay leaf and cayenne pepper.

## Cook's Notes

**Time**
Preparation takes about 30 minutes and cooking takes about 3½ hours.

**Freezing**
The recipe may be prepared in advance and frozen in rigid containers for up to three months. Allow to defrost completely before reheating. Sauce may need whisking to bring it back together once reheated.

**Serving Ideas**
Serve with freshly boiled rice or with French bread.

SERVES 4

# GRILLADES

Thin slices of beef are quickly fried and then cooked in a rich brown sauce. Add a dash or two of tabasco according to taste.

4-8 pieces frying steak, depending on size
1 tbsp oil
1 tbsp butter or margarine
1 tbsp flour
6 green onions
1 clove garlic, crushed
1 tsp chopped thyme
2 tsps chopped parsley
3 tomatoes, peeled, seeded and chopped
1 cup beef stock
Dash tabasco
Salt

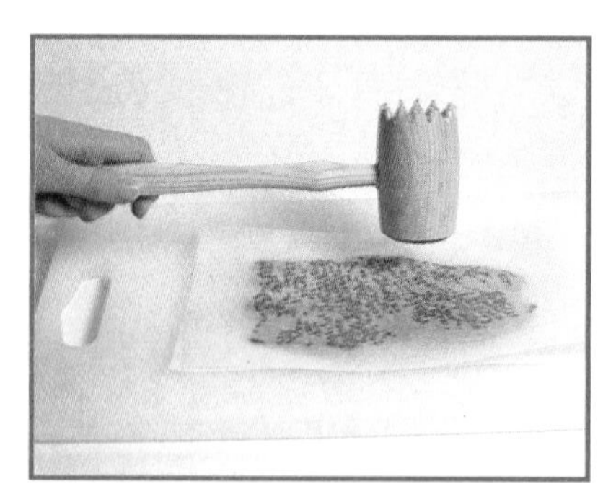

**Step 1** Pound the meat with a rolling pin or meat mallet to flatten slightly.

**1.** Place the meat between 2 sheets of plastic wrap or waxed paper and pound with a rolling pin or a meat mallet to flatten slightly.

**2.** Heat the oil in a large frying pan and brown the meat quickly, a few pieces at a time. Set the meat aside.

**3.** Melt the butter or margarine in the frying pan and add the flour. Cut the white part off the green onions and chop it finely. Add to the flour and butter, reserving the green tops for later use.

**4.** Add garlic to the pan and cook the mixture slowly, stirring frequently until it is a dark golden brown. Add the herbs, tomatoes, stock, tabasco and salt to taste and bring to the boil. Cook about 5 minutes to thicken and add the steaks. Cook to heat the meat through.

**5.** Chop the green tops of the onions and sprinkle over the steaks to garnish.

**Step 2** Press the meat against the hot pan to brown it quickly and evenly.

**Step 4** Cook the sauce rapidly for about 5 minutes to thicken. Tomatoes will break up slightly.

*Cook's Notes*

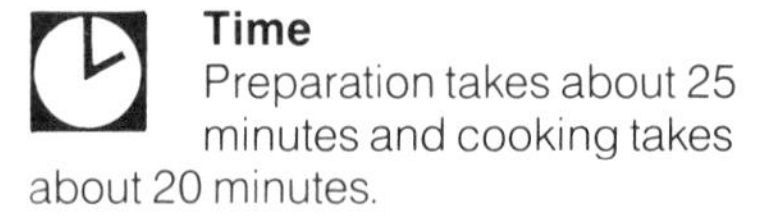

**Time**
Preparation takes about 25 minutes and cooking takes about 20 minutes.

**Serving Ideas**
Serve with rice or grits.

**Variation**
Add chopped red or green pepper to the sauce.

SERVES 4

# PANEED LEMON VEAL

Paneed means pan-fried in Creole – a perfect way to prepare this tender cut of veal that only needs brief cooking.

8 veal cutlets
Flour for dredging
Salt and pepper
2 tbsps butter or margarine
1 green pepper, seeded and thinly sliced
6 tbsps dry white wine
1 tbsp lemon juice
¾ cup chicken stock
1 lemon; peeled and thinly sliced

**Step 1** Use a flour dredger to sprinkle flour on the veal. Pat in by hand and then shake the pieces to remove excess flour.

**1.** Dredge the veal with a mixture of flour, salt and pepper. Shake off the excess.

**2.** Melt the butter or margarine in a large frying pan or sauté pan and brown the veal, a few pieces at a time. Remove the meat and keep it warm.

**Step 3** Cook the peppers briefly and remove them while still green and slightly crisp.

**Step 4** Pour the wine and lemon juice into the hot fat in the pan and scrape to deglaze.

**3.** Cook the peppers briefly and set aside with the veal.
**4.** Pour the wine and lemon juice into the pan to deglaze. Add the stock and bring to the boil. Boil for 5 minutes to reduce. Add the veal and peppers and cook 15 minutes over gentle heat. Add the lemons and heat through before serving.

## Cook's Notes

**Time**
Preparation takes about 25 minutes and cooking takes about 20-25 minutes.

**Preparation**
If the sauce is too tart, add a pinch of sugar to taste.

**Variation**
Use red pepper instead of green pepper and add chopped green onions.

SERVES 4

# Veal Jardinière

Jardin, French for garden, denotes a colorful garnish of vegetables, in this case a selection of carrots, beans, peas and tiny onions.

4 large veal chops
Oil for frying
1 tbsp butter or margarine
1 carrot, peeled and diced
12 button onions
1 tbsp flour
1½ cups beef stock
6 tbsps white wine
Salt and pepper
3oz green beans, topped, tailed and sliced
2oz peas

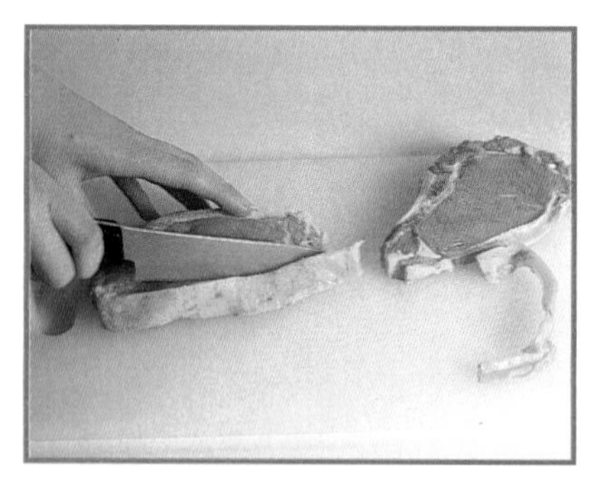

**Step 1** Use a small, sharp knife to trim away most of the veal fat.

**1.** Heat about 2 tbsps of the oil in a large frying pan. Trim the chops to remove most of the fat. Fry on both sides in the hot fat until browned.

**2.** Melt the butter or margarine in a medium saucepan. Peel the onion and add to the butter with the carrot. Cook slowly to soften. Sprinkle on the flour and cook to a good golden brown. Add the stock, wine, salt and pepper and bring to the boil. Cook until thick.

**3.** Pour the fat from the veal and pour in the sauce. Add the beans and peas and cook until the veal is tender, about 25 minutes.

**Step 2** Put unpeeled onions into a saucepan of boiling water and bring back to the boil for 1-2 minutes. Transfer to a bowl of cold water.

**Step 2** Allow to cool. Peels should come off easily.

## Cook's Notes

**Time**
Preparation takes about 25 minutes, and cooking takes about 40 minutes.

**Variation**
Serve the same sauce with beef, chicken or lamb.

**Preparation**
Brown the flour slowly, stirring constantly for an even color and to prevent a burned taste.

SERVES 4

# SPICED LAMB

French influence is evident in this dish, but the Creole touch is, too, with a good pinch of allspice and bright red peppers.

1lb lamb neck fillet
1 tsp fresh dill, chopped
1 tsp rosemary, crushed
1 tsp thyme, chopped
2 tsp mustard seeds, crushed slightly
2 bay leaves
1 tsp coarsely ground black pepper
½ tsp ground allspice
Juice of 2 lemons
1 cup red wine
2 tbsps oil
2 tbsps butter or margarine
1 small red pepper, seeded and sliced
3oz button mushrooms, left whole
3 tbsps flour
½ cup beef stock
Salt

**1.** Place the lamb in a shallow dish and sprinkle on the dill, rosemary, thyme and mustard seeds. Add the bay leaves, pepper, allspice, lemon juice and wine, and stir to coat the meat thoroughly with the marinade. Leave for 4 hours in the refrigerator.

**2.** Heat the oil in a large frying pan and add the red pepper and mushrooms and cook to soften slightly. Remove with a draining spoon.

**3.** Reheat the oil in the pan and add the lamb fillet, well drained and patted dry. Reserve marinade. Brown meat quickly on all sides to seal. Remove from the pan and set aside with the vegetables.

**4.** Melt the butter in the pan and when foaming add the flour. Lower the heat and cook the flour slowly until a good, rich brown. Pour in the beef stock and the marinade. Bring to the boil and return the vegetables and lamb to the pan. Cook about 15 minutes, or until the lamb is tender, but still pink inside.

**5.** Slice the lamb fillet thinly on the diagonal and arrange on plates. Remove the bay leaves from the sauce and spoon over the meat to serve.

**Step 1** Place lamb fillet in a shallow dish and mix with the marinating ingredients.

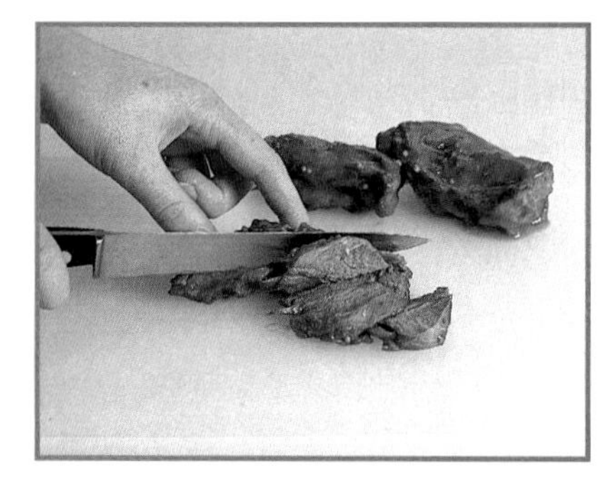

**Step 5** To serve, slice lamb fillet on the diagonal with a large, sharp knife or carving knife.

## Cook's Notes

**Time**
Preparation takes about 25 minutes, plus 4 hours marinating time for the meat. Cooking takes about 35 minutes.

**Variation**
Recipe can be prepared with pork fillet or steak.

**Serving Ideas**
Serve with rice or Pommes Noisettes (small potato balls browned in butter.)

SERVES 4

# OYSTERS ROCKEFELLER

Oysters can be purchased already opened, and you'll find the rest of this famous New Orleans dish simplicity itself to prepare.

24 oysters on the half shell
Rock salt
6 strips bacon, finely chopped
1¼lbs fresh spinach, well washed, stems removed and leaves finely chopped
1 small bunch green onions, finely chopped
2 cloves garlic, crushed
4-5 tbsps fine fresh breadcrumbs
Dash tabasco
2 tbsps aniseed liqueur
Pinch salt
Parmesan cheese

**1.** Loosen the oysters from their shells, strain and reserve their liquid.

**2.** Rinse the shells well and return an oyster to each one. Pour about 1 inch of rock salt into a baking pan and place in the oysters in their shells, pressing each shell gently into the salt.

**3.** Place the bacon in a large frying pan and cook slowly to render the fat. Turn up the heat and brown the bacon evenly.

**4.** Add the spinach, green onions and garlic and cook slowly until softened. Add the breadcrumbs, tabasco, oyster liquid, liqueur, and a pinch of salt.

**5.** Spoon some of the mixture onto each oyster and sprinkle with Parmesan cheese. Place in a preheated 350°F oven for about 15 minutes. Alternatively, heat through in the oven for 10 minutes and place under a preheated broiler to lightly brown the cheese. Serve immediately.

**Step 1** With a small sharp knife loosen the oysters from their shells to make them easier to eat. Hold over bowl to catch liquid.

**Step 2** Press the oyster shells into a baking pan filled with salt so that the shells sit level.

**Step 5** Spoon in the prepared mixture to cover each oyster completely.

## Cook's Notes

**Time**
Preparation takes about 25 minutes or longer if opening the oysters yourself. Cooking takes about 25 minutes.

**Buying Guide**
Fishmongers will sell oysters already opened on their half shell. If only shelled oysters are available, allow 6 per person and cook them 6 at a time in small baking dishes.

**Variation**
Finely chopped anchovies may be used instead of the bacon, and 3 tbsps butter or margarine substituted for the bacon fat.

SERVES 4

# Shrimp Remoulade

The shrimp in this dish 'cook' in the refrigerator in a marinade that is piquant with mustard, horseradish and wine vinegar.

1½lbs raw unshelled large shrimp
3 tbsps mild mustard
2 tsps horseradish
1 tbsp paprika
1 fresh chili pepper, seeded and finely chopped
1 clove garlic, crushed
Salt
½ cup white wine vinegar
1½ cups oil
6 green onions, sliced
2 sticks celery, thinly sliced
2 bay leaves
2 tbsps chopped parsley
Lettuce and lemon wedges

**1.** Shell the shrimp, except for the very tail ends. If desired, the shrimp may be completely shelled.

**2.** Combine the mustard, horseradish, paprika, chili pepper, garlic and salt in a deep bowl. Mix in the vinegar thoroughly.

**3.** Add the oil in a thin, steady stream while beating constantly with a small whisk. Continue to beat until the sauce is smooth and thick. Add the green onions, celery, bay leaves and chopped parsley. Cover the bowl tightly and leave in the refrigerator for several hours, or overnight.

**4.** Two hours before serving, add the shrimp to the marinade and stir to coat them well. Leave in the refrigerator until ready to serve.

**5.** To serve, shred the lettuce finely and place on individual serving plates. Arrange the shrimp on top and spoon over some of the marinade to serve, discarding the bay leaves.

**Step 2** Combine marinade ingredients in a bowl and stir in the vinegar.

**Step 3** Using a small whisk, gradually whisk in the oil until the sauce is smooth and thick.

**Step 4** Add the shrimp to the marinade and stir well to coat.

**Time**
Preparation takes about 25 minutes plus overnight chilling for the marinade and 2 hours marinating time for the shrimp.

**Cook's Tip**
After two hours' marinating, the seafood will look cooked, that is opaque and slightly firm. However, it is still raw, so absolutely fresh seafood is required.

**Variation**
Scallops, quartered or sliced, depending on the size, mussels, clams or whitefish, cut into thin strips, may be used instead of or in addition to the shrimp.

SERVES 4

# SHRIMP CREOLE

Deceptively simple, this dish combines all the ingredients that characterize Creole cooking – seafood, garlic, tomatoes, peppers, herbs, and a dash of hot pepper.

4 tbsps oil
1 large green pepper, seeded and cut into 1 inch pieces
2 sticks celery, sliced
2 medium onions, diced
2 cloves garlic, crushed
2 14oz cans tomatoes
2 bay leaves
1 tsp cayenne pepper or tabasco sauce
Pinch salt and pepper
Pinch thyme
2 tbsps cornstarch mixed with 3 tbsps dry white wine
1½lbs shrimp, uncooked

**1.** Place the oil in a large saucepan and add the vegetables. Cook for a few minutes over gentle heat and add the garlic.

**2.** Add the tomatoes and their juice, breaking up the tomatoes with a fork or a potato masher. Add the bay leaves, cayenne pepper or tabasco, seasoning and thyme, and bring to the boil. Allow to simmer for about 5 minutes, uncovered.

**3.** Mix a few spoonfuls of the hot tomato liquid with the cornstarch mixture and then return it to the saucepan. Bring to the boil, stirring constantly until thickened.

**4.** Add the shrimp and cover the pan. Simmer over gentle heat for about 20 minutes, or until the shrimp curl and look pink and opaque.

**5.** Remove the bay leaves before serving, and spoon the sauce over rice.

**Step 1** Cook the vegetables and garlic briefly in hot oil to soften slightly.

**Step 3** Mix a few spoonfuls of the hot tomato liquid into the cornstarch mixture and then return to the saucepan.

**Step 4** Add shrimp to the tomato sauce and cook until they curl up and turn pink.

**Time**
Preparation takes about 25 minutes and cooking takes about 20-30 minutes. Rice will take about 10-12 minutes to boil.

**Cook's Tip**
Do not allow shrimp or other shellfish to cook too rapidly or for too long, as this will toughen them.

**Variation**
If using cooked, shelled shrimp, cook the tomato sauce mixture for about 15 minutes and then add the cooked shrimp to heat through.

SERVES 4-6

# NEW ORLEANS JAMBALAYA

An easy and extremely satisfying dish of rice and seafood. Sometimes garlic sausage is added for extra spice.

2 tbsps butter or margarine
2 tbsps flour
1 medium onion, finely chopped
1 clove garlic, crushed
1 red pepper, seeded and finely chopped
14oz canned tomatoes
4 cups fish or chicken stock
¼ tsp ground ginger
Pinch allspice
1 tsp chopped fresh thyme or ½ tsp dried thyme
¼ tsp cayenne pepper
Pinch salt
Dash tabasco
4oz uncooked rice
2lbs uncooked shrimp, peeled
2 green onions, chopped to garnish

**1.** Melt the butter in a heavy-based saucepan and then add the flour. Stir to blend well and cook over low heat until a pale straw color. Add the onion, garlic and pepper and cook until soft.

**2.** Add the tomatoes and their juice, breaking up the tomatoes with a fork or a potato masher. Add the stock and mix well. Add the ginger, allspice, thyme, cayenne pepper, salt and tabasco. Bring to the boil and allow to boil rapidly, stirring for about 2 minutes.

**3.** Add the rice, stir well and cover the pan. Cook for about 15-20 minutes, or until the rice is tender and has absorbed most of the liquid.

**4.** Add the shrimp during the last 10 minutes of cooking time. Cook until the shrimp curl and turn pink. Adjust the seasoning, spoon into a serving dish and sprinkle with the chopped green onion to serve.

**Step 1** Cook the flour and butter roux until it is a pale straw color.

**Step 3** Add the uncooked rice directly into the sauce and stir well.

## Cook's Notes

**Time**
Preparation takes about 40 minutes and cooking takes about 25-30 minutes.

**Cook's Tip**
If the rice still has a lot of liquid left before adding the shrimp, uncover and boil rapidly, stirring once or twice, for about 5 minutes. This should evaporate excess liquid.

**Variation**
If desired, use fresh tomatoes, peeled, seeded and chopped. Add about ½ cup extra stock. Green pepper may be used instead of red pepper, if desired.

SERVES 2-4

# Crab Meat Imperial

Another of New Orleans' famous dishes, this makes a delicious warm weather salad for lunches, light suppers or elegant appetizers.

2 small crabs, boiled
2 tbsps oil
4 green onions
1 small green pepper, seeded and finely chopped
1 stick celery, finely chopped
1 clove garlic, crushed
¾ cup prepared mayonnaise
1 tbsp mild mustard
Dash tabasco and Worcestershire sauce
1 piece canned pimento, drained and finely chopped
2 tbsps chopped parsley
Salt and pepper
Lettuce, curly endive or raddichio (optional)

**1.** To shell the crabs, first remove all the legs and the large claws by twisting and pulling them away from the body.

**2.** Turn the shell over and, using your thumbs, push the body away from the flat shell. Set the body aside.

**3.** Remove the stomach sack and the lungs or dead man's fingers and discard them. Using a small teaspoon, scrape the brown body meat out of the flat shell.

**4.** Using a sharp knife, cut the body of the crab in four pieces and using a pick or a skewer, push out all the meat.

**5.** Crack the large claws and remove the meat in one piece if possible. Crack the legs and remove the meat as well, leaving the small, thin legs in the shell. Set all the meat aside. Scrub the shells if desired to use for serving.

**6.** Heat the oil in a small sauté pan or frying pan. Chop the white parts of the green onions and add to the oil with the green pepper, celery and garlic. Sauté over gentle heat for about 10 minutes, stirring often to soften the vegetables but not brown them. Remove from the heat and set aside. When cool, add the mayonnaise, mustard, tabasco, Worcestershire sauce, pimento and finely chopped tops of the green onions.

**7.** Spoon the reserved brown body meat from the crabs back into each shell or serving dish. Mix the remaining crab meat with the dressing, reserving the crab claws for garnish, if desired. They may also be shredded and added to the other crab meat. Do not overmix the sauce as the crab meat should stay in large pieces. Spoon into the shells on top of the brown body meat, sprinkle with chopped parsley and place the crab shells on serving plates, surrounding them with lettuce leaves, if desired. Garnish with the shelled crab claws and use the crab legs if desired. Sprinkle with parsley and serve immediately.

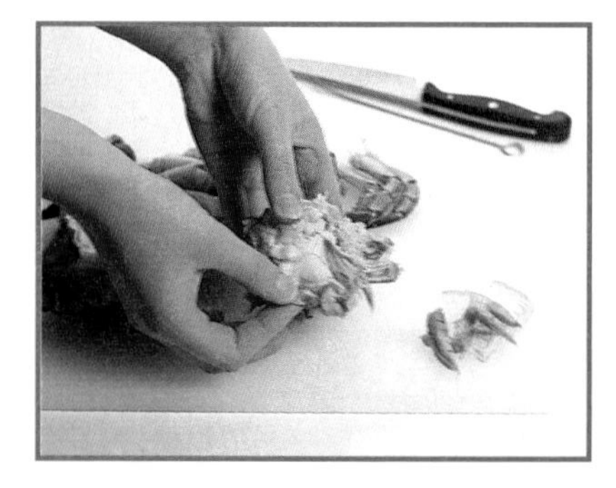

**Step 3** Discard the plastic-like stomach sack and spongy lungs. Remove brown body meat from the shell of the crab and reserve it.

**Step 4** Cut through the body of the crab with a sharp knife and pick out the crab meat with a skewer.

**Time**
Preparation takes about 45 minutes, cooking takes about 10 minutes.

**Variation**
If desired, recipe can be prepared with dressed or frozen crab meat. Allow about 3-4 oz crab meat per person.

**Buying Guide**
Precooked crabs may be purchased from fishmongers or fish markets. Use on the day of purchase.

SERVES 4

# POISSON EN PAPILLOTE

A famous New Orleans dish that cannot fail to impress at a special dinner party, this recipe demands the use of freshly prepared fish stock.

8 single or 4 double whitefish fillets
Fishbones and trimmings
1 bay leaf, sprig thyme and 2 parsley stalks
6 black peppercorns
1 slice lemon
1 cup dry white wine
1 cup water
8 large uncooked shrimp, shelled
4 crab claws, cracked and shelled
¼ cup butter or margarine
3 tbsps flour
1 onion, finely chopped
Pinch salt and pepper
2 egg yolks

**1.** Preheat the oven to 400°F. To make fish stock, skin the fish fillets and place the skin in a large stockpot along with the fish bones, thyme, bay leaf, peppercorns and lemon slice. Add the wine and water and bring to the boil. Lower the heat and simmer for 20 minutes. Strain and set aside.

**2.** Cut wax paper or baking parchment into large ovals big enough to form a parcel for each fish fillet. Fold the paper in half and lightly oil both sides.

**3.** Place the fish fillets on one half of the paper and arrange the shrimp and crab claws on top of each fillet.

**4.** Melt the butter in a heavy-based saucepan and, when foaming, add the flour. Cook over moderate heat for 2-3 minutes, stirring frequently until a pale straw color. Add the onion and cook until lightly browned.

**5.** Gradually pour on the fish stock, whisking continuously. Cook over moderate heat for about 4-5 minutes, or until the sauce thickens.

**Step 3** Place the fish fillets, shrimp and crab claws on the greased paper.

**Step 6** Spoon the prepared sauce over the fish.

**6.** Mix the egg yolks with a few spoonfuls of the hot sauce and then stir the egg yolks into the sauce. Spoon some of the sauce over each fillet and seal the parcels, folding the edge over twice and twisting the ends slightly to seal completely.

**7.** Place the parcels on baking sheets or in shallow baking pans and place in the preheated oven for about 20 minutes.

**8.** Serve the parcels unopened, to be opened at the table. Serve any remaining sauce separately.

## Cook's Notes

**Time**
Preparation takes about 40 minutes. Cooking takes about 20 minutes for the stock, 7-8 minutes for the sauce and 20 minutes to finish the dish.

**Cook's Tip**
When making fish stock, cook for only 20 minutes with the fishbones in. Overcooking will result in a bitter tasting stock.

**Preparation**
If reheating extra sauce to serve, place over gentle heat and stir constantly until heated through. Do not allow the sauce to boil or the sauce will curdle.

SERVES 4

# Creole Court Bouillon

Different from a gumbo, this is still a classic Creole soup-stew. Usually, it's prepared with redfish, local to the region, but any firm whitefish will substitute.

Fishbones
1 bay leaf, 1 sprig thyme and 2 parsley stalks
2 slices onion
1 lemon slice
6 black peppercorns
1½ cups water
6 tbsps oil
6 tbsps flour
1 large green pepper, seeded and finely chopped
1 onion, finely chopped
1 stick celery, finely chopped
2lbs canned tomatoes
2 tbsps tomato paste
1 tsp cayenne pepper
Pinch salt and allspice
6 tbsps white wine
2 whole plaice, filleted and skinned
2 tbsps chopped parsley

**Step 4** Pour the fish stock onto the brown roux, whisking constantly to form a smooth paste.

**1.** Prepare the fish stock as in the recipe for Poisson en Papillote.

**2.** Heat the oil and add the flour. Cook slowly, stirring constantly, until golden brown

**3.** Add the green pepper, onion and celery, and cook until the flour is a rich dark brown and the vegetables have softened.

**4.** Strain on the stock and add the canned tomatoes, tomato paste, cayenne pepper, salt and allspice. Bring to the boil and then simmer until thick. Add the wine.

**5.** Cut the fish fillets into 2 inch pieces and add to the tomato mixture. Cook slowly for about 20 minutes, or until the fish is tender. Gently stir in the parsley, taking care that the fish does not break up. Adjust the seasoning and serve.

**Step 4** Simmer the tomato mixture until very thick.

**Step 5** Cut the fish fillets into 2 inch pieces and add to the tomato mixture.

## Cook's Notes

**Time**
Preparation takes about 30 minutes and cooking takes about 20 minutes for the fish stock and 20 minutes to finish the dish.

**Preparation**
Fish stock can be prepared a day in advance and refrigerated. It can also be frozen.

**Variation**
Shrimp may be added if desired.

SERVES 4-6

# CREPES À L'ORANGE

This dish is an American cousin of Crêpes Suzette. It's easier than it seems, because it can be prepared in advance and reheated to serve.

1 cup all-purpose flour
1 tbsp oil
1 whole egg
1 egg yolk
1 cup milk (or more)
Oil for frying
1lb cream cheese or low fat soft cheese
½ cup sugar
Grated rind of 1 orange
4 tbsps finely chopped pecans
½ cup orange juice mixed with 2 tsps cornstarch
4 oranges, peeled and segmented
4 tbsps orange liqueur

**1.** Sift the flour into a mixing bowl and make a well in the center.

**2.** Pour the oil, whole egg and egg yolk into the center of the well and beat with a wooden spoon.

**3.** Gradually beat in the milk, incorporating the flour slowly. Set aside for 30 minutes.

**4.** Beat the cheese and sugar together with the orange rind until light and fluffy. Stir in the chopped pecans and set aside.

**5.** Heat a small crêpe pan or frying pan and pour in a small amount of oil. Wipe over with a paper towel for a thin coating of oil on the bottom.

**6.** Pour a small amount of batter (about 2 tbsps) into the hot pan and swirl the batter to coat the base evenly. Pour out the excess to re-use.

**7.** Cook until the bottom is a light golden brown and turn over. Cook the other side and stack up the crêpes on a plate. Repeat with remaining batter to make 12 small or 6 large crêpes.

**8.** Spread some of the filling on the speckled side of each crêpe and roll up or fold into triangles. Place in a warm oven while preparing the sauce.

**9.** Pour orange juice and cornstarch mixture into a saucepan and bring to the boil, stirring constantly. Boil until thickened and clear. Stir in the orange segments and liqueur. Spoon sauce over crêpes to serve.

**Step 6** Pour batter into the hot pan and swirl to coat the base.

**Step 7** When first side is brown, turn crêpe over using a palette knife.

## Cook's Notes

**Time**
Preparation takes about 30 minutes and cooking takes about 45 minutes. Prepare ahead of time and reheat about 15 minutes in a slow oven. Reheat sauce separately.

**Variation**
Use canned, pitted cherries as an alternative sauce.

**Freezing**
Unfilled crêpes can be stacked between sheets of non-stick or wax paper, placed in plastic bags and frozen for up to 3 months. Thaw at room temperature, separate and use with a variety of sweet or savory fillings.

SERVES 8

# Bread Pudding with Whiskey Sauce

A childhood pudding made sophisticated by the addition of a bourbon-laced sauce, and a stylish presentation.

½ loaf day-old French bread
2 cups milk
3 eggs
¾ cup raisins
1 tsp vanilla extract
Pinch ground ginger
Butter or margarine
½ cup butter
1 cup sugar
1 egg
4 tbsps bourbon
Nutmeg

1. Cut bread into small pieces and soak in the milk.

2. When the bread has softened, add the eggs, raisins, vanilla and ginger.

3. Grease 8 custard cups with butter or margarine and fill each with an equal amount of pudding mixture to within ½ inch of the top.

4. Place the dishes in a roasting pan and pour in enough hot water to come halfway up the sides of the dishes. Bake in a preheated 350°F oven until risen and set – about 35-40 minutes.

5. When the puddings have cooked, combine the ½ cup butter and the sugar in the top of a double boiler and heat to dissolve the sugar.

6. Beat the egg and stir in a spoonful of the hot butter mixture. Add the egg to the double boiler and whisk over heat until thick. Allow to cool and add bourbon.

7. To serve, turn out puddings onto plates and surround with sauce. Sprinkle the tops with nutmeg.

**Step 2** Soak bread until very soft and mix with other ingredients.

**Step 4** Bake the pudding until risen and set. The puddings are done when a skewer inserted in the middle comes out clean.

**Step 7** Loosen puddings from the sides of the dishes and turn out carefully.

## Cook's Notes

**Time**
Preparation takes about 40 minutes, giving bread time to absorb milk. Cooking takes about 35-40 minutes for the pudding and about 20 minutes for the sauce.

**Preparation**
If desired, cook pudding in one large dish, increasing time to 1 hour. Spoon portions onto plates and pour over sauce.

**Variation**
Sauce may be prepared with brandy instead of whiskey.

SERVES 4-6

# CHERRIES JUBILEE

This makes a special, elegant pudding, but an easy one, too. The contrast of hot brandied cherries and cold ice cream or whipped cream is sensational.

1½lbs black cherries, fresh or canned
2-4 tbsps sugar
¾ cup brandy
Vanilla ice cream or whipped cream

**Step 1** Pit cherries using a cherry pitter, vegetable peeler or small knife.

**1.** If using fresh cherries, wash them, remove the stems and pit, if desired, but leave the cherries whole. Combine them with 4 tbsps sugar in a saucepan and cook over gentle heat until the cherries soften and the juices run. If using canned cherries, combine the juice with 2 tbsps sugar and heat through to dissolve the sugar. Pit the cherries, if desired, but leave them whole and add to the juice.

**2.** Pour the brandy into a separate saucepan or a large ladle. Heat the brandy and ignite with a match. Combine the brandy with the fruit and leave until the flames die down naturally.

**3.** Spoon the fruit over ice cream or on its own into serving dishes to be topped with whipped cream. Serve immediately.

**Step 1** Cook slowly with the sugar until the cherries soften and juices run.

**Step 2** Add brandy and cook briefly.

## Cook's Notes

**Time**
Preparation takes about 30 minutes if pitting the cherries, and cooking takes about 10 minutes.

**Preparation**
If using fresh cherries, pit and cook in advance and set aside. Before adding the brandy, reheat the cherries until hot.

**Buying Guide**
Black cherries are often available already pitted in cans or bottles from larger supermarkets or specialty shops.

SERVES 4

# BANANAS FOSTER

This rich concoction originated in a famous New Orleans restaurant, but it's now a favorite on any Creole menu.

4 ripe bananas, peeled
½ cup butter
½ cup soft brown sugar, light or dark
Pinch ground cinnamon and nutmeg
4 tbsps orange juice
½ cup white or dark rum
Juice of ½ lemon
Whipped cream
Chopped pecans

**Step 1** Cut the bananas carefully in half lengthwise.

**Step 2** Combine butter, sugar and spices in a large frying pan and heat gently to form a syrup.

**Step 3** Baste the bananas frequently whilst cooking, but do not turn them.

**1.** Cut the bananas in half lengthwise and sprinkle with lemon juice on all sides.

**2.** Melt the butter in a large frying pan and add the sugar, cinnamon, nutmeg and orange juice. Stir over gentle heat until the sugar dissolves into a syrup.

**3.** Add the banana halves and cook gently for about 3 minutes, basting the bananas often with syrup, but not turning them.

**4.** Once the bananas are heated through, warm the rum into a small saucepan or ladle and ignite with a match. Pour the flaming rum over the bananas and shake the pan gently until the flames die down naturally. Place 2 banana halves on a serving plate and top with some of the whipped cream. Sprinkle with pecans and serve immediately.

## Cook's Notes

**Time**
Preparation takes about 15 minutes and cooking takes about 5 minutes for the sugar and butter syrup and 3-4 minutes for the bananas.

**Serving Ideas**
The bananas may be served with vanilla ice cream instead of whipped cream, if desired.

**Cook's Tip**
Sprinkling the cut surfaces of the banana with lemon juice keeps them from turning brown and also offsets the sweetness of the sauce.

SERVES 6

# Beignets with Apricot Sauce

French in origin, these fritters are easier to make than the classic Creole type, but just as delicious.

6 tbsps water
1 tbsp butter or margarine
6 tbsps all-purpose flour
3-4 eggs
Few drops vanilla extract
Powdered sugar

**Apricot Sauce**

14 canned apricots
1 tbsp cornstarch mixed with 4 tbsps bourbon
Dash lemon

**1.** Combine the water and butter or margarine in a saucepan and slowly bring to the boil.

**2.** When boiling rapidly, stir in the flour quickly and remove the pan from the heat.

**3.** Beat in the eggs one at a time, beating well in between each addition. It may not be necessary to add all the eggs. The mixture should be of dropping consistency and hold its shape well. Beat in the vanilla extract.

**4.** Heat oil to 350°F in a deep fat fryer or in a deep saucepan on top of the stove. Drop the batter from a teaspoon into the hot fat and cook until puffed and golden. The beignets will rise to the surface of the oil when cooked and may be turned over if necessary. Cook the beignets about four at a time.

**5.** Drain on paper towels and dust with powdered sugar.

**6.** While the beignets are cooking, combine all the sauce ingredients in a heavy-based pan and bring to the boil. Cook until thickened and then transfer to a blender or food processor and purée until smooth. Serve the sauce warm with the warm beignets.

**Step 2** Add the flour to the boiling water and butter mixture, and stir until it leaves the sides of the pan.

**Step 3** Beat in the eggs one at a time until the mixture is smooth and shiny and holds its shape.

**Step 4** Drop the batter by spoonfuls into hot fat and cook until the beignets puff and brown and rise to the surface.

## Cook's Notes

**Time**
Preparation takes about 20 minutes. Beignets will take about 2 minutes to cook per batch.

**Preparation**
The beignets are best served as soon as they are cooked. They do not reheat well.

**Serving Ideas**
Beignets may be served without the sauce with coffee or tea.

MAKES 12

# Mardi Gras Cakes

A different version of the King's cake, made to celebrate this famous Lenten carnival in New Orleans. The three colors symbolize justice, power and faith.

1 package dried active yeast
6 tbsps lukewarm water
2 tsps sugar
2 cups all-purpose flour
4 tbsps additional sugar
Pinch salt
1 tsp ground ginger
Grated rind of 1 lemon
2 eggs
6 tbsps lukewarm milk
4 tbsps butter or margarine, cut in small pieces
4oz golden raisins, currants and chopped, candied fruit

**Icing**

2 cups powdered sugar
Juice of 1 lemon
Hot water
¾ cup granulated sugar
Purple, yellow and green food colorings

**1.** Sprinkle the yeast on top of the lukewarm water and stir in the sugar. Set in a warm place to prove for 15 minutes, or until bubbly.

**2.** Sift the flour, sugar, salt and ginger into a large bowl and add the lemon rind. Make a well in the center of the ingredients and pour in the yeast. Add the egg and milk.

**3.** Beat well, drawing the flour in from the outside edge, and gradually add the butter, a few pieces at a time.

**4.** Turn the dough out onto a well-floured surface and knead until smooth and elastic, about 10 minutes. Place the dough in a large, lightly-oiled bowl and cover with oiled plastic wrap.

**5.** Leave to rise in a warm place for 1-1½ hours, or until doubled in bulk.

**6.** Knock the dough back and knead in the fruit to distribute it evenly.

**7.** Oil a 12-space muffin pan. Divide the dough in 12 and knead each piece into a smooth ball. Place a ball in each space in the pan and cover lightly. Leave in a warm place for 20-30 minutes to rise a second time. Bake at 375°F for about 20-25 minutes, or until golden brown. Allow to cool slightly and loosen the cakes. Cool completely before removing from the pan.

**8.** Place an equal portion of sugar in each of three jars and add a drop of different food coloring to each. Shake the jars to color the sugar.

**9.** Sift the powdered sugar and mix with the lemon juice. Add enough hot water to make an icing that pours easily but still clings to the back of a spoon. Spoon some icing over each cake and sprinkle the cakes with the different colored sugars before the powdered sets.

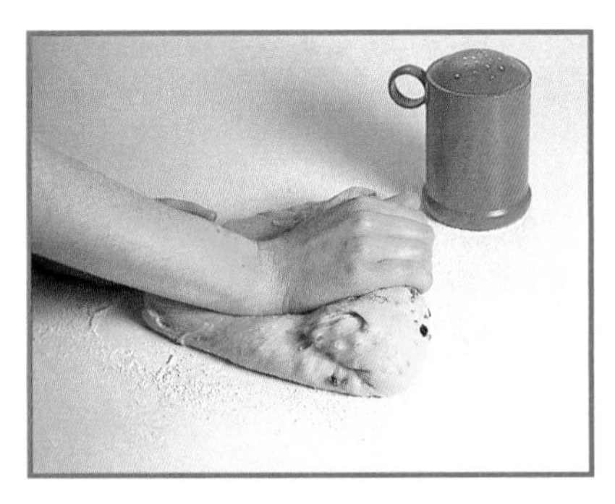

**Step 6** When the dough has risen the first time, knock back and knead in the fruit to distribute them evenly.

## Cook's Notes

**Time**
Preparation takes about 40 minutes. This does not include rising times for the yeast dough. Cooking takes about 20-25 minutes.

**Variation**
Use dried fruit such as apricots, dates or prunes, finely chopped, instead of candied fruit. Nuts or chocolate chips may also be used.

**Preparation**
The cakes may be prepared the day before and kept in airtight containers. Ice and decorate with sugar on the day of serving.

MAKES ABOUT 24

# CALAS

These small rice cakes are crisp outside, soft and light inside. They are delicious served hot with coffee or tea.

1½-2 cups long-grain rice, cooked
1 cup all-purpose flour
1 tsp baking powder
Pinch salt
½ cup sugar
2 eggs, separated
6 tbsps milk
Grated rind of 1 lemon
4 tbsps raisins
Powdered sugar

**Step 4** Beat the egg whites until stiff peaks form.

**1.** Cook the rice, rinse, drain and leave to cool completely.

**2.** Sift the flour, baking powder and salt into a mixing bowl and stir in the sugar.

**3.** Beat the yolks with the milk and add gradually to the dry ingredients, stirring constantly, to make a thick batter. Stir in the rice.

**4.** Beat the egg whites until stiff but not dry, and fold into the batter along with the lemon rind and raisins.

**5.** Lightly oil the base of a heavy frying pan and place over moderate heat. When the pan is hot, drop in about 1 tbsp of batter and if necessary, spread into a small circle with the back of the spoon.

**6.** Cook until brown on one side and bubbles form on the top surface. Turn over and cook the other side. Cook 4-6 at a time.

**7.** Repeat until all the batter is used, keeping the cakes warm. Sprinkle with powdered sugar and serve.

**Step 4** Mix a spoonful of whites into the rice mixture to lighten it. Fold in the remaining whites using a large spoon.

**Step 5** Drop the mixture by spoonfuls into a hot frying pan. Cook until brown on both sides.

## Cook's Notes

**Time**
Preparation takes about 40 minutes and cooking takes about 40-45 minutes.

**Cook's Tip**
To drain rice thoroughly, place in a colander and make several drainage holes with the handle of a wooden spoon.

**Serving Ideas**
Squeeze lemon juice over hot rice cakes, or spoon on jam. Cakes can also be served cold.

TEX-MEX
COOKING

# Introduction

The Southwestern region of the United States is vast, with the landscape and climate varying from cool mountain ranges to hot, dry deserts and sun-drenched Gulf beaches. But for all its vastness and diversity, the regional recipes show a remarkable sense of unity.

The traditional ingredients of Tex-Mex cooking – chilies, corn, dried beans and squash – appear again and again. The traditional influences of Tex-Mex cooking – Indian and Hispanic – are evident, too, their stamp recognizable on many recipes still favored today.

Tortillas, either cornmeal or flour, are important as a base for toppings and sauces or as a substitute for bread rolls. Salsas, refried beans and chili, that well-known meat stew, are all part of Southwestern and Mexican cooking alike. This is Tex-Mex style, which most often symbolizes the food of the Southwest. There is more to it than that, though. Brook trout from mountain streams and seafood from the Gulf have their places, too, as do apricots and blueberries that grow so well here. There is also hearty ranch fare like barbecue ribs and pork stew.

As elsewhere, new influences are at work making food lighter and prettier, but the ingredients that have been traditional in the region for generations still prevail, making the food recognizably Tex-Mex no matter how the style changes.

MAKES 2 cups

# Red Pepper Preserves

This sweet but hot and spicy condiment adds a bright spot of color and Tex-Mex flavor to a main course or appetizer.

5 red peppers, seeded
3 red or green chilies, seeded
1½ cups sugar
¾ cup red wine vinegar
1 cup liquid pectin

**Step 3** Add the chopped peppers and bring the mixture to the boil.

**1.** Chop the peppers and chilies finely in a food processor.

**2.** Combine the sugar and vinegar in a deep, heavy-based pan and heat gently to dissolve the sugar.

**3.** Add the peppers and bring the mixture to the boil. Simmer for about 15 or 20 minutes.

**4.** Stir in the pectin and return the mixture to the boil over high heat.

**5.** Pour into sterilized jars and seal. Keep for up to one year in a cool, dark place.

**Step 4** Stir in the pectin and return the mixture to the boil.

## Cook's Notes

**Preparation**
To sterilize the storage jars, place them in boiling water and boil for 15 minutes. Drain the jars upside down on paper towels and then fill them with the hot preserves to within about ½ inch of the top. Pour a layer of melted wax directly on top of the preserves to seal. When preserves have cooled and the wax has solidified, cover the jars with their lids. Waxed paper discs may also be used. If desired, the sealing process may be omitted and the preserves stored tightly covered in the refrigerator. Refrigerator-stored preserves will not keep as long.

**Time**
Preparation takes about 20 minutes and cooking takes about 20-25 minutes.

**Serving Ideas**
Serve as a condiment with meat, poultry, vegetable, egg or cheese dishes.

MAKES 10

# TORTILLAS

Borrowed from Mexico, these have become indispensible in Tex-Mex cooking and are used in a variety of delicious ways.

2 cups all-purpose flour (more if necessary)
2 tsps baking powder
Pinch salt
4 tbsps vegetable shortening
½-¾ cup hot water
Oil for frying

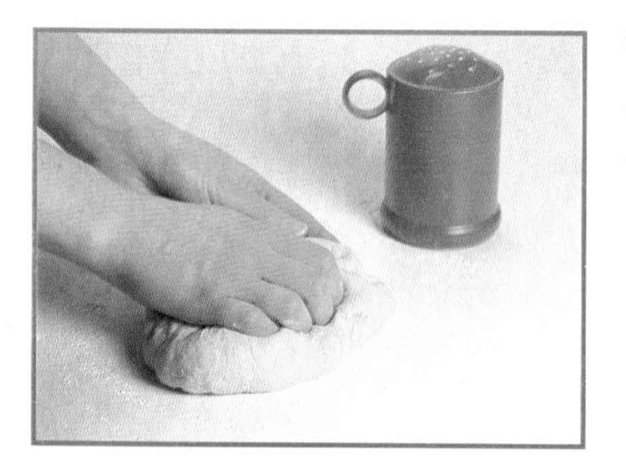

**Step 1** After water is added, knead the dough gently, adding more flour if it is too sticky.

**1.** Sift the flour, baking powder and salt into a bowl. Rub in the vegetable shortening until the mixture resembles coarse crumbs. Add water, mixing until absorbed. Knead gently and add more flour if the dough is too sticky. Cover and leave to rest for 15 minutes.

**2.** Divide the dough into ten even-sized pieces. Roll into balls on a floured surface, cover and leave to stand for 20 minutes.

**3.** Roll out each ball on a lightly floured surface to a circle 7 inches in diameter. Cover the finished tortillas while rolling all the remaining dough.

**4.** Place a lightly oiled frying pan over high heat. Fry the tortillas individually on both sides until bubbles form on the surface. Stack them as they are cooked and set them aside until ready to use.

**Step 3** Roll out even-sized balls of dough into circles on a lightly-floured surface.

**Step 4** Fry the tortillas in a lightly-oiled frying pan until bubbles appear on the surface.

Cook's Notes

**Time**
Preparation takes about 50 minutes, including 35 minutes for the dough to rest. Cooking takes about 3 minutes per tortilla.

**Freezing**
Stack the tortillas between sheets of plastic wrap or wax paper and place in freezer bags. Freeze for up to 6 months and defrost at room temperature. Use as indicated in the recipe. Tortillas may also be prepared in advance and kept in the refrigerator for several days.

**Serving Ideas**
Tortillas are used as a base for tacos, enchiladas and other Mexican or Tex-Mex dishes. They may also be served warm as an accompaniment to a main course. If desired, cut into triangles and deep-fry to serve with dips.

SERVES 4

# CORNMEAL PANCAKES

Cornmeal, either yellow, white or blue, is an important ingredient in Tex-Mex recipes. Here it's combined with corn in a light and different kind of appetizer.

1 cup yellow cornmeal
1 tbsp flour
1 tsp baking soda
1 tsp salt
2 cups buttermilk
2 eggs, separated
Oil
10oz frozen corn
Red pepper preserves
Green onions, chopped
Sour cream

**1.** Sift the dry ingredients into a bowl, adding any coarse meal that remains in the strainer.

**2.** Mix the egg yolks and buttermilk together and gradually beat into the dry ingredients. Cover and leave to stand for at least 15 minutes.

**3.** Whisk the egg whites until stiff but not dry and fold into the cornmeal mixture.

**4.** Lightly grease a frying pan with oil and drop in about 2 tbsps of batter. Sprinkle with the corn and allow to cook until the underside is golden brown. Turn the pancakes and cook the second side until golden. Continue with the remaining batter and corn. Keep the cooked pancakes warm.

**5.** To serve, place three pancakes on warm side plates. Add a spoonful of sour cream and red pepper preserves to each and sprinkle over finely sliced or shredded green onions.

**Step 2** Mix the egg yolks and buttermilk and gradually beat into the dry ingredients. Mixture will thicken on standing.

**Step 3** Fold in stiffly-beaten egg whites with a large metal spoon or rubber spatula.

**Step 4** Sprinkle the uncooked sides of the pancakes with some of the corn before turning over to cook further.

**Time**
Preparation takes about 30 minutes, including standing time for the pancake batter. Cooking takes about 3-4 minutes per pancake.

**Cook's Tip**
Allowing the pancake batter to stand 15 minutes before using it will produce a batter that is lighter and easier to use. This standing time also helps the cornmeal to soften.

**Serving Ideas**
Serve as an appetizer with the Red Pepper Preserves, sour cream and green onions or serve alone as a side dish to a main course.

SERVES 2

# DENVER OMELET

This is a quick and easy meal for busy people or unexpected company. If prepared like scrambled eggs, the mixture can double as a sandwich filling.

4 strips bacon, diced
Half a small onion, chopped
Half a small green pepper, seeded and chopped
1 tomato, seeded and diced
3 eggs, beaten
Salt and pepper
1 tbsp grated cheese
Dash tabasco (optional)
Chopped parsley to garnish

**Step 2** Cook the onion, green pepper and bacon until the vegetables are soft and the bacon is crisp.

**Step 3** Pour in the egg, tomato and cheese mixture and stir once or twice to mix thoroughly.

**Step 4** Place under a pre-heated broiler to cook the top until golden brown and slightly puffy.

**1.** Heat a medium-size frying pan or omelet pan. Add the bacon and sauté slowly until the fat is rendered.

**2.** Turn up the heat and cook until the bacon begins to brown and crisp. Add the onion and green pepper and cook to soften and finish off the bacon.

**3.** Mix the tomato with the eggs, salt, pepper, cheese and tabasco, if using. Pour into the pan and stir once or twice with a fork to mix all the ingredients. Cook until lightly browned on the underside.

**4.** Place under a pre-heated broiler and cook the top quickly until brown and slightly puffy.

**5.** Sprinkle with parsley, cut into wedges and serve immediately.

## Cook's Notes

**Time**
Preparation takes about 25 minutes and cooking takes about 10-15 minutes.

**Cook's Tip**
1 tbsp of water added to the eggs before beating will produce a lighter, fluffier omelet.

**Serving Ideas**
Serve as a light main course for supper or lunch. As an appetizer, this will serve 4 people.

SERVES 6

# CHICKEN NUEVA MEXICANA

6 chicken thighs, skinned and boned
2 tbsps mild chili powder
2 tbsps oil
Juice of 1 lime
Pinch salt

**Lime Cream Sauce**

¾ cup sour cream or natural yogurt
1 tsp lime juice and grated rind
6 tbsps heavy cream
Salt

**Corn Crêpes**

1 cup fine yellow cornmeal
½ cup flour
Pinch salt
1 whole egg and 1 egg yolk
1 tbsp oil or melted butter or margarine
1½ cups milk

**Garden Salsa**

1 large zucchini
1 large ripe tomato
2 shallots
1 tbsp chopped fresh coriander
Pinch cayenne, pepper and salt
1 tbsp white wine vinegar
3 tbsps oil

**Avocado and Orange Salad**

2 oranges
1 avocado, peeled and sliced
Juice of 1 lime
Pinch sugar
Pinch coriander
6 tbsps pine nuts, toasted

**1.** Place the chicken in a shallow dish.

**2.** Combine the chili powder, oil, lime juice and salt and pour over the chicken. Turn the pieces over and rub the marinade into all the surfaces. Cover and refrigerate for 2 hours.

**3.** Combine all the ingredients for the Lime Cream Sauce and fold together gently. Cover and leave 2 hours in the refrigerator to thicken.

**4.** Sift the cornmeal, flour and salt for the crêpes into a bowl or a food processor. Combine the eggs, oil and milk. Make a well in the center of the ingredients in the bowl and pour in the liquid.

**5.** Stir the liquid ingredients with a wooden spoon to gradually incorporate the dry ingredients. Alternatively, combine all the ingredients in a food processor and process until smooth. Leave the batter to stand for 30 minutes whichever method you choose.

**6.** Trim the ends of zucchini and cut into small dice. Peel the tomatoes and remove the seeds. Cut the tomato flesh into small dice. Cut the shallots into dice the same size as the zucchini and tomato.

**7.** Combine the coriander, cayenne pepper, vinegar, oil and salt, mixing very well. Pour over the vegetables and stir to mix. Cover and leave to marinate.

**8.** Heat a small amount of oil in a large frying pan and place in the chicken in a single layer. Fry quickly to brown both sides. Pour over remaining marinade, cover and cook until tender, about 25 minutes.

**9.** Heat a small amount of oil in an 8 inch crêpe or frying pan. Wipe out with paper towel and return the pan to the heat until hot.

**10.** Pour a spoonful of the batter into the pan and swirl to coat the bottom with the mixture. Make sure the edge of each crêpe is irregular.

**11.** When the edges of each crêpe look pale brown and the top surface begins to bubble, turn the crêpes using a palette knife. Cook the other side. Stack as each is finished Cover with foil and keep warm in a low oven.

**12.** Pour about 2 tbsps oil into a small frying pan and when hot add the pine nuts. Cook over moderate heat, stirring constantly until golden brown. Remove and drain on paper towels.

**13.** Peel and segment the oranges over a bowl to catch the juice. Cut the avocado in half, remove the stone and peel. Cut into thin slices and combine with the orange. Add the remaining ingredients for the salad, except the pine nuts, and toss gently to mix.

**14.** To assemble, place one corn crêpe on a serving plate. Place one piece of chicken on the lower half of the crêpe, top with a spoonful of Lime Cream Sauce. Place a serving of Garden Salsa and one of Avocado and Orange Salad on either side of the chicken and partially fold the crêpe over the top. Scatter over pine nuts and serve immediately.

**Preparation**
Because the dish is complicated, several of its many parts may be prepared well in advance. The chicken may be marinated longer than 2 hours in the refrigerator, overnight if desired. The Lime Cream Sauce can remain in the refrigerator overnight and so can the Garden Salsa. The Corn Crêpes can be prepared in advance and kept covered in the refrigerator. They may also be frozen with sheets of wax paper in between. Defrost at room temperature and then re-heat.

SERVES 4

# Chicken with Red Peppers

Easy as this recipe is, it looks and tastes good enough for guests. The warm taste of roasted red peppers is typically Tex-Mex.

4 large red peppers
4 skinned and boned chicken breasts
1½ tbsps oil
Salt and pepper
1 clove garlic, finely chopped
3 tbsps white wine vinegar
2 green onions, finely chopped
Sage leaves for garnish

**Step 1** Flatten the peppers with the palm of the hand and brush them with oil.

**1.** Cut the peppers in half and remove the stems, cores and seeds. Flatten the peppers with the palm of your hand and brush the skin sides lightly with oil.

**2.** Place the peppers skin side up on the rack of a preheated broiler and cook about 2 inches away from the heat source until the skins are well blistered and charred.

**3.** Wrap the peppers in a clean towel and allow them to stand until cool. Peel off the skins with a small vegetable knife. Cut into thin strips and set aside.

**4.** Place the chicken breasts between two sheets of plastic wrap and flatten by hitting with a rolling pin or meat mallet.

**5.** Heat 1½ tbsps oil in a large frying pan. Season the chicken breasts on both sides and place in the hot oil. Cook 5 minutes, turn over and cook until tender and lightly browned. Remove the chicken and keep it warm.

**6.** Add the pepper strips, garlic, vinegar and green onions to the pan and cook briefly until the vinegar loses its strong aroma.

**7.** Slice the chicken breasts across the grain into ¼ inch thick slices and arrange on serving plates. Spoon over the pan juices.

**8.** Arrange the pepper mixture with the chicken and garnish with the sage leaves.

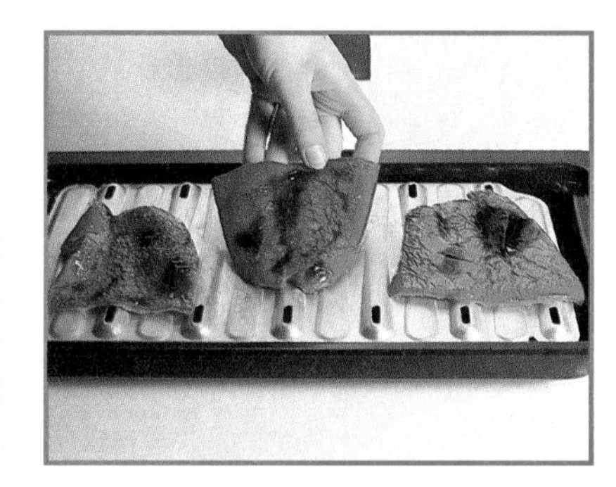

**Step 2** Cook the peppers until the skins are blistered and well charred.

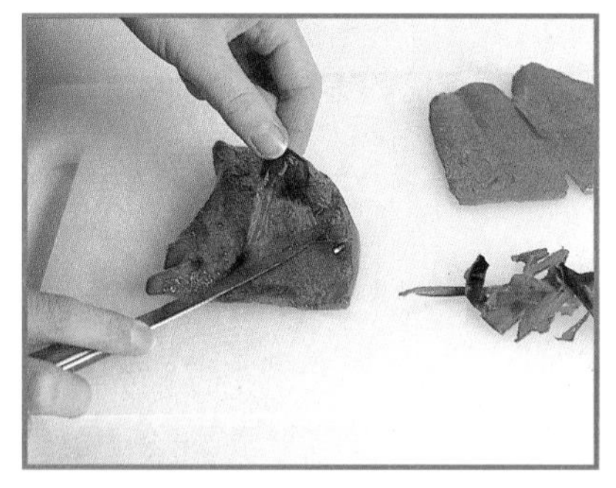

**Step 3** Peel off the skins using a small vegetable knife.

## Cook's Notes

**Time**
Preparation takes about 35-40 minutes and cooking takes about 10 minutes to char the peppers and about 20 minutes to finish the dish.

**Variation**
For convenience, the dish may be prepared with canned pimento caps instead of red peppers. These will be softer so cook the garlic, vinegar and onions to soften, and then add pimento.

**Buying Guide**
Sage is a very common herb in the Southwestern United States. If unavailable fresh, substitute coriander or parsley leaves as a garnish.

SERVES 4

# SOUTHWESTERN STIR-FRY

East meets West in a dish that is lightning-fast to cook. Baby corn, traditionally Oriental, echoes the Southwestern love of corn.

1lb sirloin or rump steak
2 cloves garlic, crushed
6 tbsps wine vinegar
6 tbsps oil
Pinch sugar, salt and pepper
1 bay leaf
1 tbsp ground cumin
1 small red pepper, seeded and sliced
1 small green pepper, seeded and sliced
2oz baby corn
4 green onions, shredded
Oil for frying

**Red Sauce**

8 fresh ripe tomatoes, peeled, seeded and chopped
4 tbsps oil
1 medium onion, finely chopped
1-2 green chilies, finely chopped
1-2 cloves garlic, crushed
6 sprigs fresh coriander
3 tbsps tomato paste

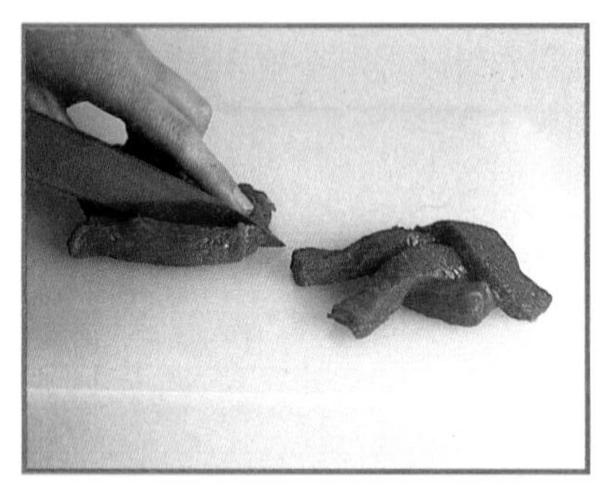

**Step 1** Slice the meat thinly across the grain.

**1.** Slice the meat thinly across the grain. Combine in a plastic bag with the next 6 ingredients. Tie the bag and toss the ingredients inside to coat. Place in a bowl and leave about 4 hours.

**2.** Heat the oil for the sauce and cook the onion, chilies and garlic to soften but not brown. Add remaining sauce ingredients and cook about 15 minutes over gentle heat. Purée in a food processor until smooth.

**3.** Heat a frying pan and add the meat in three batches, discarding the marinade. Cook to brown and set aside. Add about 2 tbsps of oil and cook the peppers about 2 minutes. Add the corn and onions and return the meat to the pan. Cook a further 1 minute and add the sauce. Cook to heat through and serve immediately.

**Step 3** Cook the meat quickly over high heat to brown.

**Step 3** Add the remaining ingredients and enough sauce to coat all ingredients thoroughly.

## Cook's Notes

**Time**
Preparation takes about 25 minutes, with 4 hours for marinating the meat. The sauce takes about 15 minutes to cook and the remaining ingredients need about 6-7 minutes.

**Preparation**
The sauce may be prepared ahead of time and kept in the refrigerator for several days. It may also be frozen. Defrost the sauce at room temperature and then boil rapidly to reduce it again slightly.

**Buying Guide**
Baby corn is available from greengrocers and supermarkets. It is also available canned in delicatessens and supermarkets that stock Oriental cooking ingredients.

SERVES 6-8

# CHILI ROJA

Red meat, red onions, red peppers, paprika, tomatoes and red beans all give clues to the name of this zesty stew.

2lbs beef chuck, cut into 1 inch pieces
Oil
1 large red onion, coarsely chopped
2 cloves garlic, crushed
2 red peppers, seeded and cut into 1 inch pieces
1-2 red chilies, seeded and finely chopped
3 tbsps mild chili powder
1 tbsp cumin
1 tbsp paprika
3 cups beer, water or stock
8oz canned tomatoes, puréed
2 tbsps tomato paste
8oz canned red kidney beans, drained
Pinch salt
6 ripe tomatoes, peeled, seeded and diced

**1.** Pour about 4 tbsps oil into a large saucepan or flameproof casserole. When hot, brown the meat in small batches over moderately high heat for about 5 minutes per batch.

**2.** Set aside the meat on a plate or in the lid of the casserole. Lower the heat and cook the onion, garlic, red peppers and chilies for about 5 minutes. Add the chili powder, cumin and paprika and cook for 1 minute further. Pour on the liquid and add the canned tomatoes, tomato paste and the meat.

**3.** Cook slowly for about 1½-2 hours. Add the beans about 45 minutes before the end of cooking time.

**4.** When the meat is completely tender, add salt to taste and serve garnished with the diced tomatoes.

**Step 2** Cook the onions, garlic, red peppers and chilies slowly until slightly softened.

**Step 2** If using beer, add it very slowly as it will tend to foam up in the heat of the pan.

**Time**
Preparation takes about 25 minutes and cooking takes about 1½-2 hours.

**Freezing**
The chili may be frozen for up to 3 months in a tightly covered freezer container. Allow the chili to cool completely before sealing and freezing. Defrost in the refrigerator and bring slowly to the boil before serving.

**Variation**
The chili may be made with pork shoulder or with a mixture of beef and pork. Although not authentic, the chili may also be made with ground beef or pork.

SERVES 6

# BARBECUED RIBS

No Tex-Mex cookbook would be complete without a barbecue recipe. This versatile sauce keeps well in the refrigerator, too.

4½lbs pork spare ribs
1 cup tomato ketchup
2 tsps mustard powder
4 tbsps Worcester sauce
2 tbsps vinegar
4 tbsps brown sugar
Half a chili, seeded and finely chopped
Half a small onion, finely chopped
4 tbsps water
Salt (if necessary)

**Step 1** Cook the ribs in a roasting pan at a high temperature for 15 minutes.

**1.** Place the ribs in a roasting pan and cover with foil. Cook for 15 minutes at 425°F.

**2.** Meanwhile, combine all the sauce ingredients in a heavy-based pan and bring to the boil. Reduce heat and simmer for about 15 minutes.

**3.** Reduce the oven temperature to 350°F and uncover the ribs. Pour over the sauce and bake a further hour, basting frequently.

**4.** Remove the ribs from the roasting pan and reserve the sauce. Place the ribs on a cutting board and slice into individual rib pieces, between the bones.

**5.** Skim any fat from the surface of the sauce and serve the sauce separately.

**Step 3** Uncover the ribs and pour over the sauce.

**Step 4** To serve, cut the ribs into individual pieces between the bones.

## Cook's Notes

**Time**
Preparation takes about 30 minutes and cooking takes about 1 hour 15 minutes.

**Variation**
The sauce is also good served on pork chops, chicken or steaks.

**Serving Ideas**
Serve with Spicy Beans and Rice or Refried Beans. Add warm tortillas and a salad.

SERVES 4

# Barbecued Pork Stew

Named for the sauce rather than the cooking method, this stew requires long, slow cooking to bring out its flavor.

2lb pork shoulder, cut in 2 inch cubes
Oil
2 medium onions, cut in 2 inch pieces
1 large green pepper, seeded and cut in 2 inch pieces
1 tbsp chili powder
2 cloves garlic, crushed
1lb canned tomatoes
3 tbsps tomato paste
1 tbsp Worcester sauce
½ cup water or beef stock
2 tbsps cider vinegar
1 bay leaf
½ tsp dried oregano
Salt and a few drops tabasco sauce

**1.** Heat about 2 tbsps oil in a large sauté or frying pan. When hot, add the pork cubes in two batches. Brown over high heat for about 5 minutes per batch. Remove to a plate. Add more oil if necessary and cook the onions and peppers to soften slightly. Add the chili powder and garlic and cook 1 minute more.

**2.** Add the tomatoes, their juice and the tomato paste. Stir in the Worcester sauce, water or stock and vinegar breaking up the tomatoes slightly. Add bay leaf, oregano and salt.

**3.** Transfer to a flameproof casserole dish. Bring the mixture to the boil and then cook slowly for about 1½ hours, covered.

**4.** When the meat is completely tender, skim any fat from the surface of the sauce, remove the bay leaf and add a few drops of tabasco sauce to taste. Adjust salt and serve.

**Step 1** Brown the pork cubes in oil over high heat in a large frying pan.

**Step 2** Combine the ingredients and stir well to break up the tomatoes slightly.

**Step 4** When the meat is tender, skim excess fat from the surface of the sauce with a spoon, or blot up with strips of paper towel.

**Time**
Preparation takes about 25 minutes and cooking takes about 1½ hours.

**Freezing**
Allow the stew to cool completely. Spoon into freezer containers, cover tightly and freeze for up to 3 months. Defrost in the refrigerator and then slowly bring to the boil to re-heat before serving.

**Serving Ideas**
Accompany with warm tortillas and serve Spicy Rice and Beans as a side dish.

SERVES 6-8

# CHILI VERDE

A chili, really a spicy meat stew, is as traditional in the Southwest as it is in Mexico.

2lbs lean pork, cut into 1inch pieces
Oil
3 green peppers, seeded and cut into 1 inch pieces
1-2 green chili peppers, seeded and finely chopped
1 small bunch green onions, chopped
2 cloves garlic, crushed
2 tsps ground cumin
2 tsps chopped fresh oregano
3 tbsps chopped fresh coriander
1 bay leaf
3 cups beer, water or chicken stock
8oz canned chickpeas, drained
1½ tbsps cornstarch mixed with 3 tbsps cold water (optional)
Salt
1 large ripe avocado, peeled and diced
1 tbsp lime juice

**1.** Heat 4 tbsps of oil and lightly brown the pork cubes over high heat. Use a large flameproof casserole and brown the pork in 2 or 3 batches.

**2.** Lower the heat and cook the peppers to soften slightly. Add the chilies, onions, garlic and cumin and cook for 2 minutes.

**3.** Add the herbs and liquid and reduce the heat. Simmer, covered, 1-1½ hours or until the meat is tender. Add the chickpeas during the last 45 minutes.

**4.** If necessary, thicken with the cornstarch, stirring constantly after adding until the liquid thickens and clears.

**5.** Add salt to taste and remove the bay leaf.

**6.** Toss the avocado in lime juice and sprinkle over the top of the chili to serve.

**Step 1** The pork should barely begin to take on color. Do not over brown.

**Step 4** If necessary, add the cornstarch mixture to thicken, stirring constantly.

## Cook's Notes

**Time**
Preparation takes about 30-40 minutes and cooking takes about 1-1½ hours.

**Variation**
Vary the amount of chili peppers, garlic and herbs to suit your own taste.

**Serving Ideas**
Serve for lunch or a light supper with warm tortillas

SERVES 4

# RIVERSIDE TROUT

Brook trout is so delicious that simple preparation is all that's necessary. Crisp cornmeal, bacon and pine nuts complement the fresh flavor.

⅓-½ cup vegetable oil
4 tbsps pine nuts
8 strips bacon, diced
1 cup yellow cornmeal
Pinch salt and white pepper
4 trout weighing about 8oz each, cleaned
Juice of 1 lime
Fresh sage or coriander

**1.** Heat 6 tbsps of the oil in a large frying pan. Add the pine nuts and cook over moderate heat, stirring constantly. When a pale golden brown, remove them with a draining spoon to paper towels.

**2.** Add the diced bacon to the oil and cook until crisp, stirring constantly. Drain with the pine nuts.

**3.** Mix the cornmeal, salt and pepper, and dredge the fish well, patting on the cornmeal. Shake off any excess.

**4.** If necessary, add more oil to the pan – it should come about halfway up the sides of the fish. Re-heat over moderately high heat.

**5.** When hot, add the fish two at a time and fry until golden brown, about 4-5 minutes. Turn over and reduce the heat slightly if necessary and cook a further 4-5 minutes. Drain and repeat with the remaining fish.

**6.** Drain almost all the oil from the pan and re-heat the bacon and the nuts very briefly. Add the lime juice and cook a few seconds. Spoon the bacon and pine nut mixture over the fish and garnish with coriander or sage.

**Step 3** Dredge the fish with the cornmeal mixture, shaking off any excess.

**Step 5** Place the fish two at a time in hot oil and fry until golden brown on one side, then turn.

**Step 6** Spoon the bacon, pine nut and lime juice mixture over the fish.

## Cook's Notes

**Time**
Preparation takes about 25 minutes and cooking takes about 15-20 minutes.

**Preparation**
When dredging fish, seafood or chicken with flour or cornmeal to coat, prepare just before ready to cook. If the food stands with its coating for too long before cooking, the coating will become soggy.

**Variation**
If desired, the trout may be dredged with plain or whole-wheat flour instead of the cornmeal.

SERVES 4

# FRIED BASS IN CORNMEAL

As a coating for frying, cornmeal is superb. It fries to a crisp crunch and adds a subtle flavor of its own.

2lb freshwater bass or other whitefish fillets
Milk
2 cups yellow cornmeal
2 tbsps flour
Pinch salt
2 tsps cayenne pepper
1 tsp ground cumin
2 tsps garlic granules
Lime wedges to garnish

**Step 3** Mix the cornmeal coating on a sheet of wax paper, place on the fish and lift the ends to toss and coat.

**Step 2** Dip the fillets into milk and then hold by one end to allow the excess to drip off.

**Step 5** Turn the fish over once it floats to the surface of the oil.

**1.** Mix the cornmeal, flour, salt, cayenne, cumin and garlic together in a shallow container or on a piece of wax paper.

**2.** Skin the fillets if desired. Dip them into the milk and then lift to allow the excess to drip off.

**3.** Place the fish in the cornmeal mixture and turn with two forks or, if using paper, lift the ends and toss the fish to coat.

**4.** Meanwhile, heat oil in a deep frying pan, large saucepan or deep fat fryer.

**5.** Add the fish in small batches and cook until the fillets float to the surface. Turn over and cook to brown lightly and evenly.

**6.** Drain on paper towels and serve immediately with lime wedges.

## Cook's Notes

**Time**
Preparation takes about 20 minutes and cooking takes about 5 minutes per batch of fish.

**Serving Ideas**
Red pepper preserves or hot pepper relish may be served as a condiment with this fish, or accompany it with either the Garden Salsa or the Orange and Avocado Salad from the Chicken Nueva Mexicana recipe.

**Variation**
If substituting another type of fish for bass, make sure that it is a firm-fleshed fish.

SERVES 4

# Swordfish with Grapefruit Tequila Salsa

Rich and dense in texture, swordfish takes very well to a tart grapefruit accompaniment with a dash of tequila.

4-6 ruby or pink grapefruit (depending on size)
1 lime
Half a green chili, seeded and finely diced
1 green onion, finely chopped
2 tbsps chopped fresh coriander
1 tbsp sugar
3 tbsps tequila
4-8 swordfish steaks (depending on size)
Juice of 1 lime
2 tbsps oil
Black pepper to taste
Coriander sprigs for garnish

**1.** Remove the zest from the grapefruit and lime with a zester and set it aside.

**2.** Remove all the pith from the grapefruit and segment them. Squeeze the lime for juice. Mix the grapefruit and citrus zests with the chilli, onion, coriander, sugar, tequila and lime juice and set aside.

**3.** Mix remaining lime juice, oil and pepper together and brush both sides of the fish. Place under a pre-heated broiler and cook for about 4 minutes each side depending on distance from the heat source.

**4.** To serve, place a coriander sprig on each fish steak and serve with the grapefruit salsa.

**Step 1** Remove the zest from the grapefruit with a zester.

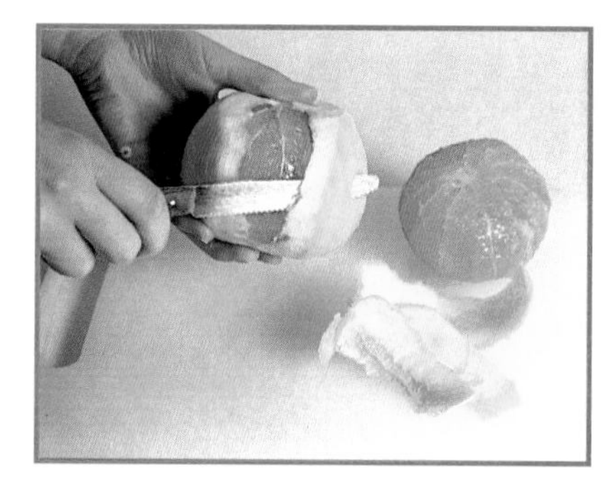

**Step 2** Use a serrated fruit knife to remove all the pith from the grapefruit.

## Cook's Notes

**Time**
Preparation takes about 35 minutes and cooking takes about 4-6 minutes.

**Variation**
If desired, substitute white rum for the tequila in the salsa or omit it altogether. The amount of sugar needed will vary depending on the sweetness of the grapefruit.

**Cook's Tip**
For extra flavor, the swordfish steaks may be marinated in a lime juice and oil mixture for up to 1 hour.

SERVES 6

# GULF COAST TACOS

Around the Gulf of Mexico, ever popular tacos take on a new look and taste with a seafood filling.

6 Tortillas (see recipe)

**Green Chili Salsa**

3 tomatillos, husks removed
1 tbsp oil
1 clove garlic
1oz coriander
2 green chilies
Juice of 1 lime
Pinch salt and sugar
½ cup sour cream

**Filling Ingredients**

8oz large raw shrimp, peeled
8oz raw scallops, quartered if large
1 tsp coriander seed, crushed
1 shallot, finely chopped
Salt and pepper
6 tbsps white wine
Water
1 small jicama, peeled and cut into thin matchstick strips
Coriander leaves and lime wedges

**1.** Prepare the Tortillas according to the recipe.

**2.** Heat 1 tbsp of oil in a small frying pan and slice the tomatillos. Sauté them for about 3 minutes to soften. Place in a food processor along with the garlic, coriander, chilies and lime juice. Purée until smooth. Fold in the sour cream, adjust seasoning and chill.

**3.** Heat oil in a deep sauté pan to a depth of at least 2 inches. When hot, place in a tortilla and press down under the oil with a metal spoon. When the tortilla starts to puff up, take it out and immediately fold to form a shell. Hold in shape until it cools slightly and sets. Repeat with the remaining tortillas. Keep them warm in an oven, standing on their open ends.

**4.** Place the shrimp, scallops, coriander seeds, shallot and salt and pepper in a sauté pan with the wine and water to barely cover. Cook for about 8 minutes, stirring occasionally. The shrimp should turn pink and the scallops will look opaque when cooked.

**5.** Fill the taco shells with the jicama. Remove the seafood from the liquid with a draining spoon and arrange on top of the jicama. Top with the salsa and decorate with coriander leaves. Serve with lime wedges.

**Step 3** Carefully fold over the tortilla to form a shell and hold in shape until it cools slightly and sets.

**Step 4** Cook filling ingredients for eight minutes, until the shrimp turn pink and the scallops look opaque when cooked.

## Cook's Notes

**Time**
Preparation takes about 1 hour, including the time to make the tortillas.

**Variation**
If desired, this recipe may be made with pre-prepared tortillas or taco shells. If using taco shells, simply re-heat in the oven, standing on their open ends.

**Cook's Tip**
Heating taco shells standing on their open ends keeps them from closing up.

SERVES 4

# CHEESE OR VEGETABLE ENCHILADAS

Many dishes in Tex-Mex cooking have Mexican origins, like these tortillas filled with a choice of fillings.

8 Tortillas (see recipe)
Full quantity Red Sauce (see Southwestern Stir-fry)

**Cheese Filling**

2 tbsps oil
1 small red pepper, seeded and finely diced
1 clove garlic, crushed
1 tbsp chopped fresh coriander
½ cup heavy cream
½ cup cream cheese
½ cup mild cheese, grated
Whole coriander leaves

**Vegetable Filling**

2 tbsps oil
1 small onion, finely chopped
1 green pepper, seeded and diced
2 zucchini, diced
½ tsp oregano
½ tsp ground cumin
4oz corn, fresh or frozen
Salt and pepper
1½ cups grated mild cheese
Sour cream
Full quantity green chili salsa (see Gulf Coast Tacos)

**1.** Prepare the tortillas, red sauce and green chili salsa according to the recipe directions.

**2.** Heat the oil for the cheese filling and cook the pepper and garlic slowly to soften. Add the coriander and pour in the cream.

**3.** Bring to the boil and cook rapidly to thicken. Add the cream cheese and stir to melt. Add the grated mild cheese, stir in and keep the filling warm.

**4.** Re-heat the tortillas wrapped in foil in a moderate oven for about 10 minutes. Place one at a time on serving dishes and spoon in the cheese filling. Fold over both sides to the middle.

**5.** Re-heat the red sauce, if necessary, and spoon over the center of two enchiladas. Garnish with coriander leaves.

**6.** For the vegetable filling, heat the oil and cook the onion to soften. Add the remaining vegetables except the corn. Add the oregano and cumin and cook about 3 minutes or until the onions are soft. Add the corn and heat through, adding seasoning to taste. Stir in the grated cheese and fill the tortillas as before, but place in a baking dish. Cook, covered, for about 10-15 minutes at 350°F, or until the cheese has melted and the filling is beginning to bubble. Serve topped with sour cream and green chili salsa.

**Step 5** Place two tortillas on a serving plate and spoon over the red sauce.

**Step 6** Place tortilla at one end of the baking dish, spoon in the filling and fold over. Repeat with the remaining tortillas and filling.

## Cook's Notes

**Time**
Preparation takes about 1 hour. Cheese filling takes about 10 minutes to cook and the vegetable filling takes 13-18 minutes.

**Serving Ideas**
Serve with Refried Beans or Spicy Rice and Beans. Add green salad or sliced avocado.

MAKES 10

# CHALUPAS

These are tortillas in another form, this time a snack with spicy meat. Create your own combination with a selection of different toppings.

Half quantity Tortilla recipe
Oil for frying
Full quantity Red Sauce (see recipe for Southwestern Stir-fry)
12oz ground beef
2 cloves garlic, crushed
1 tsp dried oregano
2 tsps cumin
Salt and pepper
3oz frozen corn
4 tbsps raisins

**Toppings**

6-8 chopped green onions
4-6 diced tomatoes
Half a small head lettuce, shredded
½ cup sour cream
1 cup shredded cheese

**1.** Prepare the tortillas according to the recipe and divide the dough in 10. After the required resting time, roll the balls of dough into 3½ inch rounds.

**2.** Prepare the Red Sauce according to the recipe instructions and set it aside.

**3.** Heat at least 2 inches of oil in a frying pan, sauté pan or medium saucepan. When hot, place in one tortilla and fry briefly until just crisp. Drain and keep them warm.

**4.** Cook the beef slowly until the fat begins to render. Add the garlic, oregano and cumin and raise the heat to brown the meat. Season to taste and then stir in enough of the Red Sauce to moisten the meat well. Add the corn and raisins, cover the pan and leave to stand for 5 minutes.

**5.** Spoon the meat onto the tortillas and drizzle over more sauce. Garnish with your choice of toppings.

**Step 4** Add enough of the sauce to moisten the meat thorougly.

**Step 5** Spoon the meat onto the tortillas and add more sauce and topping.

## Cook's Notes

**Time**
Preparation takes about 40 minutes and cooking takes about 30 seconds for the tortillas, 15 minutes for the sauce and about 15 minutes to finish the beef topping.

**Variation**
Refried Beans may be used instead of the beef topping, if desired. About half quantity of the Refried Bean recipe should be enough to top 10 Chalupas. Omit the corn and raisins and use half quantity of the Red Sauce recipe as a topping.

**Serving Ideas**
Serve as a snack or cocktail savory. For a main course, add Refried Beans or Spicy Rice and Beans as an accompaniment.

SERVES 4-6

# Indian Bread with Chorizo and Salsa

A version of this bread recipe has been baked by American Indians for hundreds of years. It's delicious served plain, too.

**Bread**
2 cups all-purpose flour
1 tbsp baking powder
Pinch salt
1 tbsp vegetable shortening
2 tsps cumin seed
¾ cup plus 2 tbsps water

**Chorizo Topping**
1lb chorizo sausage
2 medium red potatoes, scrubbed
4 green onions, chopped

**Salsa**
1 clove garlic
1oz coriander leaves
1 tsp fresh oregano
Half or less fresh red or green chili, seeded
Pinch salt and dry mustard
Juice of 2 limes
¾ cup oil
Shredded lettuce, crumbled goat's milk cheese and chopped tomatoes to garnish

**1.** Sift the flour, baking powder and salt into a bowl. Rub in the shortening until the mixture resembles coarse crumbs and then stir in the cumin seed. Stir in enough water to make a soft, slightly sticky dough. Knead several times. cover and leave to stand for 15-20 minutes.

**2.** Divide the dough into 8 pieces and roll or pat into 5 inch circles on a well-floured surface. Make a hole in the center of each with your finger and leave the circles to stand, covered, for 30 minutes.

**3.** Meanwhile, boil the potatoes in their skins in a covered saucepan. Place the chorizo in a sauté pan and cover with water. Cover the pan and bring to the boil. Lower the heat and simmer about 10 minutes, or until just tender. Remove the chorizo from the water and peel off the casings while the sausage is still warm. Chop sausage roughly and set aside. When the potatoes are tender, drain them and leave to cool. Cut the potatoes into ½ inch dice.

**4.** Place the garlic, coriander, oregano, chili, salt and mustard into a food processor and add the lime juice. Process until well blended. With the machine running, pour the oil through the funnel in a thin, steady stream. Process until smooth and adjust the seasoning.

**5.** Pour the oil for cooking the bread into a deep-fat fryer, large saucepan or deep sauté pan to a depth of about 2-3 inches. Heat to 375°F. Carefully lower in one dough circle and push it underneath the oil with a large metal spoon. Fry for about 30 seconds, turn over and fry the other side. Drain each while frying the others.

**6.** Mix the chorizo, green onions and potatoes with enough of the salsa to moisten. Arrange the shredded lettuce on top of the bread and spoon on the chorizo topping. Spoon on any remaining salsa, sprinkle with chopped tomato and crumbled cheese.

## Cook's Notes

**Time**
Preparation takes about 45 minutes – 1 hour. Indian Bread will take about 1-2 minutes to cook per piece. The chorizo topping will take about 25 minutes for the potatoes and sausage to cook.

**Preparation**
Indian Bread is best prepared, cooked and eaten on the same day. If desired, the chorizo topping and salsa may be prepared in advance and kept in the refrigerator overnight. The salsa will keep 3-4 days, but may separate slightly during storage. Simply re-process or beat vigorously to bring the mixture back together.

**Serving Ideas**
The recipe directions are for serving the dish at room temperature. For serving hot, re-heat the chorizo topping and combine with the salsa. Place directly on the hot bread, saving the lettuce to garnish the top along with the tomatoes and cheese.

MAKES 12-14

# CHURROS

These fritters can be either sweet or savory. Either way, they're a treat with a Mexican influence.

**Basic Dough**

Scant 1 cup plus 2 tbsps water
3 tbsps butter or margarine
Pinch salt
1 cup all-purpose flour
6 tbsps cornmeal
2 eggs
Oil for deep frying

**Savory Ingredients**

2 tbsps finely grated cheese
2 chili peppers, seeded and finely chopped
Parmesan cheese (optional)

**Sweet Ingredients**

4 tbsps sugar
1 tbsp unsweetened cocoa powder
1 tsp ground cinnamon
Powdered sugar (optional)

**1.** Combine the water, butter or margarine and salt in a heavy-based saucepan. If making sweet churros, add sugar as well. Cook over medium heat until the butter or margarine melts.

**2.** Immediately stir in the flour and cornmeal. Keeping the pan over medium heat, stir until the mixture pulls away from the sides of the pan and forms a ball. Take off the heat and cool slightly.

**3.** Add the eggs one at a time, beating vigorously in between each addition. It may not be necessary to add all the egg. Beat until the mixture is smooth and shiny and thick enough to pipe. Add the cheese and chilies *or* the cocoa and cinnamon with the eggs.

**4.** Spoon the mixture into a pastry bag fitted with a star tip.

**5.** Heat the oil in a deep fat fryer, deep saucepan or deep sauté pan to a depth of at least 4 inches. Pipe the dough into the oil in 10 inch strips and fry until golden brown, about 3 minutes per side. Drain on paper towels and sprinkle the savory churros with Parmesan cheese and the sweet with powdered sugar, if desired. Serve warm.

**Step 2** Cook the mixture over moderate heat, stirring until it pulls away from the sides and forms a ball.

**Step 5** Pipe the dough into the hot oil in long strips. They will curl and change shape as they cook.

## *Cook's Notes*

**Time**
Preparation takes about 25-30 minutes and cooking takes about 6 minutes per piece.

**Preparation**
As the churros cook in the hot fat, they will curl into different shapes.

**Cook's Tip**
The mixture will be easier to pipe if it is used just after preparation.

SERVES 6-8

# SPICY RICE AND BEANS

A lively side dish or vegetarian main course, this recipe readily takes to creative variations and even makes a good cold salad.

4 tbsps oil
2 cups long grain rice
1 onion, finely chopped
1 green pepper, seeded and chopped
1 tsp each ground cumin and coriander
1-2 tsps tabasco sauce
Salt
3½ cups stock
1lb canned red kidney beans, drained and rinsed
1lb canned tomatoes, drained and coarsely chopped
Chopped parsley

**Step 2** Cook the rice in the oil until just turning opaque.

**1.** Heat the oil in a casserole or a large, deep saucepan.

**2.** Add the rice and cook until just turning opaque. Add the onion, pepper and cumin and coriander. Cook gently for a further 2 minutes.

**3.** Add the tabasco, salt, stock and beans and bring to the boil. Cover and cook about 45 minutes, or until the rice is tender and most of the liquid is absorbed.

**4.** Remove from the heat and add the tomatoes, stirring them in gently. Leave to stand, covered, for 5 minutes.

**5.** Fluff up the mixture with a fork and sprinkle with parsley to serve.

**Step 3** Cook with the remaining ingredients until rice is tender and most of the liquid is absorbed.

**Step 4** Carefully stir in the tomatoes before covering and leaving to stand.

## Cook's Notes

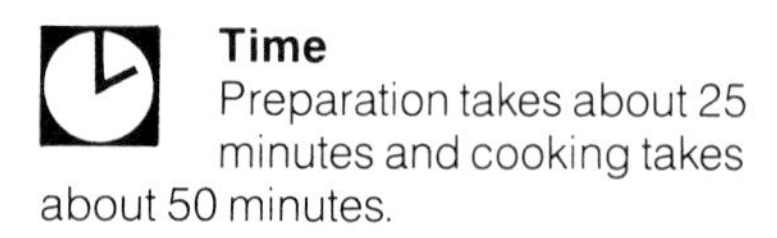

**Time**
Preparation takes about 25 minutes and cooking takes about 50 minutes.

**Serving Ideas**
Serve with warm tortillas and a salad for a light vegetarian meal. Serve as a side dish with enchiladas, meat or poultry, or cheese and egg dishes.

**Variation**
The recipe may be made with 1lb fresh tomatoes, peeled, seeded and coarsely chopped.

SERVES 6-8

# REFRIED BEANS

This is a classic accompaniment to both Mexican and Tex-Mex main courses be they poultry or meat, vegetable or cheese.

8oz dried pinto beans
Water to cover
1 bay leaf
6 tbsps oil
Salt and pepper
Grated mild cheese
Shredded lettuce
Tortillas

**Step 2** As the beans fry in the oil, mash them with the back of a spoon.

**1.** Soak the beans overnight. Change the water, add the bay leaf and bring to the boil. Cover and simmer about 2 hours, or until the beans are completely tender. Alternatively, bring the beans to the boil in cold water and then allow to boil rapidly for 10 minutes. Cover and leave to stand for one hour. Change the water and then continue with the recipe. Drain the beans and reserve a small amount of the cooking liquid. Discard bay leaf.

**2.** Heat the oil in a heavy frying pan. Add the beans and, as they fry, mash them with the back of a spoon. Do not over-mash – about a third of the beans should stay whole. Season to taste.

**Step 3** Turn the beans over when the bottom is set but not brown.

**Step 4** Sprinkle on the cheese and cook until it melts.

**3.** Smooth out the beans in the pan and cook until the bottom is set but not browned. Turn the beans over and cook the other side.

**4.** Top with the cheese and cook the beans until the cheese melts. Serve with finely shredded lettuce and tortillas, either warm or cut in triangles and deep-fried until crisp.

## Cook's Notes

**Time**
Preparation takes about 15 minutes. The beans must be soaked overnight or re-hydrated by the quick method. The beans must be cooked at least 2 hours before frying.

**Watchpoint**
Make sure the beans are completely tender and have boiled rapidly for at least 45 minutes before eating.

**Serving Ideas**
Serve the beans as a side dish with enchiladas or with barbecued meats.

SERVES 8

# CHILI RELLENOS

Organization is the key to preparing these stuffed peppers. Fried inside their golden batter coating, they're puffy and light.

Full quantity Red Sauce (see recipe for Southwestern Stir-fry)
8 small green peppers
4 small green chilies, seeded and finely chopped
1 clove garlic, crushed
1 tsp chopped fresh sage
8oz cream cheese
2 cups grated mild cheese
Salt
Flour for dredging
Oil for deep frying
8 eggs, separated
6 tbsps all-purpose flour
Pinch salt
Finely chopped green onions

**1.** Blanch the whole peppers in boiling water for about 10-15 minutes, or until just tender. Rinse them in cold water and pat them dry.

**2.** Carefully cut around the stems to make a top, remove and set aside. Scoop out the seeds and cores, leaving the peppers whole. Leave upside down on paper towels to drain.

**3.** Mix together the chilies, garlic, sage, cheeses and salt to taste. Fill the peppers using a small teaspoon and replace the tops, sticking them into the filling.

**4.** Dredge the peppers with flour and heat the oil in a deep fat fryer to 375°F.

**5.** Beat the egg yolks and flour in a mixing bowl until the mixture forms a ribbon trail when the beaters are lifted.

**6.** Beat the whites with a pinch of salt until stiff but not dry. Fold into the egg yolk mixture.

**7.** Shape 2 tbsps of batter into an oval and drop into the oil. Immediately slide a metal draining spoon under the batter to hold it in place. Place on a filled pepper. Cover the tops of the peppers with more batter and then spoon over hot oil to seal. Fry until the batter is brown on all sides, turning the peppers over carefully.

**8.** Drain on paper towels and keep them warm on a rack in a moderate oven while frying the remaining peppers.

**9.** Sprinkle with onions and serve with Red Sauce.

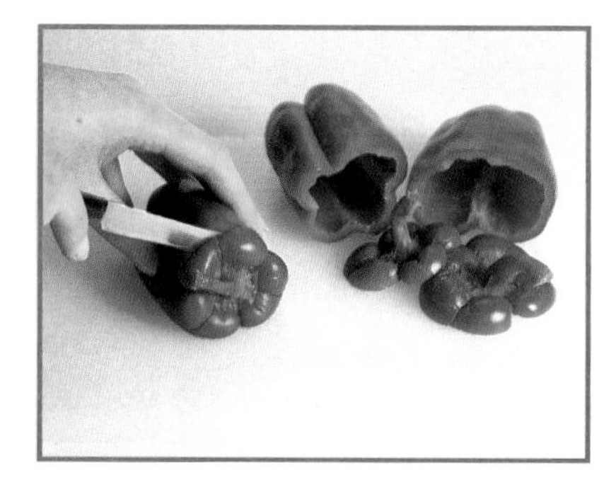

**Step 2** Carefully cut around the stems of each blanched pepper to make a top.

**Step 7** Cover the tops of the peppers with more batter and spoon over oil to seal.

## Cook's Notes

**Time**
Preparation takes about 40 minutes and cooking takes about 3 minutes per pepper. Red Sauce will take approximately 15 minutes to cook.

**Cook's Tip**
Sprinkling savory foods lightly with salt helps to draw out any excess oil. For fried sweet foods, substitute sugar.

**Serving Ideas**
Chili Rellenos may be served as a main course with a salad and Refried Beans. These also make a good appetizer served with either the Red Sauce, Green Chili Salsa or Garden Salsa.

SERVES 4

# SALAD HUEVOS RANCHEROS

Chicory is becoming popular all over the United States. This recipe puts it to delicious use with eggs and other Tex-Mex favorites – peppers, zucchini, jicama and chorizo.

4 heads chicory
1 large red pepper, roasted (see Chicken with Red Peppers)
1 large or 2 small zucchini, cut into matchstick pieces
1 small jicama root, cut into matchstick pieces
2-3 green onions, shredded
1 chorizo sausage, blanched and cut into thin strips
4 eggs
4 tbsps pine nuts

**Dressing**

1 tsp chopped fresh coriander
6 tbsps oil
2 tbsps lime juice
Dash tabasco
Salt and pinch sugar

**1.** Prepare the roasted pepper and cut it into thin strips. Blanch the chorizo as for Indian Bread Chorizo and Salsa.

**2.** Separate the leaves of the chicory and slice or leave whole if small.

**3.** Bring water to the boil and blanch the zucchini and jicama strips for one minute. Rinse under cold water until completely cool and leave to drain. Combine with the chicory. Add the strips of chorizo and set aside.

**4.** Toast the pine nuts in a moderate oven until golden brown, about 5 minutes.

**5.** Bring at least 2 inches of water to the boil in a frying or sauté pan. Turn down the heat to simmering. Break an egg onto a saucer or into a cup.

**6.** Stir the water to make a whirlpool and then carefully pour the egg into the center, keeping the saucer or cup close to the level of the water. When the water stops swirling and the white begins to set, gently move the egg over to the side and repeat with each remaining egg. Cook the eggs until the whites are completely set, but the yolks are still soft.

**7.** Remove the eggs from the water with a draining spoon and place them immediately into a bowl of cold water.

**8.** Mix the dressing ingredients together and pour half over the vegetables and sausage. Toss to coat. Arrange the mixture on individual plates in the shape of nests.

**9.** Remove the eggs from the cold water with the draining spoon and hold them over a towel for a few minutes to drain completely. Place one egg in the middle of each nest. Spoon the remaining dressing over each egg, sprinkle over the pine nuts and garnish the yolk with a coriander leaf.

**Step 6** To poach the eggs, make a whirlpool in the water and carefully pour the egg into the center.

**Step 8** Arrange the vegetable mixture in the shape of a nest on a serving plate and carefully spoon an egg into the middle.

## Cook's Notes

**Time**
Preparation takes about 45 minutes and cooking takes about 5 minutes for the eggs, 1 minute to blanch the vegetables and 10 minutes to blanch the chorizo.

**Serving Ideas**
Double the quantity of the vegetables and sausages and serve as a light lunch or supper dish. The salad may also be served as an appetizer.

MAKES 1 PIE

# Black Bottom Ice Cream Pie

Unbelievably simple, yet incredibly delicious and impressive, this pie is a perfect ending to a summer meal or a spicy one anytime.

8-10 Graham crackers, crushed
½ cup butter or margarine, melted
3 cups coffee ice cream
2oz semi-sweet chocolate, melted
4oz shredded coconut
Dark rum

**1.** Crush crackers with a rolling pin or in a food processor. Mix with melted butter or margarine.

**2.** Press into an 8½ inch false-bottomed flan dish. Chill thoroughly in the refrigerator.

**3.** Meanwhile, combine 4 tbsps coconut with the melted chocolate. When cooled but not solidified, add about a quarter of the coffee ice cream, mixing well.

**4.** Spread the mixture on the base of a crust and freeze until firm.

**5.** Soften the remaining ice cream with an electric mixer or food processor and spread over the chocolate-coconut layer. Re-freeze until firm.

**6.** Toast the remaining coconut in a moderate oven, stirring frequently until pale golden brown. Allow to cool completely.

**7.** Remove the pie from the freezer and leave in the refrigerator 30 minutes before serving. Push up the base of the dish and place the pie on a serving plate. Sprinkle the top with toasted coconut. Cut into wedges and drizzle with rum before serving.

**Step 2** Press the crust mixture into the base and up the sides of a flan dish.

**Step 4** Spread the chocolate-coconut mixture evenly over the bottom of the crust.

**Step 5** Spread the coffee ice cream carefully over the chocolate-coconut layer and re-freeze.

**Time**
Preparation takes about 25 minutes. The ice cream will take several hours to freeze.

**Freezing**
The pie may be prepared well in advance and kept in the freezer for up to 3 months. Coconut may be sprinkled on top before freezing or just before serving.

**Variation**
If desired, use vanilla ice cream in place of the coffee.

MAKES 3 cups

# Guava Mint Sorbet

When a light dessert is called for, a sorbet can't be surpassed. The exotic taste of guava works well with mint.

4 ripe guavas
⅔ cup granulated sugar
1 cup water
2 tbsps chopped fresh mint
1 lime
1 egg white
Fresh mint leaves for garnish

**Step 2** Combine the puréed guava, mint and cold syrup.

**Step 3** Freeze the mixture until slushy and then process to break up the ice crystals.

**Step 4** Process the frozen mixture again and gradually work in the egg white.

**1.** Combine the sugar and water in a heavy-based saucepan and bring slowly to the boil to dissolve the sugar. When the mixture is a clear syrup, boil rapidly for 30 seconds. Allow to cool to room temperature and then chill in the refrigerator.

**2.** Cut the guavas in half and scoop out the pulp. Discard the peels and seeds and puree the fruit until smooth in a food processor. Add the mint and combine with cold syrup. Add lime juice until the right balance of sweetness is reached.

**3.** Pour the mixture into a shallow container and freeze until slushy. Process again to break up ice crystals and then freeze until firm.

**4.** Whip the egg white until stiff but not dry. Process the sorbet again and when smooth, add the egg white. Mix once or twice and then freeze again until firm.

**5.** Remove from the freezer 15 minutes before serving and keep in the refrigerator.

**6.** Scoop out and garnish each serving with mint leaves.

## Cook's Notes

**Time**
Preparation takes about 2-3 hours, allowing the sorbet to freeze in between processing.

**Preparation**
If a food processor is not available, use an electric mixer.

**Freezing**
The sorbet will keep in the freezer for up to 3 months in a well-sealed, rigid container.

SERVES 6

# FROZEN LIME AND BLUEBERRY CREAM

Blueberries grow wild in this part of the United States and recipes to use them abound.

Juice and rind of 4 limes
Water
1 cup sugar
4oz blueberries
3 egg whites
1 cup heavy cream, whipped

**Step 3** Boil the lime juice, water and sugar rapidly once a clear syrup forms.

**1.** Measure the lime juice and make up to 6 tbsps with water if necessary.

**2.** Combine with the sugar in a heavy-based pan and bring to the boil slowly to dissolve the sugar.

**3.** When the mixture forms a clear syrup, boil rapidly to 250°F on a sugar thermometer.

**4.** Meanwhile, combine the blueberries with about 4 tbsps water in a small saucepan. Bring to the boil and then simmer, covered, until very soft. Purée, sieve to remove the seeds and skin, and set aside to cool.

**5.** Whisk the egg whites until stiff but not dry and then pour on the hot sugar syrup in a steady stream, whisking constantly. Add the lime rind and allow the meringue to cool.

**6.** When cold, fold in the whipped cream. Pour in the puree and marble through the mixture with a rubber spatula. Do not over-fold. Pour the mixture into a lightly-oiled mold or bowl and freeze until firm. Leave 30 minutes in the refrigerator before serving or dip the mold for about 10 seconds in hot water. Place a plate over the bottom of the mold, invert and shake to turn out. Garnish with extra whipped cream, blueberries or lime slices.

**Step 5** Pour the syrup gradually onto the whisked egg whites, beating constantly.

**Step 6** Fold the cream and the fruit purée into the egg whites, marbling the purée through the mixture.

## Cook's Notes

**Time**
Preparation takes about 40 minutes. The cream should be left in the freezer overnight to firm completely.

**Variation**
Substitute 2 large or 3 medium lemons for the limes. Other berries, such as raspberries, blackberries, red or black currants, may be substituted for the blueberries. If using currants, add sugar to taste.

**Freezing**
The cream will keep in its mold, well covered,in the freezer for up to 2 months. Remove from the freezer and leave in the refrigerator for 30 minutes or dip in hot water as the recipe suggests.

MAKES 10

# FRUIT EMPANADAS

Tortillas can have a sweet side, too, when stuffed with cheese and sunny apricots or exotic tropical fruit.

Full quantity Tortilla recipe
10 ripe fresh apricots, halved and stoned, or 1lb canned apricots, well drained
1lb cream cheese
Oil for deep frying
Powdered sugar

**Step 3** Place the cheese and apricots on the lower half of each tortilla.

**1.** Prepare the tortilla dough, roll out but do not pre-cook. Heat oil in a deep saucepan, sauté pan or deep-fat fryer to a depth of at least 2 inches. Oil should reach a temperature of 375°F.

**2.** Cut the apricots into quarters and the cheese into 10 even pieces.

**3.** Place one piece of cheese and an even amount of apricots on the lower half of each tortilla. Fold over the upper half and seal the edges. Crimp tightly into a decorative pattern.

**4.** Fry 1 empanada at a time until golden on both sides. Baste the upper side frequently with oil to make the tortillas puffy.

**5.** Drain well on paper towels and serve warm, sprinkled with powdered sugar.

**Step 3** Fold over the upper half and seal the edges.

**Step 3** Crimp the edges tightly into a decorative pattern.

## Cook's Notes

**Time**
Preparation takes about 40 minutes-1 hour for the tortillas and about 20 minutes to prepare the rest of the dish.

**Variation**
Other fruit may be used in the empanadas instead of apricots. Substitute fresh guava, mango or papaya cut into short strips. Sliced peaches may also be used as well as cherries, although they are not native to the Southwest.

**Preparation**
As with all deep-fried foods, fruit empanadas are best served as soon as they are cooked.

MAKES 1 LOAF

# CHOCOLATE CINNAMON MONKEY BREAD

Pull this bread apart to serve in individual pieces rather than slicing it. Savory versions substitute Parmesan and herbs for sugar and spice.

**Dough**
4 tbsps warm water
1 tbsp sugar
1 envelope dry yeast
3-3¾ cups bread flour
6 tbsps sugar
Pinch salt
5 tbsps butter, softened
5 eggs

**Topping**
½ cup butter, melted
1 cup sugar
2 tsps cinnamon
2 tsps cocoa
6 tbsps finely chopped pecans

**1.** Sprinkle 1 tbsp sugar and the yeast on top of the water and leave it in a warm place until foaming.

**2.** Sift 3 cups of flour into a bowl and add the sugar and salt. Rub in the butter until completely blended.

**3.** Add 2 eggs and the yeast mixture, mixing in well. Add the remaining eggs one at a time until the mixture forms a soft, spongy dough. Add remaining flour as necessary. Knead for 10 minutes on a lightly floured surface until smooth and elastic.

**4.** Place the dough in a greased bowl and turn over to grease all the surfaces. Cover with plastic wrap and put in a warm place. Leave to stand for 1-1½ hours or until doubled in bulk.

**5.** Butter a ring mold liberally. Knock the dough down and knead it again for about 5 minutes. Shape into balls about 2 inches in diameter. Mix the topping ingredients together except for the melted butter. Roll the dough balls in the butter and then in the sugar mixture.

**6.** Place a layer of dough balls in the bottom of the mold and continue until all the dough and topping has been used. Cover and allow to rise again about 15 minutes. Bake in a pre-heated 350°F oven for about 45-50 minutes. Loosen from the pan and turn out while still warm.

**Step 5** Roll the dough in melted butter and then in the sugar mixture.

**Step 6** Lay out the balls of dough in a prepared pan.

## Cook's Notes

**Time**
Preparation takes about 2 hours and cooking takes about 45-50 minutes.

**Cook's Tip**
Check the temperature of the water carefully. If it is too hot it can kill the yeast and then the bread will not rise. Water should feel warm when tested on the inside of your wrist.

**Serving Ideas**
Serve warm with coffee or tea, or serve as an accompaniment to a fresh fruit salad.

# CALIFORNIAN COOKING

# INTRODUCTION

As varied as its landscapes, as vibrant as its climate, California's food is innovative, but with an eye to its heritage. Nothing if not cosmopolitan, California cuisine draws heavily on the dishes of China, Mexico and Italy, from where many of the state's first citizens came. Contemporary chefs have studied French cuisine, experimented and come up with spirited versions of classics that reflect today's style of eating. California's climate and location have had a benevolent influence on its cuisine from the start. Fruits and vegetables flourish, vineyards produce grapes for wines that rival those of France, and miles of scenic coastline provide an exciting selection of seafood. All this beautifully fresh food has made the trend to healthier eating possible and very palatable.

The fresher the food, the better it stands on its own. That is why contemporary California cooks favor light sauces on simply cooked fish, poultry and meat, and light dressings for salads that let the flavors of the individual ingredients shine through. Above all, food from California is fun to eat.

Trends set here usually spread throughout the country. Given the enthusiasm and adventurous spirit of California cooks, we will have yet more to look forward to.

SERVES 6-8

# CIOPPINO

California's famous and delicious fish stew is Italian in heritage; but a close relative of French Bouillabaisse, too.

1lb spinach, well washed
1 tbsp each chopped fresh basil, thyme, rosemary and sage
2 tbsps chopped fresh marjoram
4 tbsps chopped parsley
1 large red pepper, seeded and finely chopped
2 cloves garlic, crushed
24 large fresh clams or 48 mussels, well scrubbed
1 large crab, cracked
1lb monkfish or rock salmon (huss)
12 large shrimp, cooked and unpeeled
1lb canned plum tomatoes and juice
2 tbsps tomato paste
4 tbsps olive oil
Pinch salt and pepper
½-1 cup dry white wine
Water

**1.** Chop the spinach leaves roughly after removing any tough stems.

**2.** Combine the spinach with the herbs, chopped red pepper and garlic, and set aside.

**3.** Discard any clams or mussels with broken shells or ones that do not close when tapped. Place the shellfish in the bottom of a large pot and sprinkle over a layer of the spinach mixture.

**4.** Prepare the crab as for Crab Louis, leaving the shells on the claws after cracking them slightly. Place the crab on top of the spinach and then add another spinach layer.

**5.** Add the fish and a spinach layer, followed by the shrimp and any remaining spinach.

**6.** Mix the tomatoes, tomato paste, oil, wine and seasonings and pour over the seafood and spinach.

**7.** Cover the pot and simmer the mixture for about 40 minutes. If more liquid is necessary, add water. Spoon into soup bowls, dividing the fish and shell fish evenly.

**Step 3** Place well scrubbed clams or mussels in the bottom of a large pot, sprinkling over spinach mixture.

**Step 6** Pour the tomato paste and wine mixture over the layered seafood and spinach

## Cook's Notes

**Time**
Preparation takes abut 40 minutes and cooking takes about 40 minutes.

**Preparation**
Soup must be eaten immediately after cooking. It does not keep or reheat well.

**Variation**
The choice of seafood or fish may be changed to suit your own taste and budget. For special occasions, add lobster.

SERVES 4

# Avocado Soup

Avocados feature frequently in California cooking. A cold soup like this makes an easy summer meal.

2 large ripe avocados
1½ cups natural yogurt
2 cups chicken or vegetable stock
½ clove garlic, minced
Juice of 1 lemon
2 tsps chopped fresh oregano
Salt and white pepper
Chopped parsley to garnish

**Step 1** Cut the avocados in half and twist to separate.

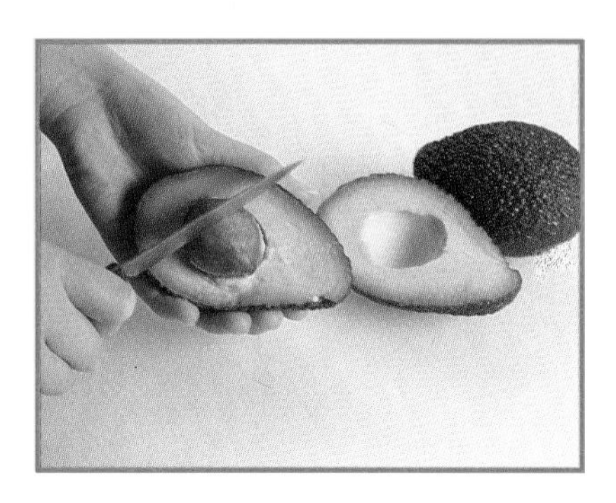

**Step 1** Tap the stone with a knife and twist to remove it.

**Step 2** Place the avocado cut side down on a worktop, score the skin and pull it backwards to remove.

**1.** Cut the avocados in half lengthwise and twist to separate. Tap the stone sharply with a knife and twist to remove.

**2.** Place the avocado halves cut side down on a flat surface. Score the skin with a sharp knife and then peel the strips of skin backwards to remove them.

**3.** Cut the avocado into pieces and place in a food processor. Reserve 4 tbsps yogurt and add the remaining yogurt and other ingredients, except the parsley, to the avocado. Process until smooth and chill thoroughly.

**4.** Pour the soup into bowls or a tureen and garnish with reserved yogurt. Sprinkle with parsley and serve chilled.

## Cook's Notes

**Time**
Preparation takes about 20-25 minutes. The soup should chill for about 2 hours in the refrigerator before serving.

**Cook's Tip**
The lemon juice, plus the slight acidity of the yogurt, will keep the avocado from turning brown. However, serve the soup on the same day it is prepared.

**Preparation**
Check the avocado skins and be sure to scrape off any flesh that remains attached to them before processing the ingredients.

# CALIFORNIAN SHRIMP AND SCALLOP STIR-FRY

Stir-frying came to California with Chinese settlers who worked on the railroads. It's the perfect way to cook seafood.

3 tbsps oil
4 tbsps pine nuts
1lb uncooked shrimp
1lb shelled scallops, quartered if large
2 tsps grated fresh ginger
1 small red or green chili, seeded and finely chopped
2 cloves garlic, finely chopped
1 large red pepper, seeded and cut into 1″ diagonal pieces
8oz fresh spinach, stalks removed and leaves well washed and shredded
4 green onions, cut in ½″ diagonal pieces
4 tbsps fish or chicken stock
4 tbsps light soy sauce
4 tbsps rice wine or dry sherry
1 tbsp cornstarch

**1.** Heat oil in a wok and add the pine nuts. Cook over low heat, stirring continuously until lightly browned. Remove with a draining spoon and drain on paper towels.

**2.** Add the shrimp and scallops to the oil remaining in the wok and stir over moderate heat until shellfish is beginning to look opaque and firm and the shrimp look pink.

**3.** Add the ginger, chili, garlic and red pepper and cook a few minutes over moderately high heat.

**4.** Add the spinach and onion, and stir-fry briefly. Mix the remaining ingredients together and pour over the ingredients in the wok.

**5.** Turn up the heat to bring the liquid quickly to the boil, stirring ingredients constantly. Once the liquid thickens and clears, stir in the pine nuts and serve immediately.

**Step 1** Cook pine nuts in oil until they are light brown.

**Step 2** Cook shellfish until shrimp begin to turn pink and scallops lose their transparency.

**Step 5** When all ingredients are added, cook briskly to thicken the sauce.

## Cook's Notes

**Time**
Preparation takes about 35 minutes, cooking takes about 8-10 minutes.

**Preparation**
Because cooking time is so short, be sure to prepare all ingredients and have them ready before beginning to stir-fry.

**Economy**
Eliminate scallops and cut the quantity of shrimp in half. Make up the difference with a firm whitefish cut into 1″ pieces.

SERVES 4-6

# Caesar Salad

Both Los Angeles and Tijuana take credit for this salad, said to have been concocted one evening from the only ingredients left in the kitchen.

6 anchovy fillets, soaked in 4 tbsps milk
1 cup olive oil
1 clove garlic, left whole
4 slices French bread, cut into ½" cubes
1 egg, cooked 1 minute
1 head Romaine lettuce
Juice of 1 small lemon
Salt and pepper
4 tbsps grated Parmesan cheese

**Step 2** Fry the cubes of French bread in the hot oil, stirring them constantly for even browning.

**1.** Leave the anchovies to soak in the milk for 15 minutes. Rinse and pat dry on paper towels. Chop roughly.

**2.** Crush the garlic and leave in the oil for about 30 minutes. Heat all but 6 tbsps of the oil in a frying pan until hot. Fry the cubes of bread until golden brown, stirring constantly with a metal spoon for even browning. Drain on paper towels.

**3.** Break the cooked egg into a bowl and beat well with the lemon juice, salt and pepper. Toss the lettuce with the remaining garlic oil and anchovies. Add the egg mixture and toss to coat well. Place in a clean serving bowl and sprinkle over the croûtons and Parmesan cheese. Serve at room temperature.

**Step 3** To make the dressing, break the egg into the bowl and mix well with the lemon juice and seasoning until slightly thickened.

**Step 3** Add the oil to the lettuce separately and then toss with the egg dressing mixture.

## Cook's Notes

**Time**
Preparation takes about 30 minutes and cooking takes about 3-5 minutes for the croûtons.

**Cook's Tip**
Soaking anchovy fillets in milk before using them neutralizes the strong salty taste.

**Watchpoint**
Remove the croûtons from the hot fat when just barely brown enough. They continue to cook slightly in their own heat as they drain.

SERVES 4

# GREEN GODDESS SALAD

Californians' love of salads and avocados combine in this fresh recipe named for its green dressing.

8 anchovy fillets, soaked in milk, rinsed and dried
1 green onion, chopped
2 tbsps chopped fresh tarragon
3 tbsps chopped chives
4 tbsps chopped parsley
1 cup prepared mayonnaise
½ cup natural yogurt
2 tbsps tarragon vinegar
Pinch sugar and cayenne pepper
1 large head lettuce
1lb cooked chicken or seafood
1 avocado, peeled and sliced or cubed
1 tbsp lemon juice

**Step 1** The dressing should be very well blended and light green after working in a food processor. Alternatively, use a hand blender.

**1.** Combine all the ingredients, except the lettuce, avocado and chicken or shellfish in a food processor. Work the ingredients until smooth, well mixed and green. Leave in the refrigerator at least 1 hour for the flavors to blend.

**2.** Shred the lettuce or tear into bite-size pieces and arrange on plates.

**3.** Top the lettuce with the cooked chicken cut into strips or cubes. If using crab or lobster, cut the meat into bite-size pieces. Shelled shrimp or mussels can be left whole.

**4.** Spoon the dressing over the chicken or seafood. Brush the avocado slices or toss the cubes with lemon juice and garnish the salad. Serve any remaining dressing separately.

**Step 3** Arrange lettuce on individual plates and top with shredded chicken or shellfish.

## Cook's Notes

**Time**
Preparation takes about 30 minutes.

**Preparation**
Dressing may be prepared ahead of time and kept in the refrigerator for a day or two.

**Serving Ideas**
The dressing may be served as a dip for vegetable crudités or with a tossed salad.

SERVES 4-6

# China Beach Salad

Named for a stretch of beach near San Francisco, this recipe reflects the Chinese heritage in California's past and its present passion for salads.

- 1lb cooked, peeled shrimp
- 1lb seedless white grapes, halved if large
- 6 sticks celery, thinly sliced on diagonal
- 4oz toasted flaked almonds
- 4oz canned water chestnuts, sliced or diced
- 8oz canned lichees or 12oz fresh litchis, peeled
- 1 small fresh pineapple, peeled, cored and cut into pieces
- 1½ cups mayonnaise
- 1 tbsp honey
- 1 tbsp light soy sauce
- 2 tbps mild curry powder
- Juice of half a lime
- Chinese cabbage or Belgian endive (chicory)

**1.** Combine the shrimp, grapes, celery, almonds, water chestnuts and litchis in a large bowl. Trim off the top and bottom of the pineapple and quarter. Slice off the points of each quarter to remove the core.

**2.** Slice the pineapple skin away and cut the flesh into bite-size pieces. Add to the shrimp and toss to mix.

**3.** Break the Chinese cabbage or endive and wash them well. If using Chinese cabbage, shred the leafy part finely, saving the thicker ends of the leaves for other use. Place the Chinese cabbage on salad plates. Mix the remaining dressing ingredients thoroughly. Pile the salad ingredients onto the leaves and spoon over some of the dressing, leaving the ingredients showing. Separate chicory leaves and arrange them whole. Serve remaining dressing separately.

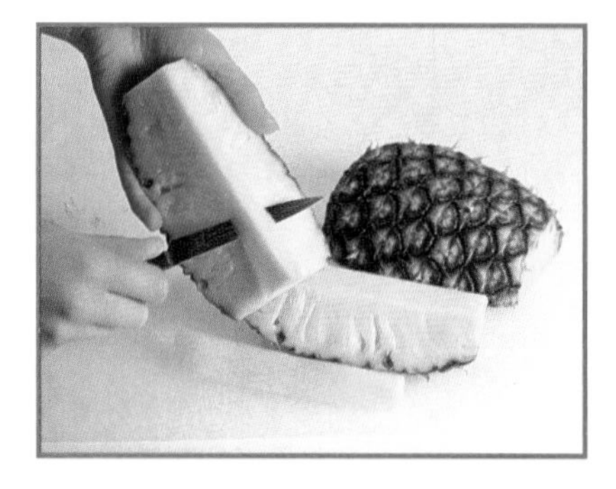

**Step 1** Trim the point of each quarter of pineapple to remove the core.

**Step 2** Use a serrated fruit knife to slice between the skin and pineapple flesh.

**Step 2** Add pineapple pieces to the shrimp and mix well.

**Time**
Preparation takes about 30 minutes.

**Serving Ideas**
Serve as a main course salad for lunch or a light dinner. Serve in smaller quantities as an appetizer.

**Variation**
Other seafood may be substituted for the shrimp. Use crab, lobster or shellfish such as mussels.

SERVES 6

# WALNUT GROVE SALAD

Walnut Grove is a town famous for its walnuts! They add their crunch to a colorful variation on coleslaw.

1 small head red cabbage
1 avocado, peeled and cubed
1 carrot, grated
4 green onions, shredded
1 cup chopped walnuts
6 tbsps oil
2 tbsps white wine vinegar
2 tsps dry mustard
Salt and pepper

**1.** Cut the cabbage in quarters and remove the core. Use a large knife to shred finely or use the thick slicing blade on a food processor.

**2.** Prepare the avocado as for Avocado Soup and cut it into small cubes.

**3.** Combine the cabbage, avocado and shredded carrot with the onions and walnuts in a large bowl.

**4.** Mix the remaining ingredients together well and pour over the salad. Toss carefully to avoid breaking up the avocado. Chill before serving.

**Step 1** Remove the core from the cabbage quarters and shred with a sharp knife or use a food processor.

**Step 4** Mixing the salad with your hands prevents the avocado from breaking up too much.

## Cook's Notes

**Time**
Preparation takes about 25-30 minutes.

**Serving Ideas**
Serve as a side dish with chicken or as part of a salad buffet.

**Preparation**
The salad may be prepared a day in advance and the avocado and dressing added just before serving.

SERVES 4

# CRAB LOUIS

This salad is legendary on Fisherman's Wharf in San Francisco. Once tasted, it is sure to become a favorite.

2 large cooked crabs
1 head iceberg lettuce
4 large tomatoes
4 hard-boiled eggs
16 black olives
1 cup prepared mayonnaise
4 tbsps whipping cream
4 tbsps chili sauce or tomato chutney
½ green pepper, seeded and finely diced
3 green onions, finely chopped
Salt and pepper

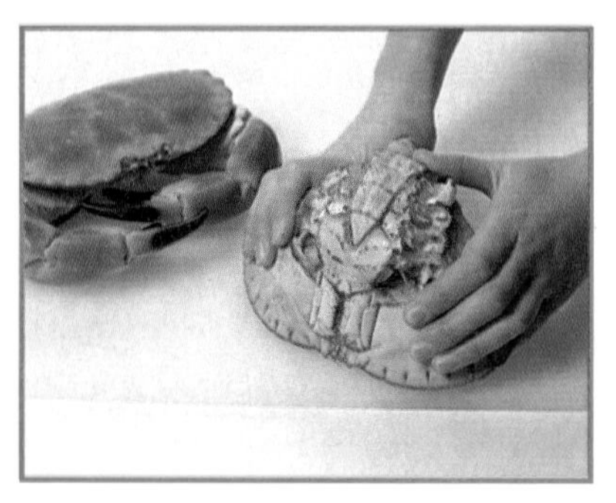

**Step 1** Turn crabs over and press up with thumbs to separate the under-body from the shell.

**1.** To prepare the crabs, break off the claws and set them aside. Turn the crabs over and press up with thumbs to separate the body from the shell of each.

**2.** Cut the body into quarters and use a skewer to pick out the white meat. Discard the stomach sac and the lungs (dead-man's fingers). Scrape out the brown meat from the shell to use, if desired.

**3.** Crack the large claws and legs and remove the meat. Break into shreds, discarding any shell or cartilage. Combine all the meat and set it aside.

**4.** Shred the lettuce finely, quarter the tomatoes and chop the eggs.

**5.** Combine the mayonnaise, cream, chilli sauce or chutney, green pepper and spring onions and mix well.

**6.** Arrange the shredded lettuce on serving plates and divide the crab meat evenly.

**7.** Spoon some of the dressing over each serving of crab and sprinkle with the chopped egg. Garnish each serving with tomato wedges and olives and serve the remaining dressings separately.

**Time**
Preparation takes about 30-40 minutes.

**Preparation**
To shred lettuce finely, break off the leaves and stack them up a few at a time. Use a large, sharp knife to cut across the leaves into thin shreds.

**Variation**
Frozen crab meat may be used instead of fresh. Make sure it is completely defrosted and well drained before using. Pick through the meat to remove any bits of shell or cartilage left behind.

SERVES 4

# Tomato and Orange Salad with Mozzarella and Basil

Juicy tomatoes combine with mozzarella and basil in this classic Italian salad given Californian flair with bright oranges.

4 large tomatoes
4 small oranges
8oz mozzarella cheese
8 fresh basil leaves
4 tbsps olive oil
1 tbsp balsamic vinegar
Salt and pepper

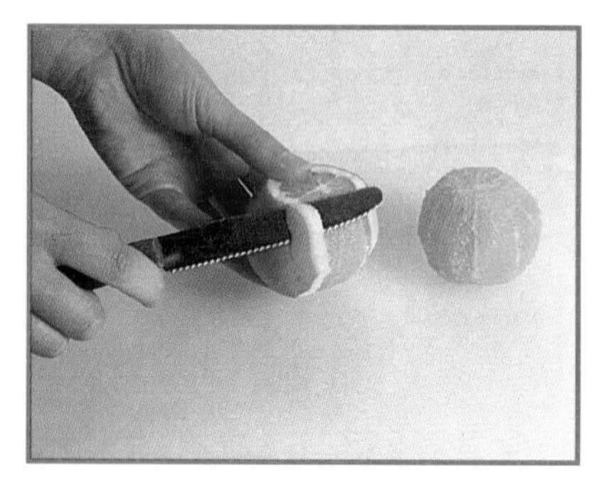

**Step 2** Peel the oranges in thin strips to help preserve the round shape of the fruit.

**1.** Remove the cores from the tomatoes and slice into rounds about ¼ inch thick.

**2.** Cut the slice from the top and bottom of each orange and, using a serrated fruit knife, remove the peel in thin strips. Make sure to cut off all the white pith. Slices oranges into ¼ inch thick rounds. Slice the mozzarella cheese into the same thickness.

**3.** Arrange the tomatoes, oranges and mozzarella in overlapping circles, alternating each ingredient.

**4.** Use scissors to shred the basil leaves finely, and sprinkle over the salad.

**5.** Mix the remaining ingredients together well and spoon over the salad. Chill briefly before serving.

**Step 3** Arrange the ingredients in overlapping circles.

**Step 4** Use scissors to finely shred the basil leaves over the top of the salad.

Cook's Notes

**Time**
Preparation takes about 20-25 minutes.

**Preparation**
Shred the basil leaves just before serving, since they tend to turn black if cut and left to stand.

**Buying Guide**
Balsamic vinegar is available from delicatessens and Italian grocers. Substitute white wine vinegar if not available.

SERVES 4

# Squash with Californian Blueberries

This vegetable dish will steal the scene at any meal, so serve it with simply cooked poultry or meat.

2 acorn squash
1 small apple, peeled and chopped
4 tbsps light brown sugar
Freshly grated nutmeg
4 tbsps butter or margarine
6oz fresh or frozen blueberries

**1.** Cut the squash in half lengthwise. Scoop out the seeds and discard them.

**2.** Fill the hollows with the chopped apple.

**3.** Sprinkle on the sugar and nutmeg and dot with the butter or margarine.

**4.** Place the squash in a baking dish and pour in about 1" of water. Bake, covered, for 40-45 minutes at 375°F. Uncover, add the blueberries and cook an additional 10 minutes.

**Step 2** Fill the hollows with apple and sprinkle on sugar, nutmeg and butter.

**Step 4** Place the squash in a baking dish and pour in enough water to measure 1 inch.

## Cook's Notes

**Time**
Preparation takes about 30 minutes and cooking takes about 50-55 minutes.

**Preparation**
If using frozen blueberries, drain them well and shorten the cooking time by about 5 minutes.

**Buying Guide**
Acorn squash are dark green with the occasional orange patch. Choose a squash that has a very hard rind on the outside. The squash will keep uncut in a cool place for about a month or two.

SERVES 6

# ZUCCHINI SLIPPERS

Italian immigrants to California made the zucchini squash a popular food item used in many delicious recipes.

6 even-sized zucchini
4oz cottage cheese, drained
4oz grated Colby cheese
1 small red pepper, seeded and chopped
2 tbsps chopped parsley
Pinch salt and cayenne pepper
1 large egg
Watercress or parsley to garnish

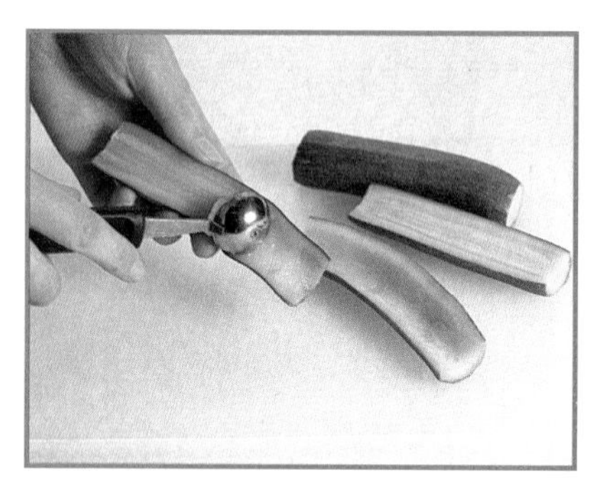

**Step 2** Cut the pre-cooked zucchini in half lengthwise and scoop out the center with a teaspoon or melon baller.

**1.** Trim the ends of the zucchini and cook in boiling salted water for about 8 minutes, or steam for 10 minutes.

**2.** Remove from the water or steamer and cut in half. Allow to cool slightly and then scoop out the center, leaving a narrow margin of flesh on the skin to form a shell. Invert each zucchini slipper onto a paper towel to drain, reserving the scooped-out flesh.

**3.** Chop the flesh and mix with the remaining ingredients.

**4.** Spoon filling into the shells and arrange in a greased baking dish. Bake, uncovered, in a pre-heated 350°F oven for 15 minutes. Broil, if desired, to brown the top. Garnish with watercress or parsley.

**Step 4** Use a small spoon to fill the zucchini neatly.

**Step 4** Bake until the cheese melts and the filling begins to bubble slightly. Grill at this point, if desired.

## Cook's Notes

**Time**
Preparation takes about 30 minutes and cooking takes about 23-25 minutes.

**Preparation**
The dish may be prepared ahead of time and kept in the refrigerator overnight to bake the next day.

**Serving Ideas**
Serve as a vegetable side dish with meat, poultry of fish. Alternatively, serve as an appetizer. Double the quantity and serve as a vegetarian main course.

**Watchpoint**
Be sure the zucchini are very well drained before filling. Baking will draw out any excess moisture and make the dish watery.

SERVES 4

# VEGETABLE RIBBONS WITH PESTO

There is no substitute for fresh basil in this sauce. Prepare it in the summer when basil is plentiful to freeze for later.

2 large zucchini, ends trimmed
2 medium carrots, peeled
1 large or 2 small leeks, trimmed, halved and well washed
1 cup shelled pistachio nuts
2 small shallots, chopped
2-3oz fresh basil leaves
1-1½ cups olive oil
Salt and pepper

**1.** Cut the zucchini and carrots into long, thin slices with a mandolin or by hand. A food processor will work but the slices will be short.

**2.** Cut the leeks into lengths the same size as the zucchini and carrots. Make sure the leeks are well rinsed in between all layers. Cut into long, thin strips.

**3.** Using a large, sharp knife, cut the zucchini and carrot slices into long, thin strips about the thickness of 2 matchsticks. The julienne blade of a food processor will produce strips that are too fine to use.

**4.** Place the carrot strips in a pan of boiling salted water and cook for about 3-4 minutes or until tender crisp. Drain and rinse under cold water. Cook the zucchini strips separately for about 2-3 minutes and add the leek strips during the last 1 minute of cooking. Drain and rinse the vegetables and leave with the carrots to drain dry.

**5.** Place the nuts, shallots and basil in the bowl of a food processor or in a blender and chop finely.

**6.** Reserve about 3 tbsps of the olive oil for later use. With the machine running, pour the remaining oil through the funnel in a thin, steady stream. Use enough oil to bring the mixture to the consistency of mayonnaise. Add seasoning to taste.

**7.** Place reserved oil in a large pan and, when hot, add the drained vegetables. Season and toss over moderate heat until heated through. Add the pesto sauce and toss gently to coat the vegetables. Serve immediately.

**Step 3** Stack several lengths of zucchini and carrot and cut into long julienne strips.

## Cook's Notes

**Time**
Preparation takes about 30-40 minutes and cooking takes about 45 minutes.

**Serving Ideas**
Serve as a side dish with broiled meat, poultry or fish and prepare larger quantities for a vegetarian main course. Parmesan cheese may be sprinkled on top.

**Preparation**
Pesto can be prepared several days in advance and kept, covered, in the refrigerator. Pesto sauce can also be frozen for up to 6 months.

SERVES 4

# Napa Valley Artichokes

The Napa Valley is wine growing country, so white wine is a natural choice for cooking one of California's best-loved vegetables.

4 globe artichokes
4 tbsps olive oil
1 clove garlic, left whole
1 small bay leaf
1 sprig fresh rosemary
2 parsley stalks
4 black peppercorns
2 lemon slices
1 cup dry white wine
1 tbsp chopped parsley
Pinch salt and pepper
Lemon slices to garnish

**1.** Trim stems on the base of the artichokes so that they sit upright. Peel off any damaged bottom leaves.

**2.** Trim the spiny tips off all the leaves with scissors.

**3.** Trim the top 1″ off the artichokes with a sharp knife.

**4.** Place the artichokes in a large, deep pan with all the ingredients except the parsley.

**5.** Cover the pan and cook about 40 minutes, or until artichokes are tender and bottom leaves pull away easily. Drain upside down on paper towels.

**6.** Boil the cooking liquid to reduce slightly. Strain, add parsley and serve with the artichokes. Garnish with lemon slices.

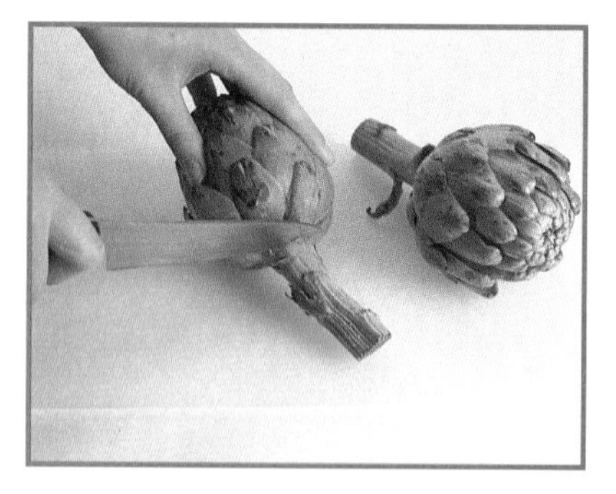

**Step 1** Trim the stems on the base of the artichokes so they sit level.

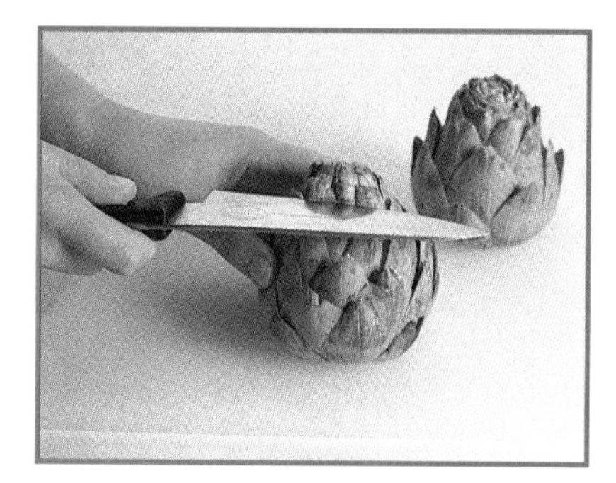

**Step 3** Use a large, sharp knife to trim the top 1 inch of the artichokes.

## Cook's Notes

**Time**
Preparation takes about 30 minutes and cooking takes about 40 minutes.

**Serving Ideas**
Place artichokes on individual plates and spoon over the sauce or serve it separately for dipping. To eat, pull off the leaves, beginning with the bottom one, and eat the fleshy thicker part at the base of each leaf. When only the fine purple leaves in the center remain, pull them off and discard them. Using a spoon, scrape away the thistle and discard it. The base may be eaten with the dipping sauce.

SERVES 4

# SAN FRANCISCO RICE

This rice and pasta dish has been popular for a long time in San Francisco, where it was invented.

4oz uncooked long grain rice
4oz uncooked spaghetti, broken into 2″ pieces
3 tbsps oil
4 tbsps sesame seeds
2 tbsps chopped chives
Salt and pepper
1½ cups chicken, beef or vegetable stock
1 tbsp soy sauce
2 tbsps chopped parsley

**1.** Rinse the rice and pasta to remove starch, and leave to drain dry.

**2.** Heat the oil in a large frying pan and add the dried rice and pasta. Cook over moderate heat to brown the rice and pasta, stirring continuously.

**3.** Add the sesame seeds and cook until the rice, pasta and seeds are golden brown.

**4.** Add the chives, salt and pepper, and pour over 1 cup stock. Stir in the soy sauce and bring to the boil.

**5.** Cover and cook about 20 minutes, or until the rice and pasta are tender and the stock is absorbed. Add more of the reserved stock as necessary. Do not let the rice and pasta dry out during cooking.

**6.** Fluff up the grains of rice with a fork and sprinkle with the parsley before serving.

**Step 2** Cook the rice and pasta in the oil until just beginning to brown.

**Step 3** Add the sesame seeds and cook until the rice, pasta and seeds are golden brown.

**Step 5** Cook until all the liquid is absorbed and the pasta and rice are tender.

**Time**
Preparation takes about 25 minutes and cooking takes about 20 minutes or more.

**Preparation**
If desired, once the stock is added the mixture may be cooked in a pre-heated 375°F oven. Cook for about 20 minutes, checking the level of liquid occasionally and adding more stock if necessary.

**Serving Ideas**
Serve as a side dish with meat or poultry. Give it an Italian flavor by omitting sesame seeds, chives and soy sauce. Substitute Parmesan and basil instead.

SERVES 4

# California Wild Rice Pilaff

Wild rice adds a nutty taste and a texture contrast to rice pilaff. It's good as a side dish or stuffing.

4oz uncooked long-grain rice, rinsed
2oz wild rice, rinsed
1 tbsp oil
1 tbsp butter or margarine
2 sticks celery, finely chopped
2 green onions
4 tbsps chopped walnuts or pecans
4 tbsps raisins
1½ cups chicken or vegetable stock

1. Heat the oil in a frying pan and drop in the butter.
2. When foaming, add both types of rice.
3. Cook until the white rice looks clear.
4. Add celery and chop the green onions, reserving the dark green tops to use as a garnish. Add the white part of the onions to the rice and celery and cook briefly to soften.
5. Add the walnuts or pecans, raisins and stock. Bring to the boil, cover and cook until the rice absorbs the liquid and is tender. Sprinkle with reserved chopped onion tops.

**Step 3** Cook both rices in butter and oil until the white rice looks clear. Stir constantly.

**Step 5** Add remaining ingredients and, if desired, transfer to an ovenproof casserole for the remainder of cooking.

## Cook's Notes

**Time**
Preparation takes about 25 minutes and cooking takes about 20 minutes.

**Serving Ideas**
Delicious served as a side dish for chicken or used as a stuffing for Cornish hens or other small game birds.

**Buying Guide**
Wild rice is not really a rice but a grain. It is fairly expensive but it can be used in small quantities. Wild rice is available in delicatessens and specialty food shops.

**Preparation**
This pilaff may also be cooked in the oven in the same manner as San Francisco Rice.

SERVES 4

# SPICY ORIENTAL NOODLES

A most versatile vegetable dish, this goes well with meat or stands alone for a vegetarian main course.

8oz Chinese noodles (medium thickness)
5 tbsps oil
4 carrots, peeled
8oz broccoli
12 Chinese mushrooms, soaked 30 minutes
1 clove garlic, peeled
4 green onions, diagonally sliced
1-2 tsps chili sauce, mild or hot
4 tbsps soy sauce
4 tbsps rice wine or dry sherry
2 tsps cornstarch

**1.** Cook noodles in boiling salted water for about 4-5 minutes. Drain well, rinse under hot water to remove starch and drain again. Toss with about 1 tbsp of the oil to prevent sticking.

**2.** Using a large, sharp knife or Chinese cleaver, slice the carrots thinly on the diagonal.

**3.** Cut the flowerets off the stems of the broccoli and divide into even-sized but not too small sections. Slice the stalks thinly on the diagonal. If they seem tough, peel them before slicing.

**4.** Place the vegetables in boiling water for about 2 minutes to blanch. Drain and rinse under cold water to stop the cooking, and leave to drain dry.

**5.** Remove and discard the mushroom stems and slice the caps thinly. Set aside with the onions.

**6.** Heat a wok and add the remaining oil with the garlic clove. Leave the garlic in the pan while the oil heats and then remove it. Add the carrots and broccoli and stir-fry about 1 minute. Add mushrooms and onions and continue to stir-fry, tossing the vegetables in the pan continuously.

**7.** Combine chili sauce, soy sauce, wine and cornstarch, mixing well. Pour over the vegetables and cook until the sauce clears. Toss with the noodles and heat them through and serve immediately.

**Step 7** Cook vegetables and sauce ingredients until cornstarch thickens and clears.

**Time**
Preparation takes about 25 minutes and cooking takes about 7-8 minutes.

**Buying Guide**
Chinese noodles, mushrooms and chili sauce are all available from Chinese groceries, gourmet food stores and larger supermarkets.

**Serving Ideas**
Use as a side dish with chicken, meat or fish, or serve as an appetizer. May also be served cold as a salad.

SERVES 4-6

# Fettucine Escargots with Leeks and Sun-Dried Tomatoes

These dried tomatoes keep for a long time and allow you to add a sunny taste to dishes whatever the time of year.

6 sun-dried tomatoes or 6 fresh Italian plum tomatoes
14oz canned escargots (snails), drained
12oz fresh or dried whole-wheat fettucine (tagliatelle)
3 tbsps olive oil
2 cloves garlic, crushed
1 large or 2 small leeks, trimmed, split, well washed and finely sliced
6 oyster, shittake or other large mushrooms
4 tbsps chicken or vegetable stock
3 tbsps dry white wine
6 tbsps heavy cream
2 tsps chopped fresh basil
2 tsps chopped fresh parsley
Salt and pepper

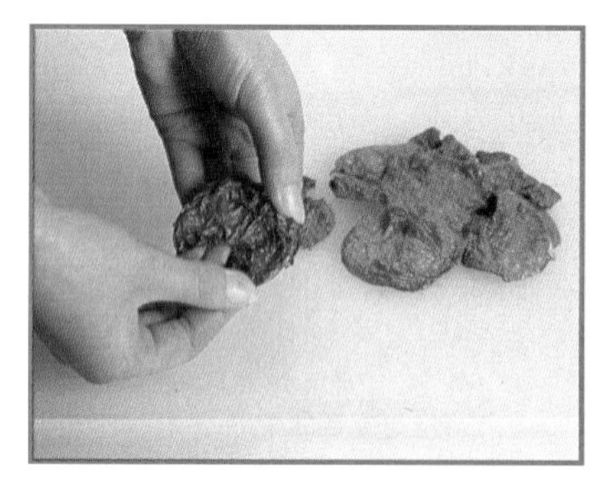

**Step 3** Properly dried tomatoes will look and feel firm, with no remaining liquid.

**1.** To "sun-dry" tomatoes in the oven, cut the tomatoes in half lengthwise.

**2.** Use a teaspoon or your finger to scoop out about half the seeds and juice. Press gently with your palm to flatten slightly. Sprinkle both sides with salt and place tomatoes, cut side up, on a rack over a baking pan.

**3.** Place in the oven on the lowest possible setting, with door ajar, if neccessary, for 24 hours, checking after 12 hours. Allow to dry until no liquid is left and the tomatoes are firm. Chop roughly.

**4.** Drain the escargots well and dry with paper towels.

**5.** Place the fettucine in boiling salted water and cook for about 10-12 minutes, or until al dente. Drain, rinse under hot water and leave in a colander to drain dry.

**6.** Meanwhile, heat the olive oil in a frying pan and add the garlic and leeks. Cook slowly to soften slightly. Add the mushrooms and cook until the leeks are tender crisp. Remove to a plate. Add the drained escargots to the pan and cook over high heat for about 2 minutes, stirring constantly.

**7.** Pour on the stock and wine and bring to the boil. Boil to reduce by about a quarter and add the cream and tomatoes. Bring to the boil then cook slowly for about 3 minutes. Add the herbs, salt and pepper to taste. Add the leeks, mushrooms and fettucine to the pan and heat through. Serve immediately.

**Time**
Preparation takes about 24 hours for the tomatoes to dry and about 15-20 minutes to finish the dish.

**Serving Ideas**
Serve as an appetizer or a main course with salad and bread. Grated Parmesan cheese may be sprinkled on top, if desired.

**Variation**
Escargots are not to everyone's taste, so substitute more mushrooms, cooked shrimp or spicy sausage, as desired.

SERVES 6

# CHICKEN MONTEREY

There's a touch of Mexican flavor in this chicken recipe with its accompaniment of colorful and spicy salsa.

6 boned chicken breasts
Grated rind and juice of 1 lime
2 tbsps olive oil
Coarsely ground black pepper
6 tbsps whole grain mustard
2 tsps paprika
4 ripe tomatoes, peeled, seeded and quartered
2 shallots, chopped
1 clove garlic, crushed
½ Jalapeno pepper or other chili, seeded and chopped
1 tsp wine vinegar
Pinch salt
2 tbsps chopped fresh cilantro (coriander)
Whole coriander leaves to garnish

**1.** Place chicken breasts in a shallow dish with the lime rind and juice, oil, pepper, mustard and paprika. Marinate for about 1 hour, turning occasionally.

**2.** To peel tomatoes easily, drop them into boiling water for about 5 seconds or less depending on ripeness. Place immediately in cold water. Peels should come off easily.

**3.** Place tomatoes, shallots, garlic, chili pepper, vinegar and salt in a food processor or blender and process until coarsely chopped. Stir in the cilantro by hand.

**4.** Place chicken on a broiler pan and reserve the marinade. Cook chicken skin side uppermost for about 7-10 minutes, depending on how close the chicken is to the heat source. Baste frequently with the remaining marinade. Broil other side in the same way. Sprinkle with salt after broiling.

**5.** Place chicken on serving plates and garnish top with cilantro (coriander) leaves or sprigs. Serve with a spoonful of the tomato salsa on one side.

**Step 1** Marinate chicken in a shallow dish, turning occasionally to coat.

**Step 2** Tomatoes peel easily when placed first in boiling water and then in cold.

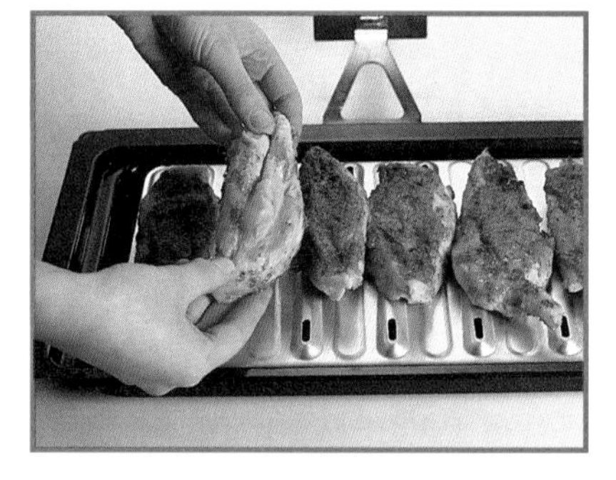

**Step 4** Broil skin side of chicken until brown and crisp before turning pieces over.

**Time**
Preparation takes about 1 hour and cooking takes 14-20 minutes.

**Preparation**
Salsa can be prepared in advance and kept in the refrigerator. It can also be served with other poultry, meat or seafood. It also makes a good dip for vegetable crudités or tortilla chips.

**Watchpoint**
When preparing chili peppers, wear rubber gloves or at least be sure to wash hands thoroughly after handling them. Do not touch eyes or face before washing hands.

SERVES 6

# Chicken Jubilee

California cooks are creative trendsetters. Trust them to change a cherry dessert into a savory recipe for chicken.

6 chicken breasts, skinned and boned
Oil
1 sprig fresh rosemary
Grated rind and juice of half a lemon
1 cup dry red wine
Salt and pepper
1lb canned or fresh black cherries, pitted
2 tsps cornstarch
6 tbsps brandy

**Step 1** Cook the chicken breasts until just lightly browned. Watch carefully, as skinned chicken will dry out easily.

**1.** Heat about 4 tbsps oil in a sauté pan over moderate heat. Place in the chicken breasts, skinned side down first. Cook until just lightly browned. Turn over and cook the second side about 2 minutes.

**2.** Remove any oil remaining in the pan and add the rosemary, lemon rind, wine and salt and pepper. Bring to the boil and then lower the heat.

**3.** Add the cherries, draining well if canned. Cook, covered, 15 minutes or until the chicken is tender. Remove the chicken and cherries and keep them warm. Discard rosemary.

**4.** Mix the cornstarch, lemon juice and some of the liquid from the cherries, if canned. Add several spoonfuls of the hot sauce to the cornstarch mixture. Return the mixture to the sauté pan and bring to the boil, stirring constantly, until thickened and cleared.

**5.** Pour the brandy into a metal ladle or a small saucepan. Heat quickly and ignite with a match. Pour over the chicken and cherries, shaking the pan gently until the flames subside. Serve immediately.

## Cook's Notes

**Time**
Preparation takes about 20 minutes if using pre-skinned and boned chicken breasts. Allow an extra 15 minutes to bone the chicken yourself.

**Serving Ideas**
Serve with plain boiled rice or California Wild Rice Pilaff. Accompany with a green vegetable such as lightly steamed pea pods.

**Preparation**
Serve the chicken dish on the day that it is cooked – it does not keep well. Add the brandy just before serving.

**Watchpoint**
When flaming spirits, always keep a pan lid handy in case the mixture flares up. In this case, quickly cover the pan and the flames will be smothered.

SERVES 4

# LAMB STEAKS ALPHONSO

Eggplant is a very popular vegetable in California cooking. Its taste is perfect with lamb marinated with garlic and rosemary.

4 large or 8 small round bone lamb steaks
4 tbsps olive oil
1 clove garlic, crushed
1 sprig fresh rosemary
Black pepper
1 tbsp red wine vinegar
1 large eggplant
Salt
1 small green pepper, seeded and cut into 1″ pieces
1 small red pepper, seeded and cut into 1″ pieces
2 shallots, chopped
4 tbsps olive oil
2 tsps chopped parsley
2 tsps chopped fresh marjoram
6 tbsps dry white wine
Salt and pepper

**Step 2** Cut eggplant in half, score lightly and sprinkle with salt.

**1.** Place lamb in a shallow dish with the oil, garlic, rosemary, pepper and vinegar and turn frequently to marinate for 1 hour.

**2.** Cut the eggplant in half and score lightly. Sprinkle with salt and leave to stand on paper towels for about 30 minutes. Rinse well and pat dry.

**3.** Cut eggplant in 1″ pieces. Heat more oil in a frying pan and add the eggplant. Cook, stirring frequently, over moderate heat until lightly browned. Add peppers, shallots and herbs, and cook a further 5 minutes.

**4.** Add the wine and bring to the boil. Cook quickly to reduce the wine. Set the mixture aside.

**5.** Meanwhile, place the lamb on a broiler pan, reserving the marinade. Cook under a pre-heated broiler for 10 minutes per side. Baste frequently with the marinade. Lamb may be served pink inside.

**6.** Serve the lamb with the eggplant accompaniment.

**Step 4** Boil the wine and vegetables rapidly to reduce the liquid and concentrate flavors.

**Time**
Preparation takes about 1 hour and cooking takes about 20 minutes.

**Preparation**
Lamb may be marinated overnight.

**Cook's Tip**
Sprinkling an eggplant with salt will draw out bitter juices and so give the dish better flavor.

SERVES 4

# TUNA BAKED IN PARCHMENT

This recipe uses a French technique called "en papillote". Californians, quick to spot a healthful cooking method, use it often with fish.

4 tuna steaks, about 8oz each in weight
1 red onion, thinly sliced
1 beefsteak tomato, cut in 4 slices
1 green pepper, seeded and cut in thin rings
8 large, uncooked peeled shrimp
2 tsps finely chopped fresh oregano
1 small green or red chili, seeded and finely chopped
4 tbsps dry white wine or lemon juice
Salt
Oil

**Steps 1-4** Layer the ingredients on oiled parchment.

**1.** Lightly oil 4 oval pieces of baking parchment about 8x10″.

**2.** Place a tuna steak on half of each piece of parchment and top with 2 slices of onion.

**3.** Place a slice of tomato on each fish and top with green pepper rings.

**4.** Place 2 shrimp on top and sprinkle over the oregano, salt and chili pepper.

**5.** Spoon the wine or lemon juice over each fish and fold the parchment over the fish.

**6.** Overlap the edges and pinch and fold to seal securely. Place the parcels on a baking sheet.

**7.** Bake for about 10-12 minutes in a pre-heated 400°F oven.

**8.** Unwrap each parcel at the table to serve.

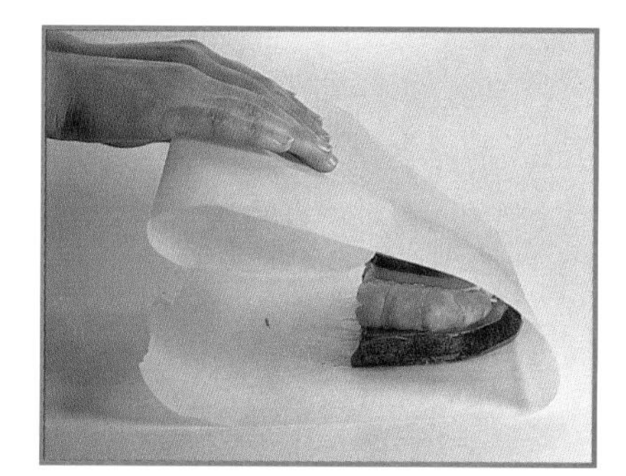

**Step 6** Overlap the edges of the parchment, but don't enclose fish too tightly.

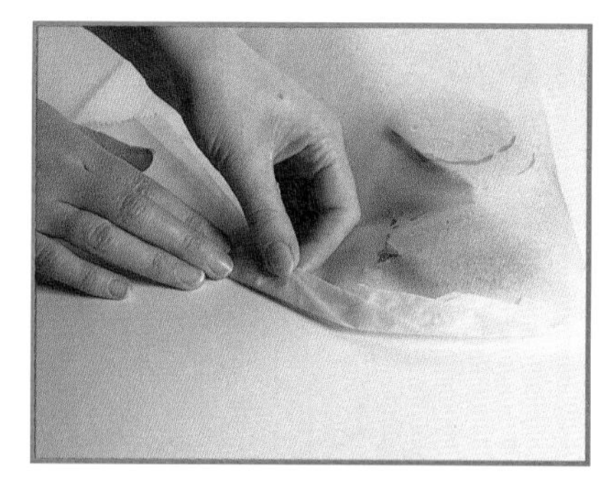

**Step 6** Use thumb and forefinger to pinch and fold the overlapped edge to seal.

## Cook's Notes

**Time**
Preparation takes about 35 minutes and cooking takes about 10-12 minutes.

**Preparation**
The dish may be prepared up to 6 hours in advance and kept in the refrigerator. Remove about 30 minutes before cooking and allow fish to come to room temperature.

**Variation**
Other fish, such as swordfish or halibut, can be used in place of the tuna. Any thinly-sliced vegetable other than potato can be used.

SERVES 4

# Trout with Chorizo

For fish with a spicy difference, try this as a dinner party dish to impress and please your fish-loving friends.

1 boned trout (about 2lb in boned weight)
8oz chorizo or other spicy sausage
Water
1 small green pepper, seeded and finely chopped
2 small onions, finely chopped
1 slice bread, made into crumbs
4 tbsps dry white wine
Lemon juice
½ cup natural yogurt
1 tsp garlic powder
2 tsps chopped cilantro (coriander)
Salt and pepper

**1.** Have the fishmonger bone the trout, leaving the head and tail on the fish.

**2.** Place the chorizo in a pan and cover with water. Bring to the boil and then cook for 10 minutes to soften and to remove excess fat. Skin sausage and chop it finely. Combine with the green pepper, onion, breadcrumbs and wine.

**3.** Sprinkle the fish cavity with the lemon juice.

**4.** Stuff the fish with the sausage mixture and place on lightly-oiled foil. Seal the ends to form a parcel and bake in a pre-heated 350°F oven for about 20-30 minutes, or until the fish feels firm and the flesh looks opaque.

**5.** Combine the yogurt, garlic powder, cilantro and seasonings to taste

**6.** Remove the fish from the foil and transfer to a serving plate. Spoon some of the sauce over the fish and serve the rest separately.

**Step 3** Sprinkle the fish cavity with lemon juice.

**Step 4** When the stuffing ingredients are well mixed, spoon into the fish on one half and press the other half down lightly to spread the stuffing evenly.

**Step 4** Seal the foil loosely around the fish.

## Cook's Notes

**Time**
Preparation takes about 25 minutes and cooking takes about 10 minutes for pre-cooking the sausage and 25 minutes for cooking the fish.

**Buying Guide**
Chorizo is a Spanish sausage that is very highly spiced. If unavailable, substitute a spicy Italian sausage or an Italian or German salami. If using salami, omit the pre-cooking.

**Variation**
Other whole fish such as sea bass or gray mullet may be used with the stuffing, however, the stuffing is too spicy to use with salmon.

SERVES 4

# SWORDFISH FLORENTINE

Swordfish, with its dense texture, is a perfect and healthful substitute for meat. Here it has a distinctly Mediterranean flavor.

4 swordfish steaks about 6-8oz each in weight
Salt, pepper and lemon juice
Olive oil
2lbs fresh spinach, stems removed and leaves well washed

**Aioli Sauce**

2 egg yolks
1-2 cloves garlic
Salt, pepper and dry mustard
Pinch cayenne pepper
1 cup olive oil
Lemon juice or white wine vinegar

**1.** Sprinkle fish with pepper, lemon juice and olive oil. Place under a pre-heated broiler and cook for about 3-4 minutes per side. Fish may also be cooked on an outdoor barbeque grill.

**2.** Meanwhile, use a sharp knife to shred the spinach finely. Place in a large saucepan and add a pinch of salt. Cover and cook over moderate heat with only the water that clings to the leaves after washing. Cook about 2 minutes, or until leaves are just slightly wilted. Set aside.

**3.** Place egg yolks in a food processor, blender or cup of a hand blender. Add the garlic, crushed, if using a hand blender. Process several times to mix eggs and purée garlic. Add salt, pepper, mustard and cayenne pepper. With the machine running, pour oil through the funnel in a thin, steady stream. Follow manufacturer's directions if using a hand blender.

**4.** When the sauce becomes very thick, add some lemon juice or vinegar in small quantities.

**5.** To serve, place a bed of spinach on a plate and top with the swordfish. Spoon some of the aioli sauce on top of the fish and serve the rest separately.

**Step 3** Pour the oil for the sauce onto the egg yolks in a thin, steady stream.

## Cook's Notes

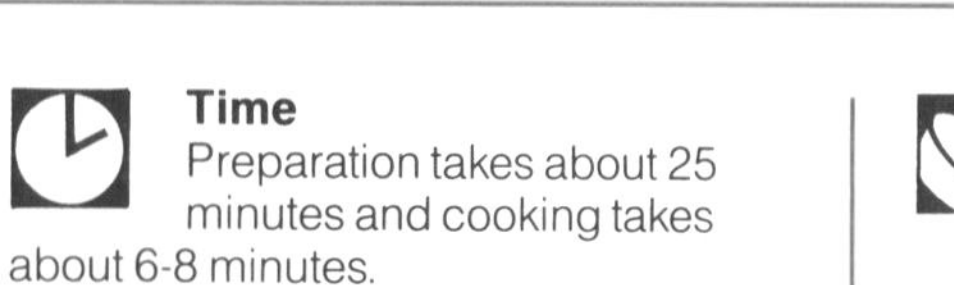

**Time**
Preparation takes about 25 minutes and cooking takes about 6-8 minutes.

**Variation**
Fresh tuna may be used in place of the swordfish.

**Preparation**
The aioli or garlic mayonnaise may be prepared in advance and will keep for 5-7 days in the refrigerator. It is also delicious served with poached shellfish, chicken or vegetables. If too thick, thin the sauce with hot water.

SERVES 6

# FLOURLESS CHOCOLATE CAKE

This is part mousse, part soufflé, part cake and completely heavenly! It's light but rich, and adored by chocolate lovers everywhere.

1lb semi-sweet chocolate
2 tbsps strong coffee
2 tbsps brandy
6 eggs
6 tbsps sugar
1 cup whipping cream
Powdered sugar
Fresh whole strawberries

**Step 5** Pour the cake mixture into the prepared pan and then place it in a bain marie.

**1.** Melt the chocolate in the top of a double boiler. Stir in the coffee and brandy and leave to cool slightly.

**2.** Break up the eggs and then, using an electric mixer, gradually beat in the sugar until the mixture is thick and mousse-like. When the beaters are lifted the mixture should mound slightly.

**3.** Whip the cream until soft peaks form.

**4.** Beat the chocolate until smooth and shiny, and gradually add the egg mixture to it.

**5.** Fold in the cream and pour the cake mixture into a well greased 9" deep cake pan with a disk of wax paper in the bottom. Bake in a pre-heated 350°F oven in a bain marie. To make a bain marie, use a roasting pan and fill with warm water to come halfway up the side of the cake pan.

**6.** Bake about 1 hour and then turn off the oven, leaving the cake inside to stand for 15 minutes. Loosen the sides of the cake carefully from the pan and allow the cake to cool completely before turning it out.

**7.** Invert the cake onto a serving plate and carefully peel off the paper. Place strips of wax paper on top of the cake, leaving even spaces in betweeen the strips. Sprinkle the top with powdered sugar and carefully lift off the paper strips to form a striped or chequerboard decoration. Decorate with whole strawberries.

## Cook's Notes

**Cook's Tip**
Cooking a delicate cake mixture in a bain marie helps protect it from the direct heat of the oven, maintains a more even temperature and gives the cake a better texture.

**Watchpoint**
Do not allow the water around the cake to boil at any time. If it starts to bubble, pour in some cold water to reduce the temperature.

**Preparation**
If desired, the cake may be prepared a day in advance and can be left well-covered overnight. This will produce a denser texture.

SERVES 4

# MANGO AND COCONUT WITH LIME SABAYON

The taste of mango with lime is sensational, especially when served with the deliciously creamy sauce in this stylish dessert.

2 large, ripe mangoes, peeled and sliced
1 fresh coconut
2 egg yolks
4 tbsps sugar
Juice and grated rind of 2 limes
½ cup heavy cream, whipped

**Step 3** Whisk egg yolks and sugar until thick and light lemon in color.

**1.** Arrange thin slices of mango on plates.

**2.** Break coconut in half and then into smaller sections. Grate the white pulp, taking care to avoid grating the brown skin. Use the coarse side of the grater to make shreds and scatter them over the mango slices.

**3.** Place egg yolks and sugar in the top of a double boiler or a large bowl. Whisk until very thick and lemon colored.

**4.** Stir in the lime juice and place mixture over simmering water. Whisk constantly while the mixture gently cooks and becomes thick and creamy.

**5.** Remove from the heat and place in another bowl of iced water to cool quickly. Whisk the mixture while it cools.

**6.** Fold in the whipped cream and spoon onto the fruit. Garnish with the grated lime rind.

**Time**
Preparation takes about 40 minutes and cooking takes about 8 minutes.

**Watchpoint**
It is important that the water under the sabayon does not boil. If it does, it can cause curdling or cook the mixture too quickly, resulting in a poor texture.

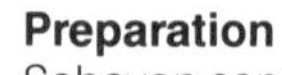

**Preparation**
Sabayon can be chilled for up to 30 minutes. After that, it may start to separate.

**Variation**
Serve the sabayon with other fruit such as papayas, peaches, pineapple or berries.

SERVES 4

# STRIPED SORBET

A tricolored iced treat that can be prepared well ahead, this is a wonderful way to end a summer meal.

2 cups water
1 cup sugar
Juice of 1-2 lemons
8 kiwi fruit, peeled and roughly chopped
4 ripe bananas, peeled and roughly chopped
1lb raspberries, fresh or well drained frozen
2 egg whites
1 banana, 1 kiwi fruit, sliced and whole raspberries to garnish

**Step 8** Pour the banana sorbet on top of the frozen raspberry sorbet.

**1.** Combine the water and sugar in a heavy-based saucepan. Bring slowly to the boil to dissolve the sugar.

**2.** When the sugar is completely dissolved, boil the syrup rapidly for about 1 minute. Allow it to cool completely and then refrigerate until completely cold.

**3.** Purée the kiwi fruit in a food processor, sieving to remove the seeds if desired. Purée the bananas and the raspberries separately. Sieve the raspberries to remove the seeds.

**4.** Divide the cold syrup in 3 parts and mix each with one of the fruit purees. Taste each and add about 1-2 tbsps of lemon juice to each fruit syrup, depending on the sweetness of the fruit.

**5.** Freeze the fruit syrups separately until almost solid, about 2 hours, then mix again in the food processor to break up ice crystals. Freeze again separately until solid.

**6.** Whip the egg whites until stiff. Process the sorbets again, separately, dividing the egg white among all three.

**7.** Pour the raspberry sorbet into a bowl or mold and freeze until firm.

**8.** Pour the banana sorbet on top and freeze again.

**9.** Finish with the kiwi sorbet and freeze overnight or until firm.

**10.** To unmold, dip briefly in hot water and invert on a plate. Garnish with the prepared fruit.

## Cook's Notes

**Time**
Preparation takes about 35 minutes. The sorbets will take at least 2 hours to freeze before their first mixing. Once layered, the sorbets should be allowed to freeze overnight.

**Variation**
Any kind of berries may be substituted for the raspberries or the kiwi fruit in the recipe. One small melon will also take the place of the kiwi fruit, if desired.

**Preparation**
The sorbets may also be prepared and frozen in an ice cream machine following the manufacturer's directions.

SERVES 4

# ORANGES IN RED WINE

Sunny California oranges look and taste beautiful in a rosy red sauce made with a good California red wine.

4 large oranges
1 cup sugar
6 tbsps water
½ cup full-bodied red wine

**Step 1** Trim the rough edges of the orange peel and then cut the peel into thin strips.

**1.** Using a swivel vegetable peeler, remove just the peel from the oranges. Be sure not to take off any white pith. Cut the peel into very thin strips.

**2.** Peel off the pith from the oranges using a small serrated knife. Take off the pith in thin strips to preserve the shape of the fruit. Peel the oranges over a bowl to catch any juice. Slice the fruit thinly and place in a bowl or on serving plates.

**3.** Place the sugar and water in a heavy-based saucepan over very low heat. Cook very slowly until the sugar dissolves completely and forms a thin syrup.

**4.** Add the strips of peel and boil rapidly for 2 minutes. Do not allow the syrup to brown. Remove the peel with a draining spoon and place on a lightly oiled plate to cool. Cool the syrup slightly and then pour in the wine. If the syrup hardens, heat very gently, stirring to dissolve again. Allow the syrup to cool completely.

**5.** Spoon the syrup over the oranges and arrange the peel on top to serve.

## Cook's Notes

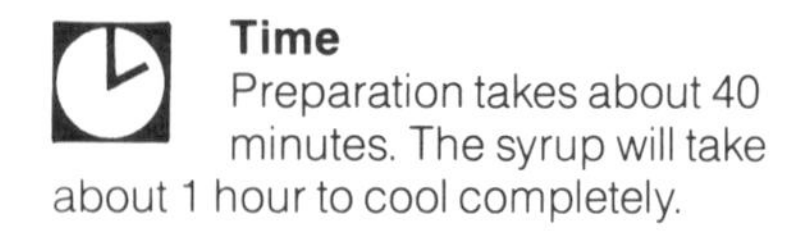

**Time**
Preparation takes about 40 minutes. The syrup will take about 1 hour to cool completely.

**Cook's Tip**
Add any juice collected while peeling the oranges to the syrup for extra flavor.

**Watchpoint**
Do not pour warm syrup over the oranges as they will cook.

MAKES 24-30

# HAZELNUT FLORENTINES

Often called filberts, hazelnuts make a good alternative to almonds in these crisp, toffee-like biscuits. They're a treat with coffee or ice cream.

1lb shelled and peeled hazelnuts
1 cup sugar
6 tbsps honey
6 tbsps heavy cream
1 cup butter
6oz white chocolate, melted
6oz semi-sweet chocolate, melted

**1.** Place hazelnuts in a plastic bag and tie securely. Tap nuts or roll them with a rolling pin to crush roughly.

**2.** Place sugar, honey, cream and butter in a heavy-based saucepan and heat gently to dissolve sugar. Bring to the boil and cook rapidly for about 1½ minutes. Remove from heat and stir in the nuts.

**3.** Brush baking sheets well with oil and spoon or pour out mixture in even amounts. Make only about six Florentines at a time.

**4.** Bake about 10 minutes in a pre-heated 375°F oven. Allow to cool on the baking sheets and, when nearly set, loosen with a spatula and transfer to a flat surface to cool completely.

**5.** When all Florentines have been baked and cooled, melt both chocolates separately. Spread white chocolate on half of the Florentines and semi-sweet chocolate on the other half, or marble the two if desired.

**6.** Place chocolate side uppermost to cool slightly and then make a wavy pattern with the tines of a fork, or swirl chocolate with a knife until it sets in the desired pattern.

**Step 3** Pour or spoon Florentine mixture into even rounds.

**Step 4** Loosen partially-set Florentines with a spatula.

**Step 6** Use a fork to make a decorative pattern in partially set chocolate.

**Time**
Preparation takes about 45-50 minutes and cooking takes about 10 minutes per batch.

**Freezing**
Store well wrapped for up to 1 month. Unwrap and defrost chocolate side up at room temperature. Store in a cool place.

**Serving Ideas**
Make in small sizes, about 1½-2 inches, for petit fours.

SERVES 6

# PEARS IN ZINFANDEL

Zinfandel has a spicy taste that complements pears beautifully. Add a garnish of crisp almonds for a California version of a French classic.

3 cups Zinfandel or other dry red wine
1 cup sugar
1 cinnamon stick
1 strip lemon peel
6 Bosc pears, even sized
4 tbsps sliced almonds
1 tbsp cornstarch mixed with 3 tbsps water
Mint leaves to garnish

**1.** Pour the wine into a deep saucepan that will hold 6 pears standing upright.

**2.** Add the sugar, cinnamon and lemon peel, and bring to the boil slowly to dissolve the sugar. Stir occasionally.

**3.** Peel pears, remove 'eye' on the bottom, but leave on the stems.

**4.** Stand the pears close together in the wine, so that they remain standing. Cover the pan and poach gently over low heat for about 25-35 minutes, or until tender. If the wine does not cover the pears completely, baste the tops frequently as they cook.

**5.** Meanwhile, toast almonds on a baking sheet in a moderate oven for about 8-10 minutes, stirring them occasionally for even browning. Remove and allow to cool.

**6.** When pears are cooked, remove from the liquid to a serving dish. Boil the liquid to reduce it by about half. If it is still too thin to coat the pears, thicken it with 1 tbsp cornstarch dissolved in 3 tbsps water.

**7.** Pour syrup over the pears and sprinkle with almonds. Serve warm or refrigerate until lightly chilled. Garnish pears with mint leaves at the stems just before serving.

**Step 3** Peel pears and remove the 'eye' on the base of each.

**Step 4** Stand the pears upright in the saucepan.

**Step 7** The syrup should be thick enough to coat the pears lightly.

**Time**
Preparation takes about 25 minutes and cooking takes about 50 minutes.

**Variation**
Use white wine to poach the pears, and flavor with cinnamon or a vanilla bean.

**Serving Ideas**
Add whipped cream, ice cream or custard for a richer pudding.

SERVES 6

# PERSIMMON PUDDING

A rich and satisfying pudding for autumn made with this plump, bright orange fruit. Spice it up with preserved or fresh ginger.

2-4 ripe persimmons or Sharon fruit (depending on size)
4 tbsps honey
Juice and rind of 1 small orange
1 egg
½ cup light cream
¾ cup all-purpose flour
½ tsp baking powder
½ tsp baking soda
Pinch cinnamon and nutmeg
2 tbsps melted butter
1 small piece preserved ginger, finely chopped, or small piece freshly grated ginger
4 tbsps chopped walnuts or pecans
Whipped cream, orange segments and walnut or pecan halves to garnish

**Orange sauce**

1 cup orange juice
Sugar to taste
1 tbsp cornstarch
2 tbsps brandy or orange liqueur

**Step 3** Gradually fold the dry ingredients in the persimmon purée using a large metal spoon or a rubber spatula.

**1.** Peel the persimmons or Sharon fruit by dropping them into boiling water for about 5 seconds. Remove to a bowl of cold water and leave to stand briefly. This treatment makes the peels easier to remove.

**2.** Scoop out any seeds and purée the fruit until smooth. Add the honey, orange juice and rind, egg and cream, and process once or twice. Pour the mixture into a bowl.

**3.** Sift the flour, baking powder, baking soda and spices over the persimmon purée and gradually fold together. Stir in the melted butter, ginger and nuts and spoon into well buttered custard cups. Place in a bain marie and bake until risen and set, about 45 minutes, in a pre-heated 350°F oven. Test by inserting a skewer into the middle. If the skewer comes out clean the puddings are set. Allow to cool slightly.

**4.** Combine the sauce ingredients and cook slowly, stirring continuously, until thickened and cleared. Stir in the brandy or orange liqueur.

**5.** When the puddings have cooled slightly, loosen them from the edge of the dish and turn out onto a plate. Spoon some of the sauce over each and garnish with whipped cream, orange segments and nuts.

**Step 5** Spoon some of the sauce over each pudding to glaze it.

**Time**
Preparation takes about 25 minutes and cooking takes about 45 minutes.

**Serving Ideas**
The pudding and sauce may be served warm or cold. If serving cold, cut the quantity of cornstarch down to 2 tsps, as the sauce will thicken on standing.

**Cook's Tip**
To prevent a skin from forming on top of a dessert sauce, sprinkle lightly with sugar to cover the top completely. If using this method, adjust the quantity of sugar in the recipe.

# INDEX